# DALEK
## *I Loved*
## YOU

# DALEK

## I Loved

# YOU

## Nick Griffiths

GOLLANCZ

LONDON

The right of Nick Griffiths to be identified as the
author of this work has been asserted by him in accordance
with the Copyright, Designs and Patents Act 1988.

First published in Great Britain in 2007 by
Gollancz
An imprint of the Orion Publishing Group
Orion House, 5 Upper St Martin's Lane, London WC2H 9EA

A CIP catalogue record for this book is
available from the British Library

ISBN-13 9 780 57507 940 3
ISBN-10 0 57507 940 1

1 3 5 7 9 10 8 6 4 2

Typeset at The Spartan Press Ltd,
Lymington, Hants

Printed and bound in Great Britain at
Mackays of Chatham plc, Chatham, Kent

The Orion Publishing Group's policy is to use papers that
are natural, renewable and recyclable products and made
from wood grown in sustainable forests. The logging and
manufacturing processes are expected to conform to
the environmental regulations of the country of origin.

www.orionbooks.co.uk

*For My Mum and Dad*

# Author's Notes

1. A few names have been changed, to protect the innocent. Annoyingly, the only name I can't change is my own.
2. These are my memories of events, some of which took place more than 35 years ago. I cannot always guarantee their accuracy (though where facts are checkable, I have done so). But this is a book about impressions that lasted. I could not put it any more perfectly than lovely Uncle Monty did, in *Withnail & I*: 'There is no true beauty without decay.'

# Foreword

'My name is Nick and I am a *Doctor Who* fan.'

Don't let that put you off me, if you're not Who-inclined. I also love David Bowie, Interpol, Boards of Canada, Godspeed You Black Emperor and swathes of electronica. I'm a Tottenham Hotspur season-ticket holder, so I do get out. I don't own any black T-shirts with rubbery sci-fi logos that smear when ironed – actually, I would never iron T-shirts, or any type of clothing frankly – nor do I wear an outsized, multi-coloured scarf.

I'm married, with a gorgeous son from a previous relationship – proof that at least two women have been prepared to do it with me – and his name is Dylan, not Gallifrey Davros Zarathustra. I don't spot trains and I don't own a single model of a Dalek.

No, hang on, that's not true. I just remembered the Palitoy Talking Dalek, which I purchased as mute and lovingly restored to its former 'Ex-ter-min-ate!' glory.

And the ancient Rolykins Dalek, which I picked up at a snip.

Equally, if you're a fellow fan, please don't think that I'd want to find a cosy corner of a convention with you, to discuss continuity errors in The Masque of Mandragora, Season 14, Production Code 4M.

(Don't be fooled: I had to look up those production

details on the BBC's *Doctor Who* website – and in doing so got sidetracked into playing Attack of the Graske featuring David Tennant. The internet is a wonderful thing. This morning, I started writing my book *and* saved the universe.)

With admirable hypocrisy, I am actually wary of other *Doctor Who* fans. There's an unwritten Nerd Scale which 'normal' people apply to fans of any science fiction/fantasy and I'd like to imagine myself around their 2 or 3 mark. (That framed set of nine Tom Baker bathroom tiles on the wall behind me suggests the truth may rank somewhere higher.)

I fear that if I mingle with Whovians – other people are Whovians; I am a *Doctor Who* fan – around the 7 or 8 mark, my own rating might creep a little higher. Of course, most other Whovians are thinking exactly the same of me. It's a tough one.

Most frustratingly, because I love *Doctor Who*, people imagine that I love every other form of sci-fi. I would sooner bed down for the night among argumentative raccoons than watch an episode of *Stargate*. *Star Trek* bores the pants off me. It's so earnest. I put all *Star Trek* fans somewhere around 8 or 9 on the Nerd Scale, again the hypocrisy not being lost on me.

The over-riding reason that I regard *Doctor Who* with such affection is that it transports me straight back to my childhood. It's my own time-travelling Tardis.

Any time I'm feeling low, or admittedly sometimes for no reason other than errant laziness, I'll draw the curtains, pull out a classic Jon Pertwee or Tom Baker story and take myself back to a time before bills addressed to me landed on the doormat and girlfriends announced that they were leaving because I was barely more liveable-with than Pol Pot.

Rarely do I tell anyone about these video trysts. *Doctor Who* fandom is definitely a badge, worn with pride among fellow admirers and hidden from view on the high street. People make assumptions about you. Not always glowing assumptions. Some of them think you want to follow them home, bleating about Zygons, then sellotape their heads to a television screen while playing The Five Doctors on the DVD.

It hasn't always been easy, remaining accepted in society.

How did I get into this mess?

People will tell you they can remember their precise whereabouts when JFK was assassinated, the moment Neil Armstrong set foot on the moon, or when they heard that Princess Diana had died. In my case, respectively: not alive; in bed asleep; and waking up after a night of cider abuse and resultant fumbling with a lovely/drunk woman in Stourbridge. That's three women who have slept with me so far. Feel free to keep a tally. Actually, don't, because the number doesn't rise significantly.

Personally, I like to tell people that I know exactly where I was when I first watched Doctor Who. I was on my parents' sofa at 63 Murray Road, Horndean, Hampshire, which I can state with certainty because I would have been four-and-a-third years old at the time and didn't get out much around dusk.

I recall the story vividly. It was Spearhead from Space, which was broadcast in January 1970 and formed Jon Pertwee's debut as the Doctor.

I remember Pertwee clowning around in his nightgown, I remember the Brigadier getting all official on his ass, but most clearly of all I remember the Autons. They were utterly terrifying. Deliciously so.

Faceless shop dummies with snap-down wrists, guns and denim suits, coming alive in shop windows, smashing their way out into the street and wreaking havoc on a defenceless small-town community. The bobby on his bike, horror-struck. I'm sure I had never seen anything like it before, death-and-destruction being low on the priority list of the writers of *Mary, Mungo and Midge* and *The Clangers*.

I was hooked. Jon Pertwee became my hero.

Did I hide behind the sofa? Since it was up against the wall and moving furniture around was frowned upon, disappointingly no. Instead, I made for the armchair in the corner and cowered behind that, peeking out at intervals to check when the coast would be clear.

Would an armchair have saved me from death-by-Auton? I certainly believed that it would.

The Silurians, the Axons, the Sea Devils – such a work of genius! – the Draconians, the Ogrons, the Daleks, inevitably . . . These are all imprinted on the relevant part of my brain and have no doubt seeped into less relevant areas which should have been reserved for Geography O-level revision.

Saturday teatime in front of *Doctor Who* became a religious experience. I devoured all of the Pertwee stories and was disturbed when Tom Baker took over. No child enjoys change and I distinctly remember my Mum voicing the opinion that Baker was 'very silly', which I initially took on board.

At least I quickly came to worship at the great man's altar of eccentricity and, as I grew older, realised that my mother was voicing the self-same opinion when we watched things like *The Young Ones* or The Smiths on *Top of the Pops*.

Contrary to popular opinion, never trust your mother.

As Peter Davison, whom I had typecast as the kindly, bumbling vet from *All Creatures Great and Small*, took over, then Colin Baker, then Sylvester McCoy, I lost interest in the new episodes of *Doctor Who*. Music had taken a hold in my life, along with an unrequited curiosity about girls.

And it might have remained that way, but for two life-changing events.

One was the discovery, in London's Free Ads paper, *Loot*, of an advertisement for home-recorded archive *Doctor Who* stories – this was in the days before the BBC's commercial versions, and before I could afford satellite television and UK Gold's re-runs – which would open up the chance to relive those seventies glory days. Not only that, but I could catch up on stories I had missed, delve into television's monochrome era to find out what William Hartnell and Patrick Troughton were really like, even revisit the likes of Baker C's Doctor, whom I had perhaps judged harshly. (As it turned out, I hadn't.)

I remember receiving the list of available stories and it was enormous. The Green Death, The Claws of Axos, The Daemons, Planet of the Daleks, Pyramids of Mars, The Talons of Weng-Chiang – episodes I was dying to see again. That was my childhood writ there, within reach.

The second life-changing event was finding myself working, as a freelance writer, for the *Radio Times*. This was in the mid-nineties, when *Doctor Who* was in abeyance, when rumours of a revival abounded but came to nought.

The BBC and the *Radio Times* march inextricably hand-in-hand, like a giant marshmallow Auntie and Uncle, down the highway of good, clean, traditional, family entertainment. The magazine and the Time Lord maintain a magnetic association that dates back to An Unearthly Child, the first *Doctor Who* story.

One of my most treasured possessions is my *Radio Times* Tenth Anniversary Special, purchased on a shopping trip to Southsea in 1973, and read so many times that its cover has fallen away and its glossy pages are smudged with the greasy thumbprints from the bedtime snacks of ages. I adored that magazine.

Amazingly, fate decreed that I myself would write swathes of 1996's 16-page Time Lord Souvenir issue, published to coincide with Paul McGann's *Doctor Who* movie, as well as the similarly sized 40th Anniversary Special.

It meant that I would interview and meet most of my heroes, Doctor and companion. I once stood and chatted to Tom Baker. And – let's not try to sound professional here – the experience was jump-around-afterwards exciting, a bold, flourished tick in the box of Achieved Ambition.

Then, out of the blue, the series returned in 2005. I would turn 40 in the same year and was allegedly too wise to become excited. Anyway, history dictated that I harboured only minor hopes for it, with so many burnt-out shells of revivals littering the show's past.

I had not reckoned on Russell T Davies and his team.

Christopher Eccleston, the new Ninth Doctor, had been in *Our Friends in the North*, fondly remembered, critically fawned-over drama which had won proper awards. He had done Shakespeare, while professing that he wasn't a big fan. That's so cool.

His companion, Rose, was to be played by Billie Piper, who at 15 became the youngest ever artist to debut at Number One, with Because We Want To (essentially a teen declaration of intent to run around a lot and play music naughtily loud, because she and her mates felt like it), and who had become an actress of note after an eye-catching performance in Chaucer's updated Canterbury Tale, The Miller's Tale, on the BBC.

She's bright, sassy and noticeably foxy. But at 40, I was allegedly too wise to become excited.

Since I still contribute to the *Radio Times*, now their unofficial *Doctor Who* Correspondent, the privilege of entering the world of Who remains.

I remember visiting the Cardiff set before the series aired, gazing at the Tardis, actually twiddling its knobs and sitting in the swish new leather seat . . . and not being that thrilled. At least, not as thrilled as I should have been.

Had my *Doctor Who* mojo died? Had it heck as like.

Later that same day I interviewed some Autons (a bizarre experience) and something inside the grey matter sparked.

The series began broadcasting and, along with most of the rest of the nation, by the time that weird old Victorian parlour-maid had risen from her death bed to walk towards the camera, moaning like a good'un, eyes all icy, in episode three, I was hooked. As, amazingly, was my son. Though you hope your progeny might follow in your footsteps, I could hardly have said to the kid, 'Here, watch this twenty-six-episode DVD box-set of The Key to Time – my American version; there isn't a British one; consider yourself lucky – then go tell your friends how cool it is.'

As luck would have it, loving the new *Doctor Who*, which entire families did, was perfectly acceptable in noughties society. Encouraged, even.

History was about to repeat itself, somehow eschewing nerdiness.

Dalek-mania came back. Only the Talking Daleks of today speak more than one word, trundle around under remote control and would probably make your tea for you, if they could only stop exterminating the cat.

Once again, I find myself having interviewed most of the cast and crew.

I have met the Tenth Doctor, David Tennant, and he used the word 'chutzpah'; I have spoken to Piper, while swooning anciently on the other end of the telephone; I have walked in the spaceship of the Sycorax and chatted with their leader in his trailer, while he changed his trousers.

And, best of all, there is more to come.

It has been an incredible ride, this life with *Doctor Who*, filled with cosiness, quarries, tolerance and intolerance, hero-worship, unnecessary purchases of memorabilia, a slag heap made of Cornflakes scattered with peppermint cream Giant Maggots, and yes, probably even a little chutzpah, once I find out what the word means.

This is how it happened . . .

## Chapter One
### *Age* 4–7

# The Joys of Being a Small Boy

*'Dreams are important. Never underestimate them.'*
The Doctor, Snakedance

Welcome to January 1970.

The sixties are over. While a nation recovers from wearing flowers in its hair, a small boy living at 63 Murray Road, Horndean, Hants, is recovering from the excitement of Christmas.

The events of 1969 have largely passed him by, which is fortunate because they had involved plenty of warring and turmoil:

America had remained ensconced in Vietnam, getting nowhere. The alleged assassins of both Bobby Kennedy and Martin Luther King had been up in court. Charles Manson and his 'Family' had committed bloody murder, British troops had entered Northern Ireland and Richard Nixon had been sworn in as the new President of the United States. Later, history records, he would be hurriedly sworn out again.

Music had had its Woodstock and The Beatles had performed their last, atop the Apple Building.

Oh, and man had landed on the moon.

Only one event of 1969 had deeply affected young Nickolas [sic] Griffiths. In July, the halfpenny had ceased to be UK legal tender. HOW ON EARTH WAS HE GOING TO AFFORD ANYTHING NOW?

Happily, Christmases chez Griffiths have always been a time of giving. What four-year-old me received that Christmas of 1969, I really couldn't tell you – it was too many years ago – but I do know that the presents would have stacked impressively, because my parents/Santa were always generous at Yuletide, and that these lovely freebies would have arrived in a gaudily coloured, thick-paper bag, because they always did.

I always thought that bag was absolutely enormous, until I came across it in the loft one day, long after said bag and my childhood had been dispensed with. When you're six foot tall, it suddenly seems much less enormous.

Note to self: consider revising opinion of parents' generosity.

Being a child is a wonderful thing. At its start, people actually wipe your arse for you. They applaud when you perform even basic functions. For ages after that, they do everything for you, and they buy you things. And for ages after that, they applaud when you perform slightly less basic functions (such as getting a job) and continue to give you cash, even though you have a job but have spent all yours on booze.

Actually, I'm being a bit unfair here. When I said 'people' and 'they' I meant 'my parents'. 'People' didn't wipe my arse for me when I was two years old. I didn't toddle out into the street and flag down passers-by, proffering my soiled bum-crack.

Note to self: consider not revising opinion of parents' generosity.

I was born in the south-coast naval city of Portsmouth in August 1965, just a week after – though no one thought to tell me – J K Rowling, and had been driven bawling back up the M3 to the nothing-town of Horndean, where I would lead the first seven years of my life.

My father, Norman, is an engineer, works manager at Tri-ang, a subsidiary of the world's biggest toymaker but which will decline into receivership, the people who make Hornby trains and Scalextric cars; my mother, Lilian (Lynne), is a housewife. They're into their forties already and my four brothers, Max (actually Norman also, but you can see why he changed it), Michael, Gordon and Brian have long since left home. I am effectively an only child. Generosity and expectations will be showered upon me. It will suit me fine.

My Dad has noticeable ears, a kindly expression and a suit for work. Sometimes people hear him speak and think he is Australian. You might imagine my Mum as one of those pre-war film stars, with her dark loose curls and bright lipstick. She also looks a tiny bit like the Queen.

I like them a lot, which is handy since they are in charge of me.


What was life in Horndean like?

I can see a back garden path framed by trellises about which roses grow. I can see pine trees lined along the back, whose branches I regularly force my way up through. I will spend a lot of my childhood up trees and am gutted when those pines are one day chopped down without my permission.

There's a muddied area out there somewhere, cordoned off with wire netting, where I will one day be allowed to keep a rabbit in a hutch.

On the patio, I will take apart a large robot which had been given to me as a present, and I won't be able to put it back together again.

In the kitchen is a table. Its legs are metallic white and its top is yellow Formica covered in a bizarre pattern of black lines and dots, with a black plastic trim. Sometimes I will shelter under there with an empty pill bottle, mixing potions in the hope of becoming a wizard, while Mum whistles as she works at the sink. Except it's not really a whistle, more a blowing through pursed lips. If you get up close, you can smell the instant coffee.

I have a breakfast cereal plate which is plastic with a colourful comic design in the centre and a rim at right angles to the base. Presumably I am a messy sod. I remember first eating Shreddies off that plate.

Murray Road itself is built on a hill, which is great for cycling down at speed on one's blue-and-yellow bike with wide white wheels. At the top is Merchistoun Hall where I attend nursery school.

Please don't concern yourself that this book is going to be filled with poo anecdotes, but my sole memory of those nursery schooldays is of finally pulling my way up on to the supporting crossbar of one of the swings, swiftly filling my pants, recognising the hopelessness of my situation, and having to ask a passing friend to get a teacher to rescue me.

I remember being cleaned up – what wages were those people on? – and being allowed to walk home down the hill on my own, and my mother expressing surprise that I am back early. I don't recall my excuses but I do recall the washing machine going.

Other early memories? Weeing on the front lawn. (Sorry.) Playing with my only friends from just up the road, Peter and Stephen. Peter is my age, his brother is a couple of years younger and I am wondering now how exactly one plays with a two-year-old. And sitting on my toy tractor in the middle of the road, while the heavens tipped buckets on my head, wondering who I was and why I was there: my first existential ponderings. I can still smell that sodden tarmac.

And my favourite anecdote: I am playing on the small triangle of unkept grasses beside the hedgerow that forms the boundary of Merchistoun Hall. A stranger arrives beside me, a small but older boy. He picks up a discarded rusty metal bucket, stuffs twigs, stones and leaves into it, and when he tips it out there is a ladybird among the rubble. 'I've made a ladybird,' he announces.

For weeks after that, when I am allowed out to play, I will return to the same spot and try to make my own ladybird. Unsuccessfully.

If you are that boy and you are reading this, please do get in touch. I'd like to punch you on the nose.

I've just looked at a Google map of Horndean, which has brought memories flooding back. The town itself is famous for one thing, a Gale's brewery that doesn't smell good: a cloying, bitter-sweet hop-scent that carries on the wind.

Nearby is Cowplain, where my dentist dwells – a defiant sadist with a syringe the size of a fire extinguisher – and where a newsagent sells multi-coloured gobstoppers in a glass dispenser, which I covet. One day my Mum will offer to pay for one, provided I ask for it. I will battle my debilitating self-consciousness and eventually walk away.

That personality trait has never left me. Try being nervous of talking to strangers while holding down a career in journalism. Every phone call I make, I first take a deep breath.

These days, when we go on holiday, I do the 'driving and hiding', my wife does the 'talking to strangers'.

My mother and I shop regularly in Cowplain or, if we are feeling adventurous, further afield in Waterlooville, which is bigger. There is a restaurant in the latter in which we often take lunch, and I am obsessed by a certain dessert cake which is a cube of sponge surrounded by chocolate wafers, with a dollop of cream on top, into which are stuck, butterfly-wing-style, two further chocolate wafers. I believe it was called the Chocolate Box.

The only problem: I am petrified of the stairs up into said eatery, which have gaps between each step, so one can see the floor way below as one rises. As we have already ascertained with the Christmas-bag incident, relative smallness can make heights and distances appear deceptively great. I have to crawl on my hands and knees up those stairs, just to reach my dessert heaven.

Fear of heights is another trait that will never leave me. Some 12 years later, I will find myself once again on hands and knees, edging petrified along the ridge towards Snowdon's peak.

What I am doing up there, fuck knows.

Crucially, into this carefree, only occasionally hair-raising existence, one day enters a tall man with a noticeable nose, wavy silver hair, friendly eyes and old-fashioned clobber, going by the name of the Doctor.

The day is 3 January 1970, the time 5.15 p.m., on BBC1. It's the first episode of Spearhead from Space, marking Jon Pertwee's debut as the nation's favourite Time Lord.

*Spearhead from Space, for the unfamiliar: Patrick Troughton has regenerated into the Third Doctor (Pertwee). He's aided by companion Liz Shaw (a boffin, though obviously rubbish compared to our hero) and bossed about without effect by Brigadier Lethbridge-Stewart (uniform, baton, moustache). The Nestene Consciousness plans to take over the Earth (a recurring theme) by controlling plastic – notably these shop dummies which come alive and are known as Autons. The same aliens would battle Christopher Eccleston's Doctor, to herald the show's triumphant return.*

★

I had never caught any Troughton stories, presumably having been deemed too young to handle the tension. Presumably also, my parents had no idea how terrifying the Autons would be. Boy, were they scary.

It had been my Dad's idea to plonk me in front of the murderous mannequins. He had watched both Hartnell and Troughton, while I slept, dreaming of bunnies or similar, and had become a fan.

*Doctor Who* has always appealed to whole families. That's one of its beauties. It gobsmacks me that at a time when the BBC were reviving the likes of *Blankety Blank*, *The Generation Game* (with Jim Davidson!) and *Ask the Family*, or airing shows hosted by Ian Wright (clearly a former footballer), they had no idea what impact the return of a well-produced *Doctor Who* would have.

Indignation over.

My Dad – who is almost 90 but wears it so well that he still has hair that isn't fully grey, albeit splendidly wispy – tells me that his mother used to make sandwiches for the beat bobbies (including his stepfather) back in the twenties, and he had to race around after them, delivering the much-needed nourishment.

Often, he says, these bobbies would hole up in a police box, exactly like the Tardis, where they could eat their sandwiches in peace.

Spotting this blast from the past in a BBC television series was one enticement for him to watch.

Mine was far less nostalgic. I had seen nothing of anything that occurred in *Doctor Who* before. It was all utterly new, a seismic blow to the mind, such a giant leap for my imagination that I was instantly hooked.

When you are that young, you don't see the joins or the wobbles – that stuff is real. And they had set it on Earth. One scene, in which the 'shop dummies' come alive, is set in a regular high street where ladies and gentlemen wear autumnal browns of low fashion sense and the days pass predictably. Forget the Earth – it might as well have been set in my house.

I cannot stress enough how much of a departure *Doctor Who* was from my previous – and would be from my near-future – televisual experiences. Here are:

## Some Things . . . I Also Remember Watching as a Small Boy

- *Andy Pandy* – Wooden puppet in stripy jim-jams has low-key adventures with a teddy bear and 'Looby-Loo', then falls asleep.
- *Mary, Mungo and Midge* – In the opening credits of this very basic animation, mouse sits on dog's nose to reach lift button; they ascend until they reach Mary's flat; what they do when they get there escapes me. Am wondering now whether it was worth their effort.
- *On the Move* – I actually remember being glued to this lunchtime programme for people who were hard of hearing, even though I wasn't.
- *Vision On* – Bizarrely, another show for the hard of hearing, in which Pat Keysell and Tony Hart did arty things or something, and a bloke invented Heath Robinson contraptions.
- *The Herbs* – Animated adventures in a herb garden. The hoot of that owl used to give me the willies.
- *The Clangers* – The closest I had previously come to watching outer-space adventures. I bloody loved *The Clangers*, and still do. My Mum knitted me one. No, not recently.
- *Pogle's Wood* – Like *The Clangers*, another Oliver Postgate and Peter Firmin creation. The men are geniuses. *Pogle's*

*Wood* captivated me. This one featured puppets (squirrel living with family in woods) in real-life settings. I watched it again a few years back, and what I didn't realise was that it was educational. These people are telling me how bees make honey! Was highly amused by Mr Pogle's 'Where's moi tea, Woife?' Mr Pogle clearly not reconstructed.

- *Joe* – Animation. Small boy, bowl haircut, large eyes. In a café?
- *Trumpton* / *Camberwick Green* / *Chigley* – I'm having problems differentiating between the three, but I recall being entranced by the musical box from which a mystery character would pop up, and of course that roll-call: 'Pugh, Pugh, Barney McGrew, Cuthbert, Dibble, Grub . . . peep!'
- *Blue Peter* – Rarely *Magpie*. We were a BBC household. Valerie Singleton, Peter Purves, John Noakes. I just loved counting down to Christmas with them, with that 'Advent Crown' made of coathangers.
- *Love Thy Neighbour* – By the time I was seven or eight, I was allowed to watch this sitcom about a bigoted white bloke living next door to a black family. Memories of weeping with laughter unforthcoming.
- *The Generation Game* – Likewise, this popular gameshow, starring Bruce Forsyth. 'Nice to see you, to see you, nice!' was his catchphrase. Adults making total fools of themselves. 'Give us a twirl, Anthea!' That conveyor belt and the inevitable cuddly toy. These things are ingrained on my subconscious. Is that a good thing?
- *Morecambe & Wise* – These two, I really did find funny. One Christmas special, I was lying on the pouffe in the lounge, laughed at a gag and my Christmas cake went down the wrong way. I choked, my parents panicked. Recall gasping, 'I don't want to die,' while becoming acutely aware of how young I was. Dad, unfamiliar with the Heimlich Manoeuvre, repeatedly whacked me on the back. I survived. Phew.

Naturally, I have watched Spearhead from Space since that original airing. A few times, in fact, given its pride of place in my past. So I must work hard to separate the memories specifically from those four Saturday evenings in January 1970.

First, of course, there was Pertwee himself. It helped that I had never seen him before. Recognising him from, say, *All Creatures Great and Small*, or his companion as, say, Bonnie Langford, that screeching infant harpy from 'talent' show *Opportunity Knocks*, would have instantly destroyed the illusion.

I had no idea that he'd been a star of Carry On films, nor that he had appeared in the likes of *Ladies Who Do*, *Nearly a Nasty Accident* or *The Gay Dog*. Neither was there ever a radio in our house, so I would have known nothing of his time on *The Navy Lark*. My Mum enjoys tranquillity and seems to regard any sort of music or performed spoken word as 'just a noise'.

So Pertwee already seemed somewhat other-worldly to me when he staggered on to the set, bulging-eyed and talking gibberish. I remember his nightshirt, which was odd because it was old-fashioned, and him staggering around corridors in it, but most of all he represented boundless wisdom and safety.

The Autons were terrifying, destructive, emotionless creatures, but Pertwee's Doctor took charge and defeated them. If he were around, everyone – and that included the viewer, because the Autons would definitely have come for me too – was safe.

Even today I am obsessed by cosiness: a bosomly, low-lit, warm environment, an emotional womb. Give me a traditional local pub over an All Bar One any day, or a country kitchen over something run by Conran. Or my home over anyone else's. Give me cushions, supersoft fabrics and a real fire, and a woman's arms to lie in, ideally while she subconsciously scratches me. Yes, it's indulgent.

*Doctor Who* provided cosiness then, and always will, because it represents nostalgia and sanctity from harm.

People who say that *Doctor Who* is too frightening for children are fools. If the Doctor and his mates regularly got wiped out by the Daleks, they wouldn't be.

What else of Spearhead from Space?

The Brigadier struck me as purely The Authority Figure; it was only later that I would recognise the man as being a well-meaning buffoon. And Liz Shaw made no impression whatsoever. Indeed, when my thoughts returned to the Pertwee era during my twenties, I could recall only Jo Grant and Sarah Jane Smith as having been his companions. Perhaps if I had been a girl – and my Mum did call me 'Nicky' for ages, until I put a stop to it – things would have been different.

But there is one image that haunts me from that story, and I can picture myself as a four-year-old watching it now. That scene where the Auton is wading through ferns and woodland, hand snapped down to reveal its gun, hunting. How scary is that? This bald bastard in its durable denim, stalking remorselessly through the British countryside, stopping as if to sniff the air, intent upon murder.

If you haven't seen Spearhead from Space, do yourself a favour and order the DVD off Amazon (or any other reputable retailer).

Will it stand the test of time? Let's find out. I'm going downstairs to watch it now, for the first time in maybe ten years, and I'm going to try to do so objectively. It's cold out, and I'm going to get the open fire going . . .

OK, so the tape was missing. Unusual, since I am a dedicated hoarder with the covetous instincts of an only child. Woe betide anyone who picks up one of my LPs by its corner, potentially creasing the cover. So I was forced to take my own advice and order the DVD off the internet – Play.com was cheaper than Amazon when I visited – and watched it instead one Sunday afternoon, with my wife, Sinead, and my son, Dylan. Be interesting, I reasoned, to see how they reacted. We didn't make it past episode three.

The action opens on two bit-part members of UNIT (United Nations Intelligence Taskforce – the 'Intelligence' part being wishful thinking) debating the identity of a formation of mysterious blips on a radar screen. The set around them is wonderfully seventies, back when computers were the size of garden sheds and lights flashed constantly to prove to viewers that everything was working.

Sadly, the director chose to show the objects in flight through the earth's atmosphere, when clearly the budget couldn't cope.

'They're so fake!' trills Dylan triumphantly.

He's eleven years old and used to high-end computer graphics. I was four years old and used to stuffed Clangers. But he is right, of course. This supposed storm of streaming energy orbs looks more like a QVC ad for rubbish perfume. I don't care. He does. Different eras.

Enter Liz Shaw, on the back seat of a limousine, accompanied by lounge music suggesting she is both sexy and cosmopolitan.

'Do you fancy her?' quips Sinead.

'No,' I mutter darkly.

Liz encounters the Brigadier.

'Do you fancy him?' quips Dylan.

This really isn't going to plan.

It turns out that 'Miss Shaw' is a bit of a brainbox. According to the Brig, she has degrees in medicine, physics and 'a dozen other subjects'. Fourteen degrees! That's enough trajectory to launch a missile! Given that 'Miss

Shaw' looks to be in her early twenties, I wonder where she found the time to play doctors and nurses.

She is the sceptic to the Brigadier's believer. Scully to his Mulder, if you will. (I accept that many won't.) He has met the Doctor twice before, so he knows. As humans have sent probes deeper into space, he tells her, 'We have drawn attention to ourselves, Miss Shaw'.

Miss Shaw scoffs audibly.

'She's like you!' Sinead accuses me, also triumphantly. 'Refusing to accept anything unless it's already proven!'

It seems, in gathering together my little reviewing panel of loved ones, that I have opened a can of worms.

Yes, my take on things is always logic-based. I did a degree in Electrical & Electronic Engineering, after all. By mistake.

But I should point out that this little set-to with my wife stems from a radio show we were listening to on Xfm (London's alternative music station), when guest Uri Geller claimed that he could make listeners' broken clocks and watches work again, if they held them next to the radio and we all shouted together, 'Work! Work! Work!'

A derisory plan.

Yet Sinead sided with Geller!

How could I know for certain, she chided, that the arch spoon-bender's techniques wouldn't work?

Well. Er. I just *did*. Put that on your exam sheet and smoke it.

Did Einstein have to put up with this sort of thing?

There are often paradoxes, being a *Doctor Who* fan. I am prepared to wallow in the existence of knobbly-faced alien life forms, while knowing with reasonable certainty that there aren't any. And the one person capable of dealing with them knows for a fact that they do exist, and deals with them in a wholly pragmatic manner.

Argue your way around that little hornet's nest.

Back to Spearhead from Space, and the Doctor is tumbling out of his Tardis into Epping Forest, conveniently the landing site of the mysterious objects from earlier.

Meanwhile, some local yokel poacher has found one of the things – a blue/pink, pulsating, misted plastic casing, housing heaven knows what, emitting a high-pitched signal – and is digging it out of the earth.

Don't do that, you fool!

Suddenly, all hell breaks loose back at UNIT HQ, where an earwigging, adenoidal cleaner has told the press about the radar blips and about the Doctor, who is by now tucked up in a cottage-hospital bed.

The Brigadier fobs off the Fourth Estate, while a dubious-looking chap with a strangely shiny face in the background takes everything in. Clearly an agent for the forces of evil.

Cut to: the Time Lord is being kidnapped by fake ambulance men, with his mouth taped shut. Ever resourceful – and I had totally forgotten this scene – he clobbers one of the kidnappers and makes his escape in a wheelchair.

In a wheelchair! How many times have you seen that on your TV screens?

UNIT men fire on the departing ambulance. 'Shoot at the tyres!' one officer barks, failing to spot the irony that his privates haven't previously managed to hit the entire vehicle.

Cut back to: the Doctor, wheelchair discarded, stumbling on foot into a small Epping Forest clearing and surprising two UNIT soldiers. One takes aim and fires. He's hit something for once! Only it's our hero.

Episode one end credits roll.

'So they've just killed him?' enquires Dylan.

I explain that the bullet probably only winged him. No one ever actually offs the Doctor. Certainly not at the end of episode one.

'What an idiot!' notes my son of the UNIT dolt.

The point, though, is that he's into it, just as I was almost four decades earlier – and we haven't even glimpsed an Auton yet. (Sinead is by now reading a magazine.)

It's alright, breathe easily: I'm not going to drag you scene-by-scene through all four episodes. These classic *Doctor Who* stories were never intended to be watched in one go, there are always lulls in the action if you try, and I am frankly grateful when Dylan asks if we can go to the park before the end of episode three – before the appearance, I am well aware, of one of the show's least-credible-ever monsters: the Nestene Consciousness.

How he and Sinead would have hooted at the sight of those rubbery octopus tentacles, sagging out of the big vat, which Pertwee had to wrap around himself while gurning, to act 'being attacked'.

What is the point in explaining to a child of today that wobbly sets and rubbery aliens were always part of *Doctor Who*'s charm? Naïvety, on the part of the viewer, is a blessing in disguise. When we lose it, a fair wodge of inner beauty dies.

I'm not the sort of person who collects hilarious tales of my two-year-old's utterings and sends them in to tabloid Letters Pages. (But here is one.)

I do remember just the one anecdote, from when Dylan was three or four. We were driving – it's all right health and safety fascists, I was at the wheel – around the Tottenham Hale one-way system and there's a car dealership on the right.

The sales bods had tied balloons to each of the vehicles, highlighting some unbeatable deal on offer. The boy spots this and says to me, 'Look, Dad! You get a free car with every balloon!'

If only it were true. We could puncture all the petrol-guzzlers shortly after purchase and spend ages batting around the air bags.

I have seen some mind-blowing sights. Many parts of the Scottish Highlands. Spurs players scoring against Arsenal. The view from the back of our hotel, when we dropped off Mexico's Copper Canyon train ride in El Fuerte, was as unexpected as it was stunning (and there were humming-birds on the porch).

But in those situations your mind is programmed what to think. 'Gosh, what a view!' – that sort of thing.

When a small child lets go of their helium balloon and it floats up into the sky, and you watch it bounce around in the thermals, the mind is set free. Where will it end up? What journey will it take and what sights will it see from that enviable vantage point?

The tot who lost the thing, assuming they are not bawling, is even better off, because their imaginings may well involve dragons and princesses and castles in the air.

It's a similar story with the message in a bottle, only we should avoid littering the sea with our empties. Plus, too many people would waste the opportunity. Imagine actually coming across a bottle washed up by the shore one day and feverishly unfurling its message to find: 'IM GONNA B FAMOS! CARLY XXXXXXXXXXXXXXXXX'

I consider myself a nailed-on cynic. In my day job as a TV writer/reviewer, you should hear me railing at the screen over plot inconsistencies or rubbish scripts. I remember when someone had a gun trained on hugely tedious doctor-detective *Dangerfield*, I was shouting, 'Shoot! Shoot!'

But I never apply the same standards to *Doctor Who*.

Why? It would be arrant madness!

The whole thing is crazy. You just have to let your mind go. Imagine thinking, 'You surely can't defeat the Daleks by reversing the polarity of the neutron flow?'

That is one of the reasons why *Doctor Who* is so great.

Of course, as a fan of the show, I do sometimes find myself marginalised and on the defensive. In response, I have developed a devil-may-care-shrug and subsequent-sulk manoeuvre.

It's funny, and this goes for any hobby that is not socially accepted – i.e. anything from the collecting of stamps or porcelain frogs to angling, as opposed to the playing of football or fighting while smoking – but you often find yourself cocooned in an artificial world of your own devising, gradually building up the courage to cry, 'I am an individual!' followed by, 'Ouch! Leave me alone!'

Until, that is, you go off and meet a group of fellow enthusiasts, when you can bask in the collective obsession, praying that cool people don't spot you.

Actually, I do have to mention the beginning of episode two.

An officer is standing over the UNIT idiots, who are kneeling, inspecting a prone, unmoving Doctor.

'Gave us no warning, sir!' says the idiot with the gun.

'How could he, with his mouth taped?' his superior points out.

'Is he dead, sir?'

*Is he dead?* Fuck me! You're the 'professional' serviceman who's been bending over him for the last five minutes!

*Doctor Who*'s writers really didn't seem to have much time for men in uniform.

Many years after Spearhead from Space went out, as fate would have it, I got to meet some Autons and chat to them. Which was odd. Not the Pertwee-era ones, but the remodelled Autons that kicked off the new series in 2005.

This was for a *Radio Times* feature to accompany a photo-shoot, which took place in a hangar cum studio on an estate outside Cardiff. Television studios are usually daunting, chilly places where technicians echo, but the wind outside was blowing a gale that could freeze eyeballs, enough to make its space feel welcoming.

And in there was the redesigned Tardis interior: all organic and curvaceous, like a heart inside an orchid. Hard metal walkways, a swish, added seat and console spattered with antiques shop detritus.

Though it looked amazing, nothing inside me stirred. It felt disconcerting. Junior Nick would have leapt up there and transported us all back to 1562 by mistake, then crapped himself while waiting dutifully for teacher's wrath. I guess I just didn't hold out much hope for the series, because of all the promises and subsequent failures of yesteryear. (All right, I did allow myself to sit in the seat, and very comfy it was too.) A new version of the show – I believed at that moment – could never recapture former glories, clutch me to its nostalgic bosom. And I had no intention of raising my hopes, only for them to be dashed once again.

As the day wore on, I spoke to make-up people, Edward Thomas, the *Doctor Who* designer, and a delightfully friendly costume designer. I saw photographs, mere tantalising glimpses, of a pig in a spacesuit, the reworked Dalek, that mad old bird who would zombie towards the screen in episode three, and finally the Autons, in real life. As it were.

There were Auton men in suits and Auton brides in full wedding fluff; their features were kitsch, well-defined, with eyelids, sexy noses and full lips. To me they didn't have the same menace as their hastily featured, hairless predecessors. Or did they?

The actors were all extras drafted in for the day. Their latex masks, which covered the entire head, had sat waiting for them, lined up on stands, while they donned their costumes – kind of Man at C&A meets Berketex.

It was hot in there, they would all report, and not overly pleasant, but none of the six had claustrophobia issues, and one chap told me that he had done NBC (Nuclear Biological

Chemical) warfare training, so he was extra-fine. Bit of a show-off. I didn't quiz him any further on the point.

Clustered pinpricks in the eyeballs of each mask allowed the wearer to see (just) and when the photographer was not snapping, straws were inserted into their mouths, to open up the air gap and allow the actors to breathe more easily.

These were the self-same masks that the actors wore during the filming itself, spreading mayhem on the streets of Cardiff.

I wouldn't say that I left that studio a fresh convert. But I had certainly allowed myself to entertain hope.

It's fair to say that my Dad isn't an adventurous holiday-maker. But then he came from a time before charter flights and cheapo airlines, when British people distrusted Spaghetti Bolognese and foreign-language skills weren't high on the curriculum.

I always thoroughly enjoyed my childhood summer holidays, I just failed to realise the minor distance we had travelled to take them, until I looked at Google maps earlier.

Shanklin is about 22 miles from Horndean, as the crow flies. Happily, for adventure's sake, there were no crows available so we had to take the ferry or hovercraft on the crossing to the Isle of Wight.

I'm not one of those people who can lie on beaches all day long. As a child that's not a problem, because there is always a rockpool to be investigated, a sandcastle to be built or a parent to be buried in sand.

Actually, I don't really like sand – and I used to hate it. We'd be down there, the English Channel lapping coldly at the shore, my parents on deckchairs, Mum in her sunhat and turquoise all-in-one, Dad in his swimming shorts (blue with white and red stripes), me in my trunks and, without fail, socks.

A large part of being a *Doctor Who* fan involves learning to stop worrying about what other people think of you.

Highlight of the day was often the evening meal, at our traditional haunt, the Cliff Tops Hotel. Or more specifically, the sweet trolley. Mum and I craved the sweet trolley, which was wheeled ceremoniously to one's table on completion of the main course, a travelling cornucopia of eye-popping confection.

She often went for the creamy concoction with sponge fingers round the outside, called something like bateau mouche. I played the field. One day I had a knickerbocker glory so tall that I had to stand on my chair to eat it, and the adults around craned in their seats to witness such cuteness.

Those were the days, though I'm glad I've moved on.

If we didn't go to the beach, rain not being unheard of on the Isle of Wight, there were the attractions. The names Godshill and Blackgang Chine are seared into my memory. They're so evocative.

Godshill was and remains a model village. I don't remember any little houses at all. What I do remember is a bloody marionette woman on a penny farthing, in a hut, which used to spook the hell out of me. So anachronistic was she that to my young eyes it was like seeing a ghost.

There may also have been some gnomes available. After the cycling woman, I don't think anything really registered.

And Blackgang Chine. What a name is that! Having always taken it at face value, I must admit to having no idea what a chine is. Allow me to consult my *Collins English* . . . which offers: 'Southern English dialect, a deep fissure in the wall of a cliff'. How about that?

Possibly then, the name refers to a band of smugglers using a certain outsized cranny to spirit away their contraband, unseen by roving customs officers. What that has to do with the dinosaur-populated adventure park of today, I have no idea.

A final memory of the Isle of Wight: Janine, chocolate-brown eyes that melted around the heart, a girl's long, dark hair, arms, legs, a one-piece bathing suit, bucket, spade and occasional harrumph. My first love. But we were only five or six and we had to get back to school.

Mrs Brown: she was my first teacher. The name of the establishment escapes me.

Mrs Brown had an impish, rounded face that was always smiling, big eyes, and light brown perhaps reddish hair. I liked her. I remember sitting cross-legged on a mat while she read us stories, and making peppermint creams in icy green, taking them home and proudly scoffing the lot.

I can recall not one classmate's face or name, though I have an image in my mind's eye of a school photograph with Mrs Brown standing back row, centre, of a group of small boys and girls with awkward haircuts, each failing to wonder where the future will take them.

How our pasts disappear as the experiences build and memory becomes selective. Presumably it's a subconscious choice, what we retain. If I were a girl, already intrigued by relationships and who said what to whom, I might have remembered a few more classmates, with whom I made daisy chains and early bonds. But I'm not and I keep stored which *Doctor Who* monsters scared me the most.

The Silurians appeared after Spearhead from Space, and I can picture them as if it were yesterday.

*Doctor Who and the Silurians, for the unfamiliar: Hibernating reptilians are awakened by nearby nuclear power station. The Doctor tries to negotiate, hoping that everyone can learn to live in harmony. Untaken by such namby-pambiness, the Brigadier blows them all up.*

★

It's funny, but I don't remember any of that peace-making aspect. I can see caves and Silurians: greeny-brown lizard men with slightly fishy faces and a third, red eye on their forehead, which glowed when they bumped people off. I was convinced they were out to kill everyone, rather than protecting their own interests.

At the age of four all aliens must seem like The Enemy, and no doubt I sided with the Brigadier. Yet *Doctor Who*, particularly when it was being scripted by hippies and Buddhists during Pertwee's tenure, preached a text of open-mindedness, conciliation and live-and-let-live. Science, logic and debate solved things, not snap decisions and explosions.

Take the classic example of the Doctor's morality: Tom Baker in Genesis of the Daleks, when he holds the two wires in his hands which, if touched together, will wipe out the Dalek race. 'Do I have the right?' and all that.

I remember thinking, 'Of-course-you-bloody-do!'

But that was the Daleks, who have no redeeming features, other than being ideal for imitating in the playground. Otherwise I would consider myself a peace-lover, with half a mind in Science and half in the Arts. I've never had a meaningful fight in my life, and I've been on a peace march – that's pretty peaceful. How much that has to do with inner soul, upbringing or a television programme, it's impossible to say, but the amount of *Doctor Who* I have watched could easily be perceived as brainwashing.

The Autons returned the following year, 1971, which was always going to be a Murray Road event. This time they wore *Hi-De-Hi* blazers and comedy heads, which made them still more sinister, but it wasn't they who made Terror of the Autons one of the scariest stories of my boyhood.

Nor was it even The Master.

★

*Terror of the Autons, for the unfamiliar: Boring Liz Shaw has been replaced by dippy hippie Jo Grant. Fellow Time Lord, The Master, Yin to the Doctor's Yang, arrives on Earth wearing black. Through the Nestenes he takes control of plastic and a series of horrible deaths occur. No guesses who saves the day, though allowing his nemesis to escape.*

This one had everything, accompanied by those bizarre synthesiser sounds, made as if by someone twiddling knobs during their death throes.

The old boy squished to death in his own inflatable armchair; the toy daffodils distributed by the Autons, which shot a plastic film over the nose and mouth of people who sniffed at them, and – most hideous of all – that devil-doll that came to life when the heating was on, and stalked some hapless victim in their own home.

That doll. It looks like a cross between Tony Hart's Morph, after eating all the pies, and Nosferatu. There is no way they would get away with that nowadays. It's scarier than Ann Widdecombe (pre-bleach-job – which surely softened the edges).

Memo to self: Contact producer of new *Doctor Who* re: possible story. The Cloning of the Widdecombe?

Those are not recollections based on later video viewing. Those costumes and special effects were the stuff of glorious nightmares. If that self-elected guardian of the national morality, Mary Whitehouse, didn't get in touch, she certainly should have done. It's too late now, of course. She's dead.

The Master deserves special elaboration, being such a stalwart of that era. According to Jon Pertwee, actor Roger Delgado was the sweetest of fellows, who wouldn't have said boo to a goose. Which was undoubtedly true, but put it this way: I wouldn't have dared approach the man in a dark alleyway and ask for an autograph.

If the devil-doll was Nosferatu, Delgado's look had more than a touch of the Draculas. His face seemed to slope forwards, like a convenient toboggan run, his eyes were unnerving black holes and his facial hair was like something concocted by, well, a BBC make-up department to make someone look the personification of all evil.

Roger Delgado would never have got a job playing Santa, and didn't five-year-old me know it.

# Some Things . . . That Give Me the Fear (Besides Doctor Who Monsters – and Heights)

- Snakes – If they really are more scared of me than I am of them, I have no idea how they function on a daily basis.
- Youths – Not all youths, obviously, but the ones with the swagger and the relaxed upper eyelids, particularly in a group. And wearing hoods. I have actually joined Middle England.
- Joining Middle England.
- Gore – I could never become a doctor. People's insides. I shrink, squealing, from the sight of any internal organ, broken bone, unreasonable gash or missing limb. Thank heavens, then, that after the toy-making business folded my Dad got a job making artificial limbs, so that he could bring home one evening, in a plastic bag, a hand, and leave it nonchalantly on the breakfast bar. I can only assume that it was an artificial one. I didn't hang around long enough to find out.
- Hospital dramas – Why would anyone want to watch these? It bewilders me. When there is no gore or death, which is the best-case scenario, everyone's lying around in rows of beds, looking ashen-faced and wondering whether they can make it to the toilet.

- Needles – I doubt I could inject myself to save my life. But more specifically, needles in the hands of . . .
- Dentists – I have no problem with them as people – although none of my best friends are dentists – but why would anyone choose dentistry as a profession? 'What would you like to do when you grow up, son?' 'I'd like to stare into people's bent gobs, sniff their decaying last meal and cause them mental, physical and financial anguish.' I've already mentioned my boyhood dentist. Hilariously, he did such a brilliant job that one wag at junior school dubbed me 'Fleabags', on account of my dodgy teeth. The Griffiths family has great hair and antibody DNA, but rubbish tooth DNA. My Dad's a bundle of false teeth and I'm pestered by crowns and fillings. I'll save the story of my tooth getting knocked out by the git at the kebab stall, and the subsequent student-dentist-with-paperclip, for a later chapter.
- Extremists – Of any persuasion. Why would anyone want to harm another human being on account of their beliefs? I shall refrain from mentioning any specific belief systems, in case they send people to come and get me.
- Politicians – What are these people on? I would laugh in the face of such formerly bullied egomaniacs, if they couldn't walk into the Houses of Parliament tomorrow and propose a law banning Nicks. Some might go into politics for all the right reasons, but by they time they've had a whiff of power, most become fawning, lying, cheating, money-grabbing monsters. Political power feels to me like a runaway train, and no one even sold me a ticket.

And so, conveniently, to the Daleks.

Many have posited theories about the Doctor's arch-enemy's popularity, all incredibly interestingly, but the main reason to me seems obvious. They were not Men in Suits.

Although *Doctor Who* has come up with a host of cracking aliens clearly bearing two arms, two legs and a head, as well as a few rather unconvincing ones – we can see you, Mister Nimon – there was no sense that the ubiquitous pepperpot tyrants had anything of the human about them.

You have to wonder what the designer's inspiration for the coloured hemispheres all over the skirt bit were, or the detail on the eye stalk, and why, after drawing up something quite so bizarre and original, he risked ruining the effect by lobbing in a sink plunger.

But the Dalek was, and remains, a design classic. If they don't have one in the Metropolitan Museum of Modern Art, they are making a mistake.

Then top that look off with that grating voice. 'Kill!', 'Murder!', 'Vanquish!', 'Maim!' – all bad. But 'Ex-ter-min-ate!', rasped out by a demented alien Domestos gargler, has such an air of ruthless efficiency about it. I would far rather be vanquished than ex-ter-min-ated.

So I can well imagine my childhood self being petrified of them, and my parents confirm that this was indeed the case.

The Daleks first troubled the Murray Road television set on New Year's Day, 1972. I would have been six-and-a-third, again recovering from the colour-blast of Christmas. Is that a Lego set in my mind's eye, from brother Max? Is that Dad's mother-in-law, sat in an armchair, all silver hair and horn-rimmed spectacles, glued to *Coronation Street*?

*Day of the Daleks, for the unfamiliar: Guerrillas from the future travel back in time to the seventies, to alter a course of history that would find the Daleks running the Earth. The Doctor helps them. Jo gets in the way.*

Ah, Jo Grant. Little Jo Grant. She wore very short skirts and I failed to notice.

I can see why they replaced Liz Shaw with her. Liz was your stiff older sister who swotted day and night and liked trad jazz. Jo was your flighty younger sister, who missed taking her O-levels because her diary was upside-down, and who bought all the latest records by anyone deemed cool and danced to them while grinning at everyone.

Jo needed constant care and reassurance. She was less use to the Doctor than a manual on cunnilingus.

I thought she was great.

But not as great as the Daleks.

Childhood duty, of course, demanded that I hide behind the sofa at their every appearance. Sadly, as the Foreword told, I was obliged to use a mere armchair. Besides the Daleks, the only thing that got me cowering there was 'Tatty-bye!'/tickle-stick comedian Ken Dodd.

I also remember their slaves for that story, the Ogrons, very clearly. Think *Planet of the Apes* meets the Mitchell brothers. They were meathead workhorses, only slightly dimmer than Jo, and a frightening presence.

People always mention this crucial weakness of the Daleks: that, in the days before computer graphics, they couldn't climb stairs. I really don't recall that holding any sway with me back then, and I think I've worked out why.

Firstly, you can't stay upstairs forever, particularly when there is school to go to. But also: people in *Doctor Who* hardly ever went up stairs! Practically, because the television cameras of the day were so bloody heavy. I bet (not very much money) that if you watched Day of the Daleks now, you wouldn't see one person going up a flight of stairs. My recollection is that they chased the Doctor, Jo and their allies around a very big house, like a slow-motion version of Benny Hill.

Also in 1972, I completed my first collection.

I don't know what it is about medium-sized boys that

cultivates their magpie instinct, but I suspect it must be their fathers: a handed-down generational thing.

Esso's Top Team Collection was a hotchpotch of the best players from each of the UK's national sides. These were thin metallic discs, featuring a photographic head-shot, and I have them here in front of me, still stuck firmly to their full-colour, fold-out collector's display. We amassed two complete sets, Dad and I. But then, we did cheat.

I had been studying the fledgling collection on the sofa one day, put them to one side, shifted my weight, and the lot slipped down the side, off a light tan leatherette cushion. Though we fished with knives and forks, they could not be retrieved.

So Dad strapped me into his white Rover and sped us down to Esso. If we'd had a siren, we would have used it.

I remember sitting in the passenger seat, literally praying.

We had lost, at most, a dozen players. When Dad came back from the cashier's, his cradled arms were filled to overflowing. What he had said, I have no idea, but it no doubt involved tears, and it had worked.

If being a father comes with a job description, that sort of thing should be in there.

Before that had come Esso's 1970 World Cup Coin Collection, but that was really Dad's, acquired 'on my behalf'. I have that set here too.

Brian Labone, Peter Simpson, Henry Newton, Keith Newton, Mick Jones . . . These names mean nothing to me.

A head of each squad player appears in relief on each lightweight, shiny coin. Brian Labone looks a bit like a Roman emperor. For all I knew, he was one.

But football interested me only vaguely as a small boy. Far more enticing had been Sugar Smacks' 'Free Dr. Who Badge' promotion.

(Sugar Smacks are basically today's Sugar Puffs, with the domestic violence element removed.)

There were six to collect and I managed five of them: Dr. Who [sic] – I am annoyingly pedantic; I would point out not only that is he 'the Doctor' not 'Dr. Who', but that 'Dr' is a contraction not an abbreviation, and therefore requires no full stop (or rather full point) – The Master, The Brigadier, Jo Grant and Bessie (the Doctor's vintage yellow roadster), each slightly lamely illustrated, as if that mattered to me at the time.

Though my sticky fingers delved desperately into the packed snow-crunch of each new Sugar Smacks box, head to one side, tongue lolling, eyes wandering, following teeny exploratory movements of sweating fingertips, the UNIT badge was fated never to emerge.

How I had coveted that bastard badge.

Five out of six. Five. Out of six.

NEVER would I let that happen again.


By 1973 I had become a big boy. Tri-ang had gone bust and Dad would have been commuting from Horndean to Basingstoke, Hampshire, to Blatchford's, the artificial limb manufacturer.

Let's have a look on Google maps. As the crow flies, it's a journey of around 25 miles – for a man who holidays at less distance, that's quite some way.

No wonder thoughts were turning to a move.

I should note in my parents' defence that they would have emigrated to Australia some years previously, with my four brothers, had paperwork wrangles not scuppered the plans.

London to Sydney, again as the crow flies, is 10,562 miles.

Alton would have to do me.

\*

Around the same time, a magazine came into my life, which I still own and treasure. It's kept in a close-fitting clear plastic bag and the cover has come off its staples, a result of the million readings it has endured, but you can tell that it is loved.

It's the *Radio Times Doctor Who Special*, 68 pages, which was bought for me on a Saturday shopping trip to Southsea. (Remember those quaint times when shops never opened on Sundays?) I can still picture myself coming out of the newsagent, gazing in fevered anticipation at its wraparound cover, which shows Jon Pertwee on an alien planet, strange gloopy sand-coloured surface and purple horizon, pursued by a queue of classic foes: Sea Devil, Cyberman, Dalek. His red tartan cape is in full swish as he spins around, startled, about to launch into some Venusian karate. The Earth hangs in the background, its moon merely a dot.

It's a fantastic, alluring cover, even by today's standards. And it promises: 'The 10th year of BBC1's great adventure series. Inside: The stars, full background, how to build your own Dalek and a chilling new Dalek story by Terry Nation.'

All that for 30p.

According to the inside blurb, nine million people were tuning in to *Doctor Who* every week. Programmes nowadays would kill for that figure – besides, of course, the new *Doctor Who*, which almost manages it and occasionally surpasses it.

Why did it mean so much to me, that magazine?

At the ages of four, five, six, seven, life goes past pretty quickly, even though you're not doing very much. That burgeoning brain is working at a hundred miles an hour, taking new stuff in, sifting fact from fiction and failing wilfully on the Santa/Tooth Fairy front – and plenty is new.

All those *Doctor Who* monsters I had lapped up would have seemed distant memories even then. That *Radio Times Doctor Who Special* brought them flooding back.

I didn't bother reading the interviews with Hartnell, Troughton and Pertwee, which were too wordy and anyway the actors really didn't matter. I made straight for the episode listings, which detailed every single story from day one – most of which I had missed seeing, several on account of not being born – with write-up and colour pictures.

Sensorites, Daleks on Westminster Bridge, early Cybermen, a Yeti, Ice Warriors and, yes!, from my era, Silurians, Axons, the Daemon, Alpha Centauri, Sea Devils, Ogrons, Draconians, Bessie, Giant Maggots!

I just stared and stared and stared. I'm not sure I have ever left those pages.

A few things are worth noting.

On page 21, in the blurb for The Tomb of the Cybermen, a sentence goes: 'Victoria saves the party from the Tombs, but the Cybermen retaliate by sending Cybermats – small'. And there it seemed to end.

Retaliate by sending Cybermats – small?! Bit of a blunt description, I thought. I remember being utterly perplexed. For years.

Looking at it now, it's just an odd line-break; you simply have to raise your eyes to the top of the next column, where it continues: 'metallic creatures – to attack them.'

On page 40, the first of a two-page, suitably futuristic illustration that ushers in Dalek creator Terry Nation's exclusive tale, 'WE ARE THE DALEKS!', I have doodled my own Dalek, in biro.

Quite why I thought my drawing skills might add anything to the vivid cityscape under attack, I have no idea. It is shit. A spindly, ill-proportioned thing that would have had trouble terrorising a death-bed geriatric.

Final mention is reserved for the 'How to Build a Dalek' feature, which fills six pages, with instructions, materials required and copious line drawings.

Approximate total cost of building Dalek: £15.

Like any boy, I was desperate to build one. Imagine owning a tame Dalek! You could get in it and scare people!

Then you look properly at the materials required. They include: 28 lb bag modelling clay, 28 lbs fast-setting potter's plaster, 4 sq yds hessian scrim, ½ pint PVA release agent, 2 oz accelerator, 2 oz catalyst, strips of glass matt . . . I could go on. In fact, I will: 6 lbs layup resin, acetone, 2 6V 0.3 amp bulbs and holders . . . Including, of course, a sink plunger.

Suddenly I wasn't so desperate. I don't know what layup resin is even now, and if you wrapped me in hessian scrim, chanting, 'This is hessian scrim! This is hessian scrim!', I wouldn't be any the wiser.

I had a toilet roll holder, one battery (dead), four boiled sweets and some fluff from the corners of a pocket. Would that do?

Approximate total cost to sanity of building Dalek: incalculable.

Wisely, Dad steered well clear.


I have never loved a magazine more. I doubt I have ever loved a book more . . . Well, one springs to mind.

Our neighbours on one side at Murray Road may have been called Owen and June. Whatever, the lady of the house one morning ushered me over and handed me a hardback tome titled *Adrift in the Stratosphere* – an incredibly sweet gesture. These days, neighbours are more likely to fornicate on your driveway then shoot you with a big gun because your driveway was a bit uncomfortable.

I still have that book, too. Somewhere.

It's a real boy's-own adventure of a journey into outer space – written by the hardly romantically named Professor A M Low (I just searched for him on Amazon and the best it could do was *Low Back Syndromes* by Craig E Morris) –

starring three lads named Peter, Philip and . . . the last name escapes me, but I suspect he was the fat one. How they managed to get into space, rockets not being generally left around, I have no recollection, but I read that book repeatedly and moaned to my parents that I wished they had named me Peter.

*Adrift in the Stratosphere*, *Doctor Who*, a few Ladybird books on planets and stars and NASA's real-life explorative efforts were giving me the serious space horn.

In a couple of years time, I would compile 'Project: Space', a handwritten research effort with iffy illustrations, as part of a bid to win a scholarship to a public school.

And as trailers for the rest of a book go, I'm not sure that can be beaten.


I have missed out one anecdote from my early years, which springs to mind. When I Tried to Dig Down to Australia.

Someone must have told me that if you dug straight down, you would eventually hit Australia. And I must have understood their every word, bar 'eventually'.

I'm there in the back garden with a red plastic, wooden-handled beach spade and it must have been summer because the earth was very dry and hard-packed. I can picture the hole, which was perhaps eight inches in diameter and no more than two inches deep. Yet I fully expected at any moment to break through a final crust of dirt, at which the ground would fall away and I would be able to peer down into what I imagined as some kind of Lost World, of blue skies, mountains and seas.

Even a bloke's head popping up through the hole, wearing a dangly-corks hat, going, 'Strewth, mate!' would have been something.

I was beginning to understand the concept of failure.

★

*Coming up: We move to Alton, a blubbing street-full of friends fails to wave me off; the Weetabix* Doctor Who *promotion makes my year; Tom Baker takes over as the Doctor; Mum offers to make some outfits for my Action Men, I accept . . .*

## Chapter Two

*Age 8–10*

# But I Don't Want a New Doctor!

*'Take the world that you've got and try to make something of it.'*
The Doctor, Invasion of the Dinosaurs

It's great when you're eight, yeah.

If I could revisit any age, I suspect this would be the one.

Your enquiring mind has worked things out and you're pretty certain you know everything you need to know. New information is merely a bonus. Your body has developed: you can run and jump and climb, and when you kick a football it doesn't flump uselessly to one side, like an aggravated tortoise.

You have a sense of humour that appreciates *The Goodies*. You wear shorts well. No one has given you revision to do, which is the curse of the schooling classes. And though 'people' have stopped wiping your bum, they remain always there for you.

And the cash keeps coming in. I don't know. I might well have been pocketing 5p a week by this stage.

I was indestructible!

★

It is autumn 1973 and the Griffiths family is on the move, to the brave new world of Alton.

As Horndean disappears in the side-view mirror, I shed no tears. To be honest, I don't remember leaving at all.

It can hardly have been a wrench.

My parents had picked out a new-build, detached three-bedroom house on a sprawling housing estate that was only just getting going. The address: 6 Princess Drive, perched atop a hill.

Its front garden is a slew of mud awaiting turf and the few houses around are incomplete. It looks a little bit like Noah's Ark, stranded on top of Mount Ararat. The analogy ends there, since we would hardly fill the place with two of every kind of animal. My only Alton pet, after much pleading, was Pebbles the kitten, which Mum took back to the shop after it repeatedly urinated in her shoes.

I haven't kept pets since.

The property has a double garage and front and back gardens, red brick with a grooved, if hardly groovy, white fascia covering its top half.

The gardens slope. In fact, most of Alton slopes. Sit at the landing window after it has snowed and you can watch, chuckling inhumanely, as the drivers slide around while braking when they reach the top of the appropriately named Highridge.

Sit on a wooden sledge in the front garden, having over-estimated the descent, and you will slide precisely nowhere, and feel like a right tool.

Outside the back gate the real adventure begins. A narrow, mudded alleyway there runs for perhaps half a mile, between Queens Road and Whitedown Lane, bordered by suburban back-garden fencing. Smells of walked dogs and rampant weeds fill your nostrils as you run.

Behind that is an abandoned nurse's home with out-buildings, plenty of green and a row of alluring conker trees.

In summer, you can throw sticks up into the foliage and hear the spiky pods land with a satisfying salvo of thuds. All year round, you can haul yourself on to the lowest, fattest branch and pick your way towards the top, becoming nervous as the vertigo kicks in. So you chicken out and save a goal for tomorrow.

Give a boy a conker tree and he will be happy. Give him a dozen and he becomes a king.

Amazingly, in all the years I lived in Alton, I never once broke into that abandoned great house. Of course the idea enticed and often I peered in through the windows, to the spooky, white-walled, nurse-free interiors, but I never plucked up the courage.

Though my parents are not remotely strict disciplinarians, I have been raised to know right from wrong, and to respect people and property. Authority terrifies me. I would sooner have gone *Doctor Who* cold turkey than speak back to anyone in uniform. Or a teacher. Or a nine-year-old, frankly.

I am a polite, well-mannered, home-haircut type of boy who finds the outside world just slightly, but noticeably, intimidating.

That said, the outbuildings – I was tempted to call them stables, which they resembled, until I conjured up an unlikely (though not unpleasant) image of massed nurses on horseback – offered a free-for-all. Their wooden, green-painted doors were dilapidated and left ajar. No vandalism required.

In there, my friend Simon Axtell and I would find our first pornographic magazine. An *H&E Monthly*. *Health & Efficiency Monthly*, I now know, was aimed at nudists. The ladies were naked and that was both funny and strange. As were the gentlemen, which was just yuck.

Happily, I failed to wonder how it had got into that rarely visited, darkened interior.

And I would build a rat trap for one outbuilding, made of wood and chicken wire. As the prey gnawed at the cheese it would unwittingly cut through an elastic band, bringing down the weighted door behind it. Ha! Trapped! Or not, since the next day the cheese was gone, with no sign of a rodent shaking its scabby fist and cursing my ingenuity.

Lucky I went into journalism rather than pest control.

The whole caboodle disappeared in the early eighties, overnight, it felt, razed to the ground and replaced by a close of new houses that lacked personality, and though the horse chestnuts remained they were suddenly on private property.

Though I had stopped conker collecting by then, it still felt like sacrilege.

Inside, our new house feels fine. I have a playroom to myself upstairs, its cupboard stacked with board games and toys, where I will while away many an hour of contented solitude, and my bedroom offers a bookshelf and bed with two whole mattresses. The extra height makes getting in and out of bed fun, so I often do so repeatedly.

Memories of that bedroom:

- Being off school sick one day, getting out of bed and fainting flat on my nose. It still looks slightly wonky.
- Lying in bed with a fever, the doctor appearing and prescribing hospital, then me lying there going, 'Ambulance! Ambulance!' while my parents fret. An ambulance man turns up, carries me to his chariot in his arms – most comforting – and I am whisked to a Basingstoke hospital. There, a nurse wakes me at an ungodly hour and asks, 'Do you want your injection in your bottom or your arm?' Show a strange lady my bottom? At this time of night? Am too weak to shriek, 'Which do you flipping think?' Having recovered the following day, am told by

another nurse that she will be bathing me shortly. Dad arrives. I demand that he takes me home.

- Preparing to lose my virginity one afternoon, when Mum is out shopping, and worrying that I'm not sure exactly where the hole is.

Downstairs are three focuses of family life: the breakfast bar in the kitchen, the same site of the Hand Incident mentioned earlier; the dining room where we eat Sunday roasts and breakfast in smart casuals every Christmas morning; and the lounge, where the television is.

We Griffiths are no strangers to the wonders of the small screen. Dad tells me that he bought one of the first televisions on the market, and no doubt if pressed further, he would tell me that everyone in their street clustered around it to watch the Queen's coronation, as everyone of a certain age did.

Of course, when moving into strange surroundings it is always heartening to be able to latch on to something familiar.

Welcome back, Jon Pertwee. Trusty Doctor. He'll save me from any monsters that lurk under the bed.

My favourite story from those formative Alton days was The Monster of Peladon, which reprised the previous Curse of Peladon and various of its monsters – a comforting double-whammy of familiarity.

*The Monster of Peladon, for the unfamiliar: The Doctor, accompanied by Sarah Jane (Elisabeth Sladen), returns to Peladon where renegade humans in league with Ice Warriors are after the planet's mining deposits. The Doctor hypnotises into docility the bear-thing in the mines, which the baddies have been using to induce terror in the minions. Another victory.*

★

The story had one star: Alpha Centauri. What madness of the mind conjured up this curious beast with its voice like a frightened lady mouse, heaven knows.

On the plus side, it didn't look like a man in a suit, so it offered that Dalek Factor. But the Dalek Factor ended there. Alpha Centauri was a fat, yellow, slug-like body, perched upright, wearing a cape, with six short, flailing clawed arms and a vast, veiny globe of a head, most of which was occupied by eyeball. I cannot help but wonder now what the Alpha Centauri actor exclaimed when presented with his costume. It could have been a mutated caterpillar – perhaps how Lewis Carroll's imagined itself after smoking that hookah – or, to the unhealthy mind, a shuffling penis.

To innocent me, it showed purely how wonderfully bizarre beings from other planets might look.

Then you had the Ice Warriors. These were men in suits – but great suits. Green, ridged carapace-like structures with tufts of hair in odd places, oval, crested skull and malevolent large eyes. They hissed as they spoke, so came with names like Azaxyr and Sskel.

The monster quotient was upped still further by Aggedor, the hairy thing that lived in the mines, terrifying the workers, a wild-boar/grizzly-bear cross which Pertwee seduced with a spinning watch.

That's a lot of monsters for your money, which in my case was nothing, since Dad paid the TV Licence. Result.

The sole disappointment was that Arcturus, effectively a head in a goldfish bowl on a trolley, had been killed in The Curse of Peladon and so was unable to reappear.

You may scoff, as I do now, but back in the seventies a head in a goldfish bowl on a trolley was about as cool as it got.

Sarah Jane Smith was the Time Lord's latest human on the side, a journalist for *Metropolitan* magazine who had become embroiled in his doings three stories previously, while impersonating her Aunt Lavinia.

A readers' poll for the *Radio Times'* 40th Anniversary Special voted her the favourite companion of all time, and only a fool would argue. Really – you don't want to get overheard debating the relative merits of *Doctor Who* companions.

(The robot dog K-9 came second, which feasibly miffed every other companion actor.)

In this Peladon story she has the line, 'There's nothing "only" about being a girl', which sums up the writers' intentions.

Jo Grant would have screamed the house down if she had spotted a ladybird set for take-off. She was to women's lib what blancmange is to a list of delicious desserts. In a fairer world, she would have become one of Slade's girlfriends and lived a life of pop lunacy, rather than trailing around the galaxy being confronted by Draconians.

Sarah Jane was altogether brighter. She had two first names, for a start, and could remember them both. And she was a brunette.

She wore sensible clothing and scoffed at the Doctor's apparent exaggerations – until they became a reality.

She could become spooked, quite reasonably, but stick a shotgun in her hand and she would gamely pull the trigger, while looking as though she had never fired a gun in her life.

Sarah Jane was incredibly endearing.

I didn't bump into Elisabeth Sladen on my *Radio Times* travels until the 2006 photoshoot for the cover that ushered in series two of new Who, featuring a queue for the Tardis of: the Doctor, Rose, Sarah Jane, K-9, Sister of Plenitude, male clockwork droid, female clockwork droid, Cyberman. Old Uncle Tom Cobley not pictured. It was a fold-out.

No surprises that Sladen had been chosen as the

companion to cross over into new Tenth Doctor, David Tennant's world, accompanied by K-9, in the episode School Reunion.

I was excited. It was like collecting another trading card for your set, only for real. I'm enough of a fan of Elisabeth Sladen that I had bought at a *Doctor Who* convention – yes, I attended one, on a professional basis, representing *Radio Times*; no, I am not being defensive – a copy of *Homes & Savings Magazine Incorporating the Home Owner: The Halifax Building Society Magazine*, dated Summer 1984, because it featured her on the front cover.

The coverlines promise: 'Investing a lump sum', 'Living with colour', 'Insuring your home' . . . you get the idea. Makes the heart race, doesn't it?

The photograph is of Sladen on her landing, hands tucked into tracksuit bottoms, smiling. Behind her is a doorway framed by bookshelves and, if you hunt as I did, on one wall is a framed poster for the spoken-word album, Doctor Who and the Pescatons. Her landing is violently orange.

I remember expecting the feature inside to be somehow enlightening, a window into the private life of the *Doctor Who* icon.

It turns out that Sladen is only one subject of an 'Ideal Homes' piece, alongside the likes of *Call My Bluff*'s Frank Muir (now deceased), *Desert Island Discs* presenter Roy Plomley (now deceased) and Mike Davies (hopefully still alive and kicking), sales manager of *New Ideal Homes*.

Her copy runs for just half a column, alongside a photograph of the actress in the kitchen, in which she reveals that she prefers older properties but that hers has a heating problem.

The pulled quote, the one supposed to make you desperate to read the piece, runs: 'The craftsmanship and materials are so much more interesting'. Than what?! Cabbages?

★

Elisabeth Sladen is tiny in real life. When I first spotted her she had her back to me, had long, thick brown hair, and I assumed her to be a young girl visiting the studio.

I accepted her dainty handshake, led her down the wrong corridor and eventually we found her dressing room, which was uninviting.

Talking to her was odd. We sat a little too far apart, and she was the woman who played Sarah Jane Smith for all those years, while I did some growing up.

Meeting celebrities in the flesh rarely fazes me. It's when I have to phone them, or worse, when I have to wait for them to phone me, that I can fret. Don't ask me why.

(One time, the phone rang at home and it was Tony Benn. I wasn't even expecting a call.)

I have interviewed a . . . what is the collective noun for celebrities? A glitz of celebrities? A glitch of celebrities? A talent? A desperation? Anyway, I've interviewed plenty. Some seem genuinely lovely, some merely professional. Just a few are complete gits.

And before you clamour, yes, I have met Andi Peters.

Obviously, it never hurts to meet someone you admire.


Which clearly includes Sladen. Her partnership alone of both Jon Pertwee and Tom Baker, my favourite Doctors, qualifies her. That she made a woman who travels through time and space in a phonebox with a bloke bearing Jelly Babies seem real to me . . . well, bless her.

We talked about her unexpected return to the series, memories of Sarah Jane and of working with the fresh incumbents, while a tangible air of edginess drifted around the room like something from *Ghostbusters*.

Neither of us settled into comfort. Although she had filmed her scenes already, it must have been a daunting experience, even for the seasoned pro, walking into that studio full of everyone, like revisiting your old school with no wrinkled friends from your own year in tow.

But she laughed occasionally and we muddled through, and when the interview was over I admitted sheepishly that I was a fan and the ice cracked. Then we parted company. Perhaps I should have admitted as much at the very start? I just didn't want to come across as nerdy.

It got worse. I bumped into Sladen on the platform at Cardiff station, waiting for the train back to London. She was sitting, peering up the dusky line, somehow unrecognised and unpestered, and there I was again: clearly now a professional stalker.

I considered scooting past but caught her eye and she ushered me over. Chatting staccato, we discovered that she was in First Class and I among the plebs. Phew. No doubt she dreaded my company for three hours or whatever, and I had no intention of being that company. But she was sweet enough to bemoan the missed opportunity.

'I'd only have bored you,' scuttled out of my gob.

'I'd only have bored you'?!

Talk yourself up, son.

Mercifully, the train arrived.

She got on.

## Some Things . . . I Love About My Job

- Working with words – Just sit me in solitary confinement and let me shape sentences. Pig in shit. (Not necessarily that sentence.) Sometimes I don't set foot outside the house all day, and when I do the sky surprises me.
- Getting to meet heroes – Tom Baker, David Bowie, John Thaw. After I met Bowie, I danced up the road.
- The dress code – There isn't one, unless I have to attend some sort of launch (see below), which is a boon for the lover of soft fabrics. Smart clothes can be terribly stiff. I have spent entire days in a dressing gown,

which is fine until you have to answer the door to the Parcelforce man mid-afternoon. Luckily my dressing gown has a hood.

- The hours of work – Generally, I can get up when I like. I'm not great in offices. My record for lateness is 2.30pm, some years back. Uninspired by the job, I wanted to be fired. They keenly obliged.
- The atmosphere – I can get away with murder. Usually someone complains if you get bored and start playing with yourself in the office. Not here! I once bought myself a mini water cooler and stood by it with myself, just talking rubbish for ages. No one batted an eyelid.
- The variety – Recently, I had to write an advertisement feature about lingerie, while looking at photographs of models wearing some. It isn't all television programmes.

## Some Things . . . I Hate About My Job

- The cash flow situation – A regular gig is the holy grail of the freelance writer's life. My life-saving, long-standing weekly date is with the *Daily Mail*, writing their Thursday and Friday TV previews. Otherwise the cheques arrive in dribs and drabs while the bank balance and my face become increasingly red.
- The necessity to accept rubbish jobs – Because of the cash flow issue, I rarely say no if someone offers me work. Lordy, the dullness I have endured. I've interviewed someone whose business was aftershave, written a feature on personal finance (as if I am the expert) and researched the facilities of Basingstoke. I realise there are worse jobs – it's all personal hells.
- Being asked who I work for – Within my usual social circle of *Guardian* readers and Labour-voting types, very few people pat me on the back, spluttering delightedly,

and offer to buy me a large drink when I say, 'The *Daily Mail*'. The best I can hope for is, 'My Mum reads that.' I always point out that I write for the television pages and that the TV desk are all kind, funny people. Occasionally we do pub quizzes together and the conversation has never once turned to hosepipe bans or jobless families of 26 demanding a new council house.

- Having to attend launches – I loathe journalistic gatherings with a passion. That's me in the corner. Losing my religion? I'm losing my tiny mind. I'll be skulking anonymously, nursing a free cocktail, dreading the prospect of small talk with a total stranger, heart pounding. Drag me into a conversation, my tongue will run away with me and I'll say the wrong thing. Mind you, there was one occasion . . .

I used to work freelance for *The Times Magazine*, writing their now defunct That Was the Week That Was column. It was an events diary and supposedly funny, but I was banned from using puns, or indeed a host of comedy devices, so it was usually less funny than contracting gout.

You try finding a punchline to the Farnborough Air Show in 75 words.

Anyway, I had a couple of friends among the staff so I accepted an invitation to their Christmas party a few years back, in an Italian restaurant.

I was standing making awkward chat with a couple of newly introduced magazine executives, when I recognised a woman slinking down the stairs. It was a famous TV chef, or rather cook.

She made straight for our little group, stopped and went, 'Who is this gorgeous young man before me?' Meaning me!

I'll give you a clue: it wasn't Delia. Or Fanny Cradock.

Beaten for a suave or witty riposte, I turned to look behind me one way and then the other, as if seeking the gorgeous young man in question.

No one laughed.

They talked among themselves, ignoring me while I floundered in social ineptitude, and eventually I walked away feeling sheepish.

Later, buoyed by the compliment and having recovered from being ignored, I was motioning towards the same TV chef/cook, boasting to a colleague about what had been said, when she turned and caught me pointing at her like a goggle-eyed schoolboy.

Doubly sheepish, I got my coat.

Little did I know that The Monster of Peladon was to be Pertwee's penultimate tale. Children of the seventies had no internet or mothers reading *Heat*. Stuff just came as a shock.

What made his departure in Planet of the Spiders worse was that we had recently become friends.

I had written to Pertwee via the BBC – though I must admit to having no recollection of doing so – and he had replied.

I certainly remember being handed the envelope. For a start, I never received any post outside of birthdays and Christmas. No one writes to small boys. Letters flopping through the postbox were an adult domain, like double beds and conversation that droned.

I have the signed postcard here. (I am such a careful magpie, and my Mum was so fastidious, that you should assume anything I accumulated with pride, I still possess.)

It's a black-and-white head shot, the man's mouth and eyes smiling, laughter creases skirting his actorly features. He looks utterly content. Beneath the photo is printed, 'Jon Pertwee Dr. Who BBCtv' – proof that even the BBC don't know their punctuation – and it is signed in black felt-tip: 'To Nickolas. With thanks! Jon Pertwee'.

As an eight-year-old you have little knowledge of the workings of the postal system – although you might imagine miracles are possible, given that you could address a letter to

'Santa Claus, North Pole' and via some postie in a cagoule, Santa invariably replies.

But I doubt very much that I expected a reply from Pertwee. He was the Doctor. I was one of millions of kids in Britain. Why should he bother? How would he even find the time?

But he did and I can only imagine my excitement.

Then he left the show.

I had to wait half a year before *Doctor Who* returned to the BBC, having already glimpsed the new man during the regeneration scene at the end of Planet of the Spiders.

Pertwee's Time Lord had, in my eyes, died. Replaced by an impostor who looked nothing like him – who, in other words, looked nothing like the Doctor. The new bloke had brown curly hair. That wasn't right.

Of course there was hope. Better that the show continued than disappear and blight my delirium overnight. But it was small hope.

As a family, we sat to watch Tom Baker's debut in Robot, on 28 December 1974, with grim anticipation . . .

I didn't enjoy it very much. I have watched it again, once, a few years back, and it didn't make much of an impression then, either, other than the memory that it was Baker's first story.

As I mentioned in the Foreword, Mum thought him silly, and so did I initially. Him prancing around in a series of daft costumes, until he found one that suited. It was played for comedy. Pertwee's stories had humour but it wasn't overt. This was like letting a big kid loose with the dressing-up box.

The so-called Giant Robot never seemed that giant. And I am sure I would have recognised the Action Man Scorpion Tank that an effects department plainly strapped for cash had used as a UNIT attack vehicle.

No, Robot simply wasn't great *Doctor Who*.

That toothy grin with its bug eyes and electrostatic curls would need a better vehicle than that to grab my imagination. But, oh, how it would.

My first school in Alton was a primary state school which I won't name because it has probably improved since.

All I remember of my education there was being given Cuisenaire rods to play with. I've just checked on Google and they still exist.

The ones I had were colour-coded rectangles of wood. The longest, red perhaps, corresponded to ten. Then you had fives and twos and ones, or something. Two blue fives would be the length of the red ten, and so on. It's mathematics, but basic. We used them enough that I began to find them boring. I do remember telling my parents about these Cuisenaire rods, and a heavy discussion ensuing.

The next thing I know, my mother has turned up unexpectedly at the school, had words with my teacher, collected my bag from my locker, grabbed my hand and home we went.

The following day I started at the Alton Convent.

Blue cap, light grey jumper with two blue stripes around the collar, blue and grey striped tie, charcoal shorts, nervous expression. You could have worn long trousers, but my Mum always plumped for shorts. I imagine she was still calling me 'Nicky' at the time, and would even today ache with joy to see me dressed the same.

How Mum and Dad wangled it, I have no idea, because surely a Convent school takes in Catholic pupils. We weren't even religious. At that stage, I hadn't even been to a church wedding.

Miss Hayden was my first teacher and she petrified me more than any Dalek. Her classroom had a high ceiling, muted colours and an outsized crucifix on one wall. Voices echoed. Especially hers. She sat up front, a small, grey-haired woman of advancing years, with pursed lips and a no-nonsense approach to education.

She used to threaten to send naughty pupils to kinder-garten. Having never even heard of such a thing, I always thought she was saying 'kinder garden' and conjured up an image – genuinely – of a large dry-mud pit somewhere outdoors, dotted about with unhappy children.

Unlike the bosomly lady-teachers to whom a young child often becomes accustomed, Miss Hayden was bony, strict and snapped, and scared me so much that my parents spoke to her after-hours on more than one occasion, returning with tales of a teacher who had my best interests at heart. In the aftermath, she would smile at me and attempt to be comforting, which only concerned me further.

I could not wait for that year to end.


For some reason, all the classes were girl-heavy. We were five boys to 25 girls, which held no significance back then, other than a feeling of being outnumbered.

We congregated as a gender, playing conkers and marbles, and somehow scraped together a football team from the various forms, all boy-lite, for our games teacher. Mr Chalmers was robust with silver hair and looked like he might once have been in the RAF.

We played just one competitive tournament, for which I was substitute, and my spectating parents had to have a word before I got a game.

In the summer we also did athletics.

I was, and remain, hopeless at any jumping event. Invari-ably, the high jump saw me eliminated first and holding the rope for the girls to leap effortlessly over.

I won just one annual school sports day – otherwise always beaten into second place by David Coppin, with whom I am still friends – and the photograph of me being presented with an Airfix kit of a Wellington bomber by a chief nun, resides today on my mother's dressing table.

I enjoy studying it. The look on my face – sod smiling for the camera – as I gaze in wonderment at the freebie; I loved Airfix kits, so this was perfect happenstance. Focus on the crowd of 'schoolmates' in the background and you can see two boys clearly bitching about my having somehow won the glittering prize.

White T-shirt, white shorts, head that looks slightly too big, and a green ribbon pinned to my chest, denoting my house, St Chantal's. Let's have a look on the internet and find out what she is the patron saint of . . . How disturbing. The catholic-forum.com's extensive patron saint database doesn't offer a St Chantal.

Sports at the Alton Convent, however, remain significant to me for two rather unsporty reasons.

I well remember looking at the girls in their T-shirts and body-hugging blue shorts and thinking, 'They aren't shaped like us'. Down there, they sort of curved backwards. It got me wondering.

Another time, on the way up the path through the trees towards the football field, I was accompanied by William Hartnett (no, not Hartnell, that would have been too much to ask), who said the word 'Fuck'.

I might have known of its existence, but never dreamed it would actually be used.

That evening, when my parents and I sat down for dinner at the breakfast bar, I dropped my fork and, because of the glaring assonance, went, 'Oh, fuck'.

My world briefly caved in. I was forbidden from ever using the word again, and obeyed for several years.

These days, partly inspired by its brilliantly comedic use in Bruce Robinson's film *Withnail & I*, I bandy 'fuck' about far too often.

I consider the swear words to be among the most potent

and glorious in the English language. Sure, there are times when they sound purely ugly, and they do usually work better spoken than written. But when emphasis and emotion are required, sometimes 'Fuck' and its derivatives, bounded only by the imagination, simply cannot be beaten – though like my parents I would prefer to give them an 18 certificate. You have to know what you're doing.

(Actually, my Mum would probably like to give them an 80 certificate, but I really couldn't wait that long.)

Shock interlude: The Doctor said 'Hello!' to me yesterday! Not just 'Hello!' but 'Hello! How you doing?'

I had met David Tennant for a second time last week – having first interviewed him for the 2005 The Christmas Invasion special – for a *Radio Times* Readers' Q&A. They emailed in the questions, I put them to him. A decent monkey could do it.

He is fabulous. Smiley, charming, unpretentious, friendly, funny, quiffed. Am I getting carried away? To hell with dignity.

We sat in shabby-chic Soho House while he played raconteur with ease. I plan to talk him up still further – alongside the equally lovely Piper – at a later stage, so suffice to say here that he happily signed autographs for Dylan and a friend's two boys (and their Dad) and that I am hooked.

Anyway, I was in Newport at the same *Doctor Who* studios where the Tardis set resides and where the Autons were snapped, standing outside in the galling wind and drizzle, chatting to a member of the crew, when Tennant breezes past in his natty brown pinstripe Who suit.

'Hi!' he says to said Second Assistant (also a friendly chap). 'Hello! How you doing?' he says to me.

I swivel and reply, 'Hello. Yeah, fine thanks,' or something, while flying inside. I would never have offered a greeting first, lest he think me over-familiar. I worry that some people mistake this reluctance for arrogance.

It's pathetic, really. I'm 40 years old, a journalist of however many years, with a wife, a son, a mortgage, a favourite pair of cords I rarely remove, Sun-In in my hair, fear of both weight gain and exercise, and memories of sticky-back plastic – and I am over the moon that an actor six years my junior has acknowledged my existence. It made me wonder whether he is the nicest man on the planet, even though that can't be possible. What is it about our personal attachments to celebrated strangers? There are people out there who would be delighted to meet Eddie 'The Eagle' Edwards. Good luck to them. We all need someone that sets the mind to Happy.

It isn't that Tennant is 'famous' – celebrity is so very tedious – it's that he is the Doctor. It all trails back to childhood again.

That man I watched and adored aged four said 'Hello' to me 36 years later.

Wow.


When you aren't old enough to frequent pubs, towns can be dreary places. The situation is preferable before your teenage years, when you don't expect fun to seek you out and are prepared to use your imagination, or to settle for mere minor thrills.

Alton offered a central Market Square, with pubs on two sides, an auction room (which my mother became addicted to) and weekly stalls. Nothing for me there.

Up the High Street hill was the local Curtis Museum, then back towards the green which had no goalposts and busy roads to cross. Ditto.

More to my tastes were the park, with its swings, roundabout, see-saw and bandstand with ne'er a band, and Ackender Wood, which I knew as Anstey Woods for reasons I cannot recall.

In the park was a drinking fountain, one of those with a stainless steel bowl and spout. I supped from that one summer's day and a passing boy felt compelled to point out that I should use the tap, which made fresh water come out, rather than drinking from the bowl that everyone spat into.

The memory still makes me feel queasy.

Anstey Woods were far less hazardous, disease-wise. Hang a left out of the back gate, take the alley to White-down Lane, cross over the brief common, slide down the chalk slope on your behind, across the Basingstoke Road, looking right, left and right again, and the woodland opens up before you.

This was in the days before paedophiles lurked on every corner of a parent's concerns, so I was allowed to venture there alone if necessary.

You could either walk to the right of the trees, along a farmland border, or take the path straight through the centre. The latter, delving into the heart of the matter, had a more alluring, exploratory feel.

My favourite haunt was the fallen tree, a few minutes in, off and down to your right, but you could keep heading inwards until the stile, after which the path became wider and grassy, and the woods either side more dense.

The sense of isolation in there. You could stand still, draw a breath, hemmed in by nature, the cackles and caws of birds in your head, sun on your cheeks, and not a soul would disturb your existence. I am no loner, but because of my family circumstances I am easy in my own company. My childhood memories are crammed with such solitary, life-affirming sensations.

Feeling inquisitive, you could just keep on going until the path fizzled out and you found yourself picking your way between tree-trunks, through undergrowth. Somewhere in there, you might come across the broken brick structure, a former abode seemingly with no links to nearby humanity.

Were the trees allowed to grow around it after it was abandoned? Or did someone purposefully build it there, and if so, for what possible reason? Picturing it now, it brings to mind the setting for the buttock-clenching climax to *The Blair Witch Project*. Back then, I turned tail and ran all the way home.

Trapped indoors, weather not permitting, regularly on my tod, obsessions were allowed to build. It was time to start collecting.

Music would come later, though I should mention buying – or rather, getting my Mum to buy – my first single. Notably, the woman is less at home in a record shop than the average badger.

Terry Jacks' Seasons in the Sun came out in early 1974 and went to Number One. I must have heard it on *Top of the Pops* and can remember singing it quietly to myself in the Alton Convent playground.

Seasons in the Sun's tale begins with a boy the singer has known since they were 'nine or ten', with whom he used to climb 'hills and trees', which would have sounded right up my street. What I failed to realise was that said boy is now a man dying of cancer and this is the singer's sad farewell.

It obviously had a lasting effect. Check out my extensive LP/CD collections and you will find far more that you can weep to than dance to.

The Esso coins and Sugar Smacks *Doctor Who* badges of previous years had made more of an immediate impact.

I imagine every Who fan of a certain age remembers Weetabix's 'Doctor Who and his Enemies' promotion. It began in April 1975.

After the ignominy of missing out on the UNIT badge, I made sure that I collected the lot and then some. Swaps? Coming out of my ears. It was the first collection that really mattered to me: it was my favourite show, the illustrations were really cool, evocative and lifelike, and there were 24 to collect (in strips of four), so it took persistence.

Usually, I would only eat two Weetabix for breakfast, and

sometimes just the one. Suddenly I was wolfing down three and being told that I couldn't have any more. Mum had to start buying the family box, which had two free sets of Who strips. It all made perfect sense.

The cereal packet had a cut-out diorama on the back, so you could gaze at that, revelling in the detail, while chewing. Tardis interior, alien planet, volcanic landscape, underground caverns, alien forest, alien city. I never used them. I just stared.

There is something primevally delicious about ripping open packaging and rummaging inside, desperate to find a certain part of a collection. The horrible sense of disappointment when they are swaps (replaced later by a feeling of hope that another collector will need them, with your keenly eyed bounty in his own stash). The violent elation when they are not! And with perfect mathematics, that elation rises in direct proportion to the size of your collection.

Picture it. You need just the strip featuring two Tom Bakers (one running), Sarah Jane and a Dalek. You slide your hand down inside, between new box and 'bix. You clutch the plastic envelope with fingertips. You close your eyes, pull it free. Open them. It's two Tom Bakers, Sarah Jane and a Dalek! Endorphin rush! You jump up and down around the kitchen, crying, 'Yes! Yes! Yes!'. Your mother comes in, hoping the celebration is something to do with school results. You explain that it isn't. You've just completed your 'Doctor Who and his Enemies' Weetabix collection. She smiles unknowingly. You part company, you to play, she to wash up.

'What about your breakfast?' she calls out, spotting the unopened cereal.

'I've gone off Weetabix,' you call back.

Check out www.cuttingsarchive.org.uk and hit the Miscellaneous link. There they all are. As if it were yesterday.

Alpha Centauri, whom we know and love; Daleks, six of them; Lynx the Sontaran from The Sontaran Experiment; Ogron; Sea Devil; Silurian; Axon monster; Cyberman; Draconian; White Robot (from Patrick Troughton's The Mind Robber, which I had never seen – all the more alluring); Giant Robot; Ice Warriors (two); Aggedor . . .

You pushed out each perforated figure from its cardboard surround and placed a bent piece of card through two slots in its base, so that it could stand up. In theory. They weren't the most stable of figures.

To make matters worse, I usually played with them on the landing, where the orange and yellow carpet had furrows, which they could easily fall into. An Ice Warrior seems somehow less macho when it trips over the carpet.

It's funny how children play. I would pick up Tom Baker, hop him over towards a Dalek, put him down, shriek 'Exterminate!', pick up Baker to have him jump out of the way, grab an Ogron. The Ogron fires. 'Ptchoo! Ptchoo!' He misses! Shuffle in Alpha Centauri. 'Oh, Doctor!' Etc.

Let's be honest, it feels lame. Kids of today with their X-Boxes and PSPs would laugh me out of town. But it's all in your head, and there is the crux. Again, Doctor Who has fired the young imagination. This is your very own adventure, and it looks far better in your mind's eye than it would to the casual spectator.


Being so small and disposable, that collection disappeared into time's mists.

So I started collecting them again. Bonus. Except that now they cost money.

According to David J Howe and Arnold T Blomberg's – what is it with these sci-fi people? I could no more refer to myself as Nickolas J Griffiths, than I could Nick the Dick – marvellous Howe's Transcendental Toybox, which gathers together seemingly every item of Who promotion, merchandise and memorabilia ever issued, with photographs, original price and current values, even chocolates and thimbles, each figure is worth £6.50 in near mint condition.

Only this morning, I received in the post from an eBay seller, nine Weetabix Who figures, frustratingly four being doubled up as swaps. The cost? Just £3.20.

The pleasures of collecting are manifold, but none so great as the feeling when I held each one in my gaze and, despite all the intervening years, tingled with recognition.

I now have 13 of the 24, with a host of swaps if anyone is interested. I shall not rest until the remaining 11 are in my grasp. Then I shall store them in their plastic wallet, alongside the Doctor Who Typhoo tea cards, sweet cigarette cards and Sky Ray ice lolly cards (all complete). Though I will look at them only sporadically, the comfort and assurance that they are safely in my possession will follow me all the way to my grave.

## Some Things . . . I Have Collected

- Butterflies – Yes, it makes me feel a bit disturbed too. We had a butterfly bush in our front garden, which regularly attracted Pink Ladies, Red Admirals, Large Whites, as well as the odd Comma. Anstey Woods was a handy haunt, too. Between them, my parents made me a special, outsized butterfly net, and Dad added a vast cigar box, with custom-made perspex lid, so that I could display the things properly. I hasten to add that I only ever collected two of each species (to show front and back, natch) and that I never even saw anything remotely rare. Snufkin from Tove Jansson's Moomintroll books used to collect butterflies, maybe that's where it came from . . . Nope, no amount of excuses can stop it from feeling wrong.
- Tove Jansson's Moomintroll books – I have the lot. Her writing and illustrations define 'delightful'. I adore the

woman. I also managed to read complete sets of: The Hardy Boys, The Three Investigators, Jennings, William – I shall never forget when Dad came home from work clutching *William and the Space Rocket* – Willard Price's Adventure books, Sven Hassel, Flashman, Colin Dexter's Inspector Morse, the Columbo novels . . . and I think that's it. I read a lot as a kid and wish that were still the case. It surely propelled me towards a writing career (after several false starts).

- PG Tips cards – We drank a lot of tea. I'm more the Earl Grey sophisticate now. PG Tips used to give cards away in each box, featuring illustration and educational blurb, in a changing run of subjects. The first one I collected was The Race into Space. The Sea Our Other World, Prehistoric Animals, Inventors & Inventions . . . If you had given me a book on these subjects, I would have expressed some interest. Factor in the collectability, plus the special collector's albums, and I couldn't be grappled away from the things by monkeys. My education from them still comes in useful at pub quizzes. When I discovered that you could send off for complete archive sets, well, light my blue touch paper and stand well back! Even The Trees of Britain.

- Matchsticks – When I was in the second year at public school, I told my housemaster, who smoked copiously, that I planned to make a matchstick model of Junior House. God knows why. Delighted, he collected thousands for me. I stuck about two dozen together, which promptly bowed, and abandoned the idea.

- *Bullet* comic – Featuring secret agent Fireball. Catriona Klangsberg – that was his nemesis. All useful memories. My brother Max bought me the first issue in 1976 and I was hooked. I joined the Fireball club – arch rivals, those Warlord clubbers – and had the special Fireball pendant. Then, as a student, I started collecting DC Comics, which took me into specialist shops, where *eau de nerd* pervaded the air and quiet young men in dark attire studied the racks, avoiding each other's gaze. I should know, I was one of them.

- Stamps – Never really got into that one. More my parents' idea, no doubt part of a master plan to breed the brilliant uber-geek.
- Airfix soldiers – The small ones and the large ones, of all sorts of nationalities. The Germans always looked the coolest. I have a photograph of me, sitting proudly before a patiently set-up battle scene featuring hundreds of the buggers.
- Concert programmes – Until I realised what a rip-off they were.
- Concert T-shirts – Ditto. I still have my blue Big Country one from the Crossing the Country tour of 1983.
- The *Sun* – I read it avidly as a student and amassed hundreds. It wasn't so much a collection as laziness. Suddenly there were piles of tabloid all over my room and the prospect of throwing the lot away became daunting.
- Magazines – *Sounds* and *Select* (whom I wrote for), *Q*, *Record Collector*, *Smash Hits*. One day, wondering what the point was of these hefty piles of outdated information, I put the lot out with the bins. (In the days before recycling.)
- Action Men – More on those very shortly.
- Hats – Inspired by David Bowie. I didn't look as good in them as he did. Frankly, I looked like a tit in a hat.
- Tazos – Nope, me neither.
- Records and CDs.
- Video games.
- Musket balls.
- I think I'll leave it there.

I received my first Action Man on a birthday, my eighth or ninth. It was probably my only present. We were far bigger on Christmas.

But the effect it had.

Let's look at that Action Man dispassionately. It's a doll. In some trousers, boots, shirt and jumper, with a rubber beret. No socks. He has a scar on his cheek and a slightly perplexed look in his eyes. Why, we are not told.

His hair is the same flocking you find on the occasional Indian restaurant wall.

Take his kit off and he's all ball joints and rippling muscle, yet with no manhood. Mine, pointedly, came from the days before gripping hands. There never was an Action Woman.

And I had been given just the one of them, with his gun. No enemies to shoot at, no armoured vehicle to swan around in. Just me and him. 'Ptchoo! Ptchoo!' Bullets off into the ether of his solitude. (And mine.)

I know exactly why I loved Action Man so much – because there were so many more of them out there, just waiting to be amassed.

On the side of each box was printed a certain number of stars; the bigger the buy, the greater the number. Stick these tokens on to your collector's card for freebies. It was an early loyalty system.

According to the 1973 version I just found on the internet, ten stars (plus 10p P&P – how quaint) got you a guard dog; 12 stars, a sentry box; 15 stars, an Action Man tie (life size); 18 stars, a Mountie uniform; and, for 21 stars, top prize, the undressed Action Man.

I remember receiving in the post the guard dog, which had no moving limbs, it just stood there, and a free guy, naked as the day he was made.

For a few years, all I wanted was Action Men. Numerous birthdays and Christmases later, I had the Jungle Fighter (Aussie hat and machete), Talking Commander ('Action Man patrol, fall in!'), German storm trooper, French resistance fighter, Red Devil parachutist, whom I used to lob off the garage roof, British infantryman, machine-gun nest (with sound and flashing LED in muzzle), Scorpion Tank (the same one from Tom Baker's Robot), helicopter, chap with metal detector . . . There were others.

One pre-Christmas, when I went into the under-stairs cupboard to fetch Dad a tool, I spotted in the gloom a Scorpion Tank box. I must have sussed the Santa conspiracy by then and was happy that I would soon own such a craved vehicle, but gutted that I had found out.

Surprise is everything. Without it, you have stuff; with it, you have stuff plus wonderment.

So I told my Dad and he explained, thinking quickly, that it was actually some saucepans for Mum, which the shop-keeper had packaged for him in an Action Man Scorpion Tank box.

The likeliest of stories.

Yet I was so desperate to believe it that when I un-wrapped the present on Christmas morning, it was at least a partial surprise.


Still the oodles of official merchandise available weren't enough. I wanted more. So Mum offered to knit them some cardigans.

And I said yes, please.

It was so sweet of her, measuring up those man-dolls and getting out her needles. Several hundred knit-one, pearl-ones later, I had two reasonably fitting cardies, one in yellow ochre, one in vibrant green.

Then I took them to school. Show them off.

My friend David (the one who usually won sports day) and I were Action Man freaks. I forget – well, wouldn't you? – I suppose we just stood them up against one other and argued over whose had died first.

A teacher one time told us to write a poem and I penned mine about the Action Man Jungle Fighter. I remember it being praised, to my surprise, since poetry was for girls not me, and bizarrely I can recall one couplet, when our soldier hero spots a tiger:

'The jungle fighter comes along / And cracks a stick to scare it'.

Hardly a case of 'Watch out, William Blake'.

But those cardigans.

There is no way around it: I was the proud owner of the first and only Action Man Val Doonican.

When I see vintage Action Men, as those of my era are now called, my heart sings a short song. It's like *Doctor Who* – except that you really would look silly playing with a doll at my age – a nostalgia thing, a direct connection via the memory banks back to a time when cares were short.

To actually gaze at the same object you once owned, three decades previously, is like staring at a snapshot in a family album that had been lost in the attic. Boy, the thoughts tumble amid the mists.

I did visit a specialist Collector's Fair back in the late nineties and picked up a limited edition England World Cup 1966 Action Man. And the Action Man spaceman I never had. Yes, and his Space Capsule.

Leave it.

The worst aspect of that visit was spotting items that I had once owned, some valued at over £100, and which my Mum had put on her stall in the bric-a-brac market, to sell for a pittance. Anyone who knew what they were doing in there would have picked up the job lot and departed, cackling like a megalomaniac.

If you are that megalomaniac, I'd like my stuff back.

Not long after I started collecting Action Man, the Denys Fisher company began releasing their *Doctor Who* action figures, featuring: Tom Baker, his Tardis, companion Leela, Dalek, Giant Robot, K-9 and Cyberman. AND I NEVER EVEN KNEW ABOUT IT.

Was no one keeping their ear to the ground? Did these people not advertise in *Bullet* comic? Or *Whizzer & Chips*?

So once again, many years later I would have to start a collection from scratch, looking like a nerd, and to give you an idea of how painful it was, the *Howe's Transcendental Toybox* entry for the Giant Robot notes an original price of £2.95 and a near-mint value now of £325.

I don't have that item.

I shall talk about my *Doctor Who* collection later – I have the Cyberman, fear not, among a host of goodies – because here in our chronology the point is different: They Were Making Tom Baker Dolls. Though a ton of Dalek ephemera existed, no one had bothered to manufacture a William Hartnell doll or a Patrick Troughton doll or a Jon Pertwee doll. (The numbskulls.)

Something had happened.

*Doctor Who*, increasingly popular BBC entertainment, had become essential national family viewing. Tom Baker had become a God.

Alright, that's too hyperbolic. Tom Baker was becoming an institution.

That's fair enough.

During my first *Doctor Who* consciousness, an average of 7.5 million Brits were watching the show.

By Baker's final story of 1975, The Android Invasion, the audience had reached almost 12 million.

After that dodgy debut in Robot, the man had come up trumps. Everyone in the know remembers The Ark in Space with reverence. Only his second story. Such a turnaround. Within weeks, he had made the role his own. He was fabulous.

The goggle-eyes and giant grin, at first dumb, had become a trademark expression you longed to see. The hat, which he slapped on to his head as if there were never enough time, and the scarf that billowed behind him as he ran. The way he spoke. That sonorous drawl, the clipped bark, the portentous growl.

He could be the harbinger of all wisdom or the loudest chuckling of all pranksters.

If Pertwee was a father figure, Baker was your favourite uncle, the one who joined in, thought himself into your bonkers adventures.

And he was loving it.

I read that he had been plucked from a building site to play the Doctor. In fact, thinking back, I had read of it before he even hit the small screens. And it hadn't provided much hope – an actor reduced to labouring, offered one of the greatest roles in the universe.

Suddenly, his performances made perfect sense. He knew too well what he was capable of, but had never been given the chance to prove it. And now he was off and running. Unstoppable.

Among the stories of Tom Baker's early tenure are some nailed-on classics: Terror of the Zygons, Pyramids of Mars, The Brain of Morbius. Genesis of the Daleks, among the greatest of them all, was only his fourth tale. But let's begin nearer the beginning.

*The Ark in Space, for the unfamiliar – The Doctor, Sarah Jane and Harry land on Nerva Beacon, essentially an endless circular corridor. The crew, the remainder of the human race held in suspended animation, are being bumped off by giant walking wasps (the Wirrn) and their gross larvae. But it's the Doctor who has the sting in the tail: luring the baddies into an escape pod and launching them into outer space. Suck on that, wasp thing!*

*

*Doctor Who* has a thing for characters rolling up their sleeves, only to find some ghastly infection engulfing their arm. Jo Grant had done it in Planet of the Daleks, the icy scientist would shortly do so in The Seeds of Doom, and a hapless crew member does it here, after being infected by the Wirrn.

I remember being revolted by the luminous green trail of slime left behind by . . . well, you dreaded, gleefully, to think. Now here it was all over this man's arm, and there was something truly chilling about that.

Advance on a man and he runs away. Shoot him and he falls over. But infect him – that's so close to home. He is dying, but worse than that, he is slowly changing from normal human being into hideous alien. The very thing that horrifies him. And there is nothing he can do about it, other than watch.

Imagine if you woke up one morning, glanced in the mirror and half your head looked like, say, John Prescott's. You try to speak. 'What's happening . . . I don't do foreign food . . . to me?'

By midday, all you can say is 'Where's me Jag?' and your whole head has been engulfed by Prescott's.

I think you get my point.

Mention should be made of Baker's new companion, Harry.

He was sensible but a bit dithery, and a man. Somehow male companions don't work as well with the Doctor. Too same-sex.

I wasn't that bothered.

Fans of the new series will be thinking, 'What about Captain Jack?'

You're right. Captain Jack is glorious. He has knowledge, style, kinkiness and guns the size of bathtubs.

But the classic (as the differentiation goes) and the new *Doctor Who* are very different beasts. Though the basic elements remain – Tardis, Time Lord and companion, sonic screwdriver, Daleks – the Doctor now views his companions less patronisingly. As equals.

I never thought that Sarah Jane or Jo or any of the others from the past, who rose to a challenge, mollycoddled, were cool. Rose and Captain Jack are. You would happily be one of them in the playground if someone more alpha had already bagged the Doctor.

I devoured and loved every story from this Tom Baker era. Certain moments will always stand out, the ones that inhabit my memory in vivid Technicolor, which still party in my head like it's 1974–5.

## Genesis of the Daleks

Any appearance of Davros. What a creature. Half Dalek, half mummified man, with the PVC perv-jacket, the wires in the head, the third eye and the spindly fingers at his switches of doom.

Yes, there is the scene with the two wires – can Baker allow himself to wipe out the entire Dalek race, despite its nastiness? – but to the child that is merely compelling wordage.

Davros was so utterly evil and so incredibly ugly-beautiful.

The Daleks were bad enough. Here was the thing that created and controlled them. How powerful is that?

Yet he also looked so frail. That Dalek base he slides around in might look swish, but it's inescapably a wheel-chair. His skin looks so papery, his wizened, blind head looks as though it might pop like a dried seed pod if you pricked it.

I wanted to run over and punch him in the face, because I just knew it would hurt him. But I would have been way too scared to do so.

## Revenge of the Cybermen

Unbelievably, Pertwee's Doctor never once encountered the Cybermen during his original run (meeting the tin psychos only during his one-off return in The Five Doctors of 1983, fact fans). They were the final monster that William Hartnell faced and cropped up four whole times during Troughton's run – including an iconic appearance from London's drainage system, while St Paul's Cathedral loomed in the background – yet Pertwee didn't so much as glimpse them during his Tardis reign.

Heads should have rolled.

So this was my first view of Cybermen in action, and thrilling as that was, it isn't my most abiding memory from the story.

I see caves, dark, Gaudi-cathedral structures in rock, with pools of water, and I hear echoes. Voices sound tinny and reverberate. The Doctor isn't there and neither are the Cybermen. No, warring factions of the same alien race are facing each other off among the rocks, shooting guns that look like something out of Jules Verne.

They are the Vogans, and they look bizarre. They have arms and legs and oddly historical fancy dress; it's their heads. Bald, sculpted, elongated bonces with old man's white hair sprayed around the back, yellowy-green skin and eyebrows up to heaven.

The combination of all those factors in that scene . . . I can hear it now. Pttiiiing! Ptttoooow! Shuffle. Ptttiiiing! Groan.

I also remember that the Cyber Leader had black 'ears' and 'handlebars' on his head, where all the others were silver. He was the best one.

## Terror of the Zygons

If the makers of new Who don't one day bring this lot back, they are missing a trick. (And the Sea Devils, please.)

In repeated cutaways from the Doctor/companion action, we are offered tantalising glimpses of some kind of underground lair, orange, organic and knobbly, in which a grotesque hand belonging to an unseen thing gently squeezes controls in the shape of suckers.

Something bad is going on, and right near the Doctor. But what the heck is it? And when the Zygon is finally revealed . . . Imagine a flame-coloured foetus that got up and walked, and grew to eight feet tall, while fighting with an octopus. You're pretty much there.

## Pyramids of Mars

What a cracker this was.

Those Mummies are a work of genius. Great hulking brutes, wrapped in greying bandage, as if wrapped around WWF wrestlers. It was the sunken pools where the eyes would be, and the way the lower half of the chest became a perfectly flat slope. And that swaying, unremitting walk.

Any of the Mummy scenes lodge in the mind. The one where Sarah aims the shotgun at the pyramid spaceship while the Doctor, dressed as a Mummy, hovers at her shoulder. And, of course, the bit where the two Mummies walk into each other, sandwiching to death the poor poacher/gamekeeper/whatever-he-was.

## The Brain of Morbius

Again it's the monster. Well, what child wouldn't?

This was *Doctor Who*'s take on the Frankenstein story – and if you thought that thing was a monstrosity . . .

I remember lots of dark brown fur, almost a werewolf's

body, and that claw. Utter madness. The designer must have sketched a crab-like pincer and some bigwig looking over his shoulder went, 'Bigger. No, bigger. Bigger than that. Bit more. Bit more. Bit more. THAT'S IT!'

It is huge.

And the head. Another goldfish bowl – nothing wrong with that, as we have ascertained – with these ridiculous mismatched eyestalks, like something out of a crazed optician's lab.

This thing crashed around the lab, sweeping bottles and potions aside, lunging at the Doctor.

To remind myself of the plot I have just dipped into the BBC's *Doctor Who* website – essentially mad scientist wants the Doctor's head, to replace that ill-functioning goldfish bowl – and checked out one of the video clips.

The mad scientist, Solon, has just drugged the Doctor and Sarah Jane. The obligatory scientist's assistant, a meathead lunk with mono-brow named Condo, steps towards our unconscious hero and goes [grunting thicko voice]: 'We take head now?'

'We take head now?' Brilliant.

Slowly, very slowly, I made some friends in Alton.

Remember how I wouldn't approach a shopkeeper for a gobstopper, even though I was gagging for one? And how my lovely wife Sinead does all the talking to strangers on holiday, while I drive and hide? That sort of thing doesn't help when it comes to making friends.

It's hardly a bonus when you're trying to 'meet' girls, either. I don't recall ever approaching an attractive female stranger with a view to engaging her in conversation. (Yes, 'chatting her up' is the common vernacular, but in my case it would have been 'chatting her down'.)

Fear of rejection? Lack of self-confidence? Basic scaredy-cat? All those and more.

Once, in a blue-moon instance, I was in a club and one

particular girl kept looking over at me. When she and her friends huddled to gab, clearly about her bizarre choice of suitor, it couldn't have been more obvious that she was interested had she knitted a big quilt emblazoned with the words, 'DO YOUR WORST'.

Over the course of an hour, I danced closer to her in minute increments, my head pounding like a bouncing pig.

'Go on, just do it!' kept running through my mind.

'Don't be a fool!' my good sense demurred.

'But what have you got to lose?'

*'Where do you want me to start?'*

Every now and again her eyes would seek me out, gauging my progress towards her in nanometres, exasperation creeping in.

When I reached spitting distance, the lights came up.

I happened to walk past her on the way out and she sort of grimaced.


David Coppin, my best friend at the Alton Convent – I did use to abbreviate it simply to 'the Convent' but that would look weird here in writing, like I was planning to become a monk – lived near Basingstoke, which was way beyond cycling distance, and the few other boy-classmates, I hadn't bonded with well enough to mix with at weekends.

So I was obliged to hunt among the neighbourhood and fortunately Mum did the legwork for me, making friends with Mrs Jansen and Mrs Axtell along Highridge, both of whom had sons my age.

Actually, Mrs Jansen, who was Dutch, had three sons: Eric the eldest (that's my description, he wasn't a king from the Middle Ages), Ian and Rinus. Although Eric was nearest my age, I tended to favour Ian who was slightly younger, though I liked them both. Rinus was too young to bother with. No doubt he's the Dutch Prime Minister now, or something.

Simon Axtell was more of an influence on me. He had

two older sisters, so was more worldly wise than the Jansen brothers.

For a start, he was the one who told me the facts of life. (My parents would never have dared. I am dreading them reading certain parts of this book.)

We were in Anstey Woods at the time, swinging on a rope, and he just dropped it into conversation.

Far from being fascinated, I was appalled. If it were true – and I was deeply sceptical – it was so . . . biological. Why would anyone even want to do that, I wondered.

It was Simon, also, who introduced me to music.

My parents' record collection, housed in their hilariously ancient 'stereogram', which offered not only 78 r.p.m. but 16 r.p.m., was small and consisted of a series of musicals (*Oklahoma!*, for one), a genre I loathe to this day, a few singles (memorably The Beatles' I Feel Fine and Engelbert Humperdinck's Les Bicyclettes de Belsize, which I played repeatedly, in the absence of anything else decent), and an orange-vinyl version of Old MacDonald Had a Farm. Cheers.

Simon, via his sisters, had Fleetwood Mac's Rumours and Pink Floyd's Dark Side of the Moon.

I remember looking inside the Rumours gatefold sleeve – presumably after I had swallowed the facts of life – with its photos of the group members hugging, and Mick Fleetwood wearing his strange dangly balls, and thinking, 'There's something sexual going on here'.

Although I had developed a junior crush on the girl off ITV's *Black Beauty*, it was my first sense of proper titillation and I didn't quite understand what was happening.

Simon and I were obsessed with making camps. Perhaps it was because neither of us had been Cubs.

Anstey Woods was handy with all its foliage, but best was the side of his house, which had become a narrow storage space for tools and things, in the absence of a garden shed.

We put old carpet on the ground, used a frame of chicken wire for the roof, which we waterproofed with tarpaulin, and accessed the area via a disguised opening of clutter.

We had call signs. He would open wide his gob and go 'Aaaah-uh!' and I would reply with 'Uh-owww!', like we were distracted Tarzans.

Great times.

One of our favourite games was Grab the Farmer's Weekly.

Simon's father sold veterinary supplies, I think, and subscribed to the magazine. We would throw it on to his lawn then both dash for it and brawl while ripping the publication to shreds.

I have no idea what that was about.


I have a great photo of us from around this period. We're standing side by side on the driveway at Princess Drive. My hair is very blond and I have on my favourite *Six Million Dollar Man* T-shirt. He's lankier than me, blue shirt, reddish-brown flares, darker hair. We're both eating ice lollies.

You can see it in our faces: we are gorging on summer holiday and freedom. When the shutter is released, we'll be gone – the time it takes to line up a snapshot, a hindrance to our innocent desperation to make every fleeting moment count.


At least when no one else was around, I could occupy my time quite happily.

In January 1975, teenager Lesley Whittle was abducted from her parents' home and a nationwide hunt began, with huge press coverage. Her kidnapper – murderer, as it sadly turned out, Donald Neilson – was known as the Black Panther, and in all sincerity I decided to track him down and find the girl.

The influence of the Hardy Boys and The Three Investigators is hard to avoid.

I remember sitting in the car on one journey home from Southsea, and pointing out to my parents that there was a young girl in the back seat of the vehicle in front. Perhaps it was Lesley Whittle?

To my frustration, Dad didn't overtake, cut the driver up, slam on his brakes and send both vehicles skidding into the verge, so that I could whip open the car door and make a daring rescue of one of the four million young girls in the UK.

So I took it upon myself to become a secret agent.

I modified the box for my Gola football boots, which was orange and black and conveniently had a carry-handle. I made holes in the base, through which I threaded elastic, to hold in place essential secret-agent equipment such as: magnifying glass, toy gun, notepad, pen and torch.

Then I went off to Whitedown common and started hunting among the grass for clues, while keeping an eye on passing cars on the Basingstoke Road. (Swirling cigarette smoke and brooding dames, not shown.)

In the end it was the police who caught the bastard and, like my career as a rat-catcher, the detective agency fizzled out.

I had also developed a knack for swimming, so the Alton Sports Centre was a regular haunt.

Sadly, that was still being constructed when I learnt to swim, so I was forced to endure the Alton Open Air Swimming Pool.

Do you have any idea how cold an English open-air pool is in May?

It was no coincidence that I also took my Bronze and Silver Survival courses there. If you got out alive, you were happy. Sod the 100 Metres patches.

Neither was it the sort of place you would want to visit to pose in trunks, to impress the girls.

★

Not being that fussed about girls at the time, it was the venue chosen for my tenth birthday celebration.

Presumably Simon, Eric and Ian were unavailable that August, as it was Peter and Stephen plus mother, from Horndean, who drove up to accompany Mum and I.

It was a sunny day and the place was pretty rammed. There's a grassy area at the back with paddling pool for the toddlers and climbing frame, where we set out our picnic.

First, a boy challenges me to a fight when neither of us will concede access on the monkey bars. I imagine he is kidding until he punches me in the face and makes my nose bleed.

Then I tread on a bee which stings me between my toes.

To complete the celebrations, I suggest to Peter, who is still learning to swim, that we swim across the big pool. It isn't that wide, I urge him. Just doggy-paddle.

It is my mistake.

Halfway across, he starts panicking.

What the heck am I supposed to do?

He is splashing his arms manically in six feet of water and no one else has noticed. It is down to me. And I am too embarrassed to draw attention to myself and call for help.

Debilitating self-consciousness is fine until someone's life is at stake.

There is nothing for it but to swim under my friend and keep his head above water.

It is horrible. In his panic, he keeps pushing me under when I try to surface for air. Still no one has noticed.

I manage to push him off and begin swimming towards the side, but he is still floundering out there and I can't just leave him. Equally, I can't shout for help because people will stare at me. So I swim back.

I am expecting it all to end swiftly and without fuss, but that isn't happening.

Underwater for the umpteenth time, pressed beneath Peter's weight, I began panicking myself. I remember realising how serious the situation was becoming – far more serious than anything I had ever experienced, way off my young scope.

Though I am some distance from death's door, it doesn't seem that way, feeling his limbs battering against me, watching his torso writhe and the air-bubbles skitter upwards through my goggles. My time on earth doesn't flash before me – mercifully, as the popcorn would have been the best bit – and there is no corridor of blinding light.

Finally, I surface and there's a woman treading water next to us, looking concerned.

'Help!' I manage to blurt out, as I gulp in air and am plunged beneath the surface again, now way past the embarrassment stage.

I feel an arm around me and movement through the water.

A lifeguard pulls us out of the pool. Everyone stops and stares. This is more fun than swimming, they think.

The lifeguard sends Peter away and lectures me on not going into the main pool if I can't swim. Everyone earwigs.

What?! I am the one who can swim! I'm in the Alton Swimming Club, for flip's sake!

But I am too shocked and embarrassed to argue – it was entirely my fault, after all – and in my fug I fail to thank him for being the speediest, most eagle-eyed lifeguard I have ever encountered. I walk away, my entire body blushing.

My tenth birthday party.

I never saw Peter again. Sorry, Peter.

Next year I will be eleven years old. Ripe for senior school. Forced out of short trousers. And it doesn't feel as though I am remotely ready.

One moment, you think you know everything. The next, that assurance crashes. It's a dangerous world out there, where bad things even happen on birthdays.

How to cope?

Once again, I was grateful for *Doctor Who*. I have no religious faith. My peace of mind came from my parents and the sanctity offered by certain television programmes. And, admittedly, my soft-toy collection – Biggy (big), Whitey (white), Rupert (looks like Rupert) and Orinoco (a Womble, name already fixed, hence its incongruous originality) – with whom I have formed the TBA (Teddy Bear Association), who hold torchlit meetings under my bedsheets.

Unexpectedly, the BBC has done me a favour. While Tom Baker plays the Doctor, I can still get my comfort-fix of Jon Pertwee, who is currently installed as presenter of *Whodunnit?*

Anyone remember that gameshow? It was an earlier version of *Cluedo*, which ran in the early nineties, hosted most notably by Chris Tarrant.

Back then, Pertwee was the host and a panel of guest celebrities – Anoushka Hempel and Patrick Mower, among the regulars – was shown a brief, naff crime drama and invited to determine whodunit.

Doctor meets detective. Result, given that I had aspirations to being both.

According to an imdb.com user, *Whodunnit?* used to air on Monday evenings, perfect post-weekend fare. I was among its addicts.

I don't remember Pertwee wearing assorted safari suits, as another user mentions, nor his jokily referring to a 'past life' (as the Doctor). But I do, distinctly, remember being just so happy that he had not disappeared from my life altogether.

It must be a humbling point in certain actors' lives when they realise the power they can wield over the populace.

Pertwee, ever twinkling of eye on screen, seemed to revel in it.

★

It was time to plan my continuing education. I think because my parents had had no choice but to put my brothers through the comprehensive system, with this last crack of the whip they decided to throw their savings at mine. Public school it would be, then. I just went along with it.

There was a small hope of discount. If I passed a scholarship, it would mean £100 per year off the fees.

I entered. Or rather, I was entered.

The exam comprised written test and project.

'PROJECT SPACE By Nickolas Griffiths. Section 1 = Space. Section 2 = Man into space.' Handwritten. With a felt-tip drawing of a rocket passing over the moon.

Within the opening paragraph I had misspelt miniature ('minature') and put an apostrophe in 'camera's'. Though I was only ten years old, current me cannot help tutting.

Most of the research came from Ladybird books, a great book I still have called *The Apollo Story*, and from NASA.

I had written to the National Aeronautics and Space Administration in Washington DC, the people who put Neil Armstrong on the moon, and they had sent me an envelope stuffed full of factsheets and photographs. Among them was one of the Apollo 11 crew which is actually autographed by Armstrong.

I would love to know whether that is an original signature. A man who travelled a quarter of a million miles, who set foot on that shining circle in our night sky, might have taken a pen and connected with a piece of card that I own. That it would make it worth far more on eBay is immaterial. Really, I could never sell it.

Project Space is pretty startling stuff. Did you know, for instance, that 'The sun has been shining for thousands of millions of years and has enough hydrogen left to shine for many more'? (Many! Phew.) Or that 'The Americans had sent a lot of animals into space, 0 American animals were recovered alive but the Russians had 2 recovered alive'?

My favourite, though, is: 'Although I have studied many

books little is known about Apollos 7, 8 and 9'. What, no one at NASA bothered to write anything down about those missions? Or maybe their pencil leads broke? What I meant was, 'There isn't much on those missions in *The Apollo Story*, and I don't have any other Apollo books.'

Despite that, I passed the scholarship.

I remember taking the exam, in the Gavin Hall, where the assemblies and events are held at Lord Wandsworth College. It was intimidating, being deposited on that sprawling estate, where big boys did their learning and the teachers were called 'Sir', and sitting down to an exam paper, eight miles up the road from everything I knew.

David Coppin was among the seven of us, and would pass too and remain a schoolfriend.

The question paper went on forever, you just answered as many as you could. And when I got out, I had to ask my Dad what 'Apartheid' meant.

*Coming up: My first day at public school, I blub; the budding writer starts to pen his own* Doctor Who *story; Howard Jones'* What is Love *reduces me to tears; Tom Baker saves my sanity; and it's the Queen's Silver Jubilee Year, I get a free mug . . .*

## Chapter Three

*Age 11–12*

# Packed off to Public School

*'The definition of the word humanity is always . . . rather complex.'*
The Doctor, The Time Warrior

As luck would have it, Jon Pertwee returned to the small screen in yet another guise, come 1976, fronting a campaign for the Green Cross Code. Obviously, if you want someone the kids will trust, call a Doctor.

Google 'Splink' – for that was its name – and you may be fortunate enough to come across archive footage of the public information film. I was. And it all came flooding back. The action finds three young children of the seventies, boasting ice cream cones and carefree hair, planning to cross a road.

Pertwee's voice cuts in: 'Here's how to remember the Green Cross Code!'

If only that were true.

'Find a safe place to cross then stop. Stand on the pavement near the kerb. Look all round for traffic and listen. If traffic is coming, let it pass. When there is no traffic coming, walk straight across the road. Keep looking and listening while you cross.'

Can you find a Splink in there? That looks to me like Fsliwk.

Still no?

Alright, it's here, hidden away in: Safe, Pavement, Look, If, No, Keep.

It sounds like a Spaniard trying to offload pavements on English tourists.

At the end, Pertwee himself appears, silver curls akimbo, in brown shirt and jacket with outrageous collar.

'Well, now we'll all remember the Green Cross Code,' he declares wishfully. 'And use it!' Then he cries 'Splink!' so expressively that his facial muscles appear to have gone into spasm.

Should you have needed any further encouragement to love the man, there it was, right there.

He adored Britain's children. This was his way of paying them back for their dedication to his Doctor, once again keeping them safe from harm. It wasn't his fault that he was the face of perhaps the only public information message that ever required revision.

People mock the seventies, but I grew up in them and have few complaints.

The Sweet, Mud, Slade and Wizzard on *Top of the Pops*, in stack heels, flares for three and the sort of hair your mother wore.

Shang-a-lang? Why on earth not?

This was a time when blokes dressed as Wombles could sing about Banana Rock, and it not be considered a novelty record.

The hippies of the sixties had decided to become a little less earnest and that was cool for me.

My childhood had been pretty idyllic. Cosseted away by my parents from any working-class realities, my personal traumas involved punctured footballs and the prospect of stew for dinner. I had glimpsed the miners' strikes on television, the picket violence and the red-headed rhetoric of union leader Arthur Scargill, but that scariness had seemed a world away.

Children on documentaries these days talk of anger and depression. I doubt I even knew what the latter meant. So I was one of the lucky ones, allowed to have a childhood. But there was growing up to be done and it helps if you have a sense of the outside world.

Where was I off to?

An upstanding educational micro-community, cordoned off from society, where the only females for miles around served you glop that passed for curry in the dining hall.

On the positive side, I was so wonderfully naïve that I failed to realise it.

I have here a prospectus for Lord Wandsworth College which, given its black-and-white nature and the look of the pupils in its photographs, must have been the one that Mum and Dad pored over before becoming sold on the place back in the mid-seventies.

It is a terribly grand name, Lord Wandsworth College, which I have been obliged to play down on countless occasions. This was no Eton or Harrow, even if this marketing tool of the time seems rather austere.

Open the first page and you have a map of the school, spread out over 1,200 acres. The senior houses, gymnasium, Junior House, dining hall / master's common room, Headmaster's study / bursar's offices, miniature rifle range . . .

Among the Governing Body number: Sir Humphrey Prideaux, OBE, Lieutenant-Colonel The Lord Wigram, MC, John fforde and Hugh Podger. In that sort of company, the remaining two, Robert Marsh and Timothy Edwards, sound a little out of place.

The section titled 'Discipline' promises prefects but no 'fagging', punishments being restricted to 'minor intrusions on the offenders' time'.

There is the chemistry lab, overseen by a teacher I would come to know as 'Wig'; there, Mr Webb (Physical Education) on the athletics field, chest out, javelin in hand, looking exactly like someone from the army (which I believe he was); there the Gavin Hall on Founder's Day, the final day of the school year, when teachers took to the stage in their graduation gowns and parents of prize-winners waited in expectation, the ladies a smattering of expansive hat brims.

I am glad I was never shown it before I started there, because I would have run to Anstey Woods and hidden in the undergrowth, to live off beetles and grubs for the foreseeable future.

The summer of 1976 had disappeared into the diaries: the one that people remember as the long hot summer, of hosepipe bans and cracked earth. I can't pretend that I do, or only to step in line with the rest of my peers.

All of my summers were long and hot. Eight weeks off from school? Which grouch would conjure up an image of rainclouds and solemnity?

But now it is late September and I am in my Dad's white Rover. A vast metal trunk fills the boot, packed with rugby shirts and underwear, with 'NJG' stencilled on top. (It's now on top of my wardrobe, filled with paint tins.) On the back seat is my 'tuck box' – an entirely alien concept, since sweets usually travelled in pockets.

In the passenger seat sits me, eyes fixed ahead, petrified.

I am to weekly board, which means home at weekends, so there is light at the end of the tunnel, but that is of little comfort right now.

We arrive at Junior House as the evening descends, having negotiated the switchback country lane that runs through Long Sutton off the Odiham Road. I really don't want to get out of the car.

My Dad is with me, always a reassuring presence, but this

is part of the grand plan, for my benefit, and there is no going back.

Others are here, offloading their own trunks. Everyone seems to be talking in murmurs. Teachers mingle, smiling, encouraging. Making it worse. This clearly isn't home.

My tuck box is stored in the Common Room, among rows of other similar wooden boxes. I have never witnessed a scene like it in my life. So many boys my age, so much uniformity.

You can tell the First Years from the Second Years easily: they are the ones in shock. The Second Years are outside by the pool, or already in the Table Tennis Hut, cocky in their experience.

I know it's coming. And then it does.

My Dad says he has to leave.

I'm not sure I have ever felt more lonely.

## Some Things . . . that Could Reduce Me to Tears

- Certain songs – Often in conjunction with relationship trauma. All these (and more) have sent the salt-wash running: Bongwater's Psychedelic Sewing Room, Mad World (Gary Jules version), Billy Bragg's St Swithin's Day covered by Dubstar, Interpol's Untitled, Your Ghost by Kristin Hersh, She Just Wants To Be by REM, Springtime by Leatherface and, er, Howard Jones' What Is Love?
- The suicide of Stuart Adamson – The Skids/Big Country singer hanged himself in his hotel room at the Best Western Plaza in Honolulu, having battled alcoholism and become estranged from his family. I wished I could have told him how I saw his band a dozen times, wore a tartan headscarf without shame, punched the air, went 'Cha!' in all the right places.

- My Dad's hospitalisation – He hadn't wanted to tell me but Mum thankfully let it slip. Having breathing problems, he had been taken into Margate hospital. He was fine, she said, but it sounded serious enough to me. I got straight into the car and set off from North London to Thanet, and for the first ten miles I could hardly see because the tears would not stop. As it turned out, the other poor buggers in his ward were far worse off and I took him home that evening.

- Just thinking about my parents – Sometimes it sets me off. I've grown up knowing they are older than the average parent, so it's always there. The thought of losing them hangs like a dread sense in my subconscious and rises easily. Brilliantly, it hasn't gone away because they remain very much alive and kicking.

- Kindness shown to a stranger – I know it sounds naff, but there is way too little humanity in this world. When I see someone help somebody else out of difficulty, purely because they can, well . . . my cynicism just folds. Documentaries, the *News*, children in hospital, *Nanny 911* – it doesn't take much.

- Dylan's wedding speech – Unannounced, at the age of 11, after we speech-givers had all stood up and been frankly hilarious, my son took the microphone and said how happy he was for Sinead and I, then wandered away as if nothing had happened. It wasn't just me; several grown men were touched to tears. The kid will go far.

- The Rush concert that wasn't – Having failed my Duke of Edinburgh expedition – how I hate hill-walking and tents – I was obliged to retake on the same day that Rush (yes, Rush) played Wembley. When I returned, exhausted, my so-called friend Richard came into my room with two Rush tickets. Not thinking straight, I imagined he had bought them for us, for another date – until I noticed the missing stubs. He had gone without me. Elation turned to

94

despair. When my Dad picked me up, I couldn't speak, so exquisite were my sobs. Yes, it does seem odd.

- *The Dish* – I almost forgot this, the most pertinent instance. Anyone seen that 2000 movie, *The Dish*, starring Sam O'Neill? It's set at a tracking station in the Australian outback – think giant satellite dish and bush (plus obligatory romance) – where tiny-town technicians are being relied upon by NASA to beam back pictures of the Apollo 11 moon landing. They fail, the world won't see Armstrong and Aldrin. It's based on a true story. Normally when I cry, I know why. This one completely flummoxed me. When the actual moon-landing footage was shown at the end of the film, tears were streaming down my face, which refused to stop for many minutes. No noise, just rivulets, tickling my lips and soaking into my cloth-covered chest. Why? I can only guess, because those scenes had clearly touched something deep, deep down inside me. Perhaps what *The Dish* did was to bring home how bloody touch-and-go that moon mission was: inspired yet mere human beings – in 1969, back when a toy robot that talked could bring the neighbours out on to the porch – using transistors, tin-foil and tightly crossed fingers, sending three men a quarter of a million miles into the sky, for two of them to actually set foot on that shining, pitted dream-orb. Forget the tawdry politics behind the scheme. Forget the obscene billions spent. As a single act, it was the most audacious, outrageous, courageous, downright incredible, romantic, staggering and beautiful thing man has ever done. I had seen the Armstrong footage after the event; maybe no one had properly put it into perspective for me until then.

That first night in Junior House, I slept in a dormitory: foreign beds in rows with red blankets and white sheets, either side of one long room. We were all a long way from home but this was no holiday.

Though there was muted chatter, we were well aware of the time available to get to know each other. I do recall a forced conversation with one fellow First Year, Paul Adolph, who was shy like me but amiable, and nothing like his noticeable wartime namesake.

When a teacher appeared, to turn the lights out with a cheery 'Goodnight!', the place fell silent. If you had listened really carefully you might have heard 20 hearts thumping inside 20 middle-sized ribcages.

What the flip was I doing there? Where were my Mum and Dad? Why wasn't I back in Alton, watching telly and eating crisps? It felt surreal, not in a good way. Eventually, longing for home, I fell asleep.

Ahead of us lay this: regime, routine, posh clothes, all-male teachers with no bosom at all, discipline, more strange faces, school dinners, rugby, new smells (I shall come to the sewage farm shortly), a medical, bells. Oh yes, the bells.

At least it didn't take long to settle in. The young are easily adapted.

Being in an exclusively male environment wasn't the hardest part. Having just turned 11, I was only lately working out that you didn't always have to go 'Euugh!' when a girl appeared, and run away to play team sports or war games.

Neither was it the company of strangers. I already knew David 'DC' Coppin, although we would drift into different factions; of the others, some appealed, some didn't. The choice was wide enough.

Even our overseers, the House Tutors, seemed reasonable. Among them numbered: Mr Smith (maths), a grinning, well-built type known to the cognoscenti as 'Brick'; Mr Watson the chemistry teacher ('Louie', though his first name was Peter); Mr Webb ('Johnny the Webb'), the afore-mentioned PE teacher, whose (considerable) bark was far worse than his bite; and at the top of the pile there was the House Master, Mr Matson. 'Gin'.

He still used the cane. The very prospect made me vow to myself never to feel its nasty, archaic sting. Luckily I had always been a bit of a square.

Though it may sound daft, for this wide-eyed pupil, one of the worst aspects of new public-school life was the uniform.

Long black trousers, black leather shoes, white or blue long-sleeved shirt with collar, tie (black with thin red and yellow diagonal stripes) and jacket. Tweed in the winter, charcoal grey thing in the summer.

If there is an itchier fabric in the universe than tweed, I have yet to encounter it. Sore wrists, sore neck, where the lining didn't reach. And the weight. Every morning, when you hefted it on, it was like giving a boar a piggyback – and only got worse as you grew out of it.

The trousers were stiff or harsh or both and chafed my delicate skin; even the shirts, usually the cheaper polyester/cotton ones, failed to billow. They crinkled. Constricted around the arm by that bastard jacket, feeling like formerly screwed-up wrapping paper.

I even recognised which material my shirts were made from, craving pure cotton, and dreaded ripping a new plastic-mix thing out of its packaging, so that it could sit there, bolt upright on the bed, flaunting stupid creases a giant couldn't have ironed out with a boulder.

Your idea of soft and mine may well differ. Remember: it's the idiosyncrasies that maketh the man. Or in my case, the mithering wimp.

I loathed that uniform.

Every morning, a teacher would appear at an ungodly hour, ringing a sodding bell, with a cod-jovial cry of 'Wakey-wakey!'

The place had a bell for every occasion, morning, noon

and night. I suppose most educational establishments do; it's just that it feels rather like being one of Pavlov's dogs. (Again, not that I realised it at the time. 'Clang-clang-clang-clang!' Off I would dash, shiny-faced and desperate not to be late.)

So we Juniors would get up, perform our ablutions, peel on those clothes, have breakfast, then head off on foot up the 'Cinder Track' to the main school – a hefty trek away – to the Gavin Hall and Assembly.

Lord Wandsworth College is actually based within farmland. Occasionally you would have to avoid being run over by a tractor. And every morning, on the 'Cindy' – even crap roads could not escape un-nicknamed – I would pass the school's dedicated sewage farm. Two large circular tanks of treated . . . waste. Sometimes it wouldn't smell; other times, it was like ramming your head into the toilet bowl pre-flush.

You would cover your nose with your jacket and sprint.

No doubt it was all character-building.


Weekends were my Holy Grail during that time of adaptation. I craved home and that panacea: familiarity.

If there was no rugby match – and I was dim enough to have landed myself in the under-12s team – my Dad could pick me up after morning lessons on a Saturday. (Yes, we became educated at weekends, too.) Otherwise, he'd meet me post-match, which could mean into the evening if we had played away.

I had been looking forward to it since Monday.

Getting into the car and being driven away, back towards Alton and my settled environment, of favourite cushion, Action Men and *Doctor Who* . . . Aaaaand exhale.


Was Basil Brush on Saturday evenings during this time? My mind's eye is showing Basil Brush then *Doctor Who* on a Saturday teatime, BBC1.

'Ah-ha-ha! Boom! Boom!' Daft story featuring Dirty Gertie from Number 30. Then that awesome theme tune. 'Wuh-duddly-do wuh-duddly-do wuh-duddly-do wuh-duddly-do . . . Wuh-oooooooooo-ooh!' Or thereabouts.

Is it the greatest TV theme tune of all time? It's certainly up there. I would not dare try to put these in any order other than alphabetical, but my top three would be (and look what comes out highest):

- *Doctor Who*
- *The Persuaders*
- *The Sweeney*

I enjoyed *The Persuaders*, but it was just a little too daft, all that backwards-glancing at ladies' bottoms. The theme tune combined with those opening credits – Lord Brett Sinclair and Danny Wilde's formative years, told through colour-washed newspaper cuttings – were a marriage that knocked into a cocked hat anything that followed.

Composer John Barry, also the man behind the James Bond themes, could have eked sex, intrigue, sophistication and longing out of two stones knocked together.

*The Sweeney* was a show that I quickly became addicted to, though it was on late, a little racy, and I wasn't always allowed to stay up.

To me, its theme tune was a siren song. Were I lying in bed, unable to sleep, it would drift up from the lounge and draw me out on to the landing, where I would sit in my pyjamas, calling, 'Dad? Dad?' softly and then more audibly, in the hope of being allowed back downstairs.

Of the three, *Doctor Who*'s is easily the most iconic. You could probably play it to someone in Taiwan and they would dutifully hide behind a sofa. Here in Britain, it must be up there with Happy Birthday and God Save the Queen in terms of recognition.

Ron Grainer was the composer – for years I was convinced he was Ron Grainger – and it was 'played' by Delia Derbyshire. Ron. And Delia. Concocted that banshee wail. How had they even known where to begin?

It is feasible that with something less startling and downright unsettling, the show might never have made the impact it did. It surely grabs your attention, makes you wonder. One woman wrote to the *Radio Times* and complained that the *Doctor Who* theme tune 'petrified' her son.

When I was researching this book, asking friends to reminiscence about our shared Who pasts, one told me that she used to have to listen to it from another room.

It disturbed me, too.

It's the combination with those abstract, swirling visuals that hits home, the way the incumbent Doctor's face appears from within the feedback, but that electronica simply drills into your gut and puts it on spin cycle while the echoes mess with your mind.

I love it.

With the Fates perhaps feeling sympathy, that first term weathering the induction into Lord Wandsworth College coincided with some of the best *Doctor Who* stories ever.

That batch from season 14 (I had already looked that up for the Foreword) involves: The Masque of Mandragora, The Hand of Fear, The Deadly Assassin, The Face of Evil, The Robots of Death and The Talons of Weng-Chiang.

To appreciate how amazing that selection is, I have to list my Top Ten *Doctor Who* stories ever. Classic series only. How many of the above will make an appearance?

This may take some time, though you need not notice – not only am I deciding for the first time ever, having stupidly avoided such a thrill previously, but I plan to rank them in order.

Hang on, I'll time myself . . .

★

Thirty-eight minutes, 12 seconds. It could have taken far longer, but you don't want to dwell on these things: that way madness lies.

My process? Look down the lists of story names for each Doctor in the BBC website's episode guide, conjuring up recollections (if warranted) and noting down the most vivid. I admit to not even glancing at Colin Baker or Sylvester McCoy's tenures; I have visited both Doctors on video, my reactions ranging from mild enjoyment and surprise to unadulterated outrage.

I ended up with a shortlist of 22: no William Hartnell (his Doctor was such an ancient grouch, for my tastes, and the stories too monochromatic in my mind, though major respect is due for the man who started it all off), two Patrick Troughton (black-and-white, yes, but the 'edutainment' of Hartnell's reign had, come Troughton, made way for some serious iconography and surrealism), five Pertwee, 14 Tom Baker and one Peter Davison (whom we shall come to).

And here – curse this writing lark which lacks the long-trumpet soundtrack of fanfare – hang on, try this – 'Toot-de-poot-de-toot!' – is . . .

## Nick's Top Ten Doctor Who Stories Ever

1. The Deadly Assassin
2. The Talons of Weng-Chiang
3. Pyramids of Mars
4. The Robots of Death
5. The Daemons
6. Horror of Fang Rock
7. Terror of the Autons
8. Genesis of the Daleks
9. The Android Invasion

10. The Mind Robber
(I have to honourably mention 11 and 12, The Sea Devils and State of Decay, which I had a hell's own job discarding.)

Seven of those are Tom Baker's, despite my adoration of Pertwee, whose stories can drag in retrospect. At least his classic The Daemons (devil worship, Morris dancers and a walking gargoyle which UNIT actually hit but fail to wound) hits a spot, just above some obligatory Autons. And that's Pat Troughton's mind-bogglingly weird trip into storybook-land, The Mind Robber, scraping a spot.

Now, I make no bones about this: everyone on the planet should watch those ten stories. Among them is some of the greatest escapist entertainment you will ever witness.

The sets may wobble on occasions, the monster costumes may have glaring joins or feature some noticeable silver-painted kitchen equipment, certain performances might be slightly pantomime and the special effects will most definitely look outdated – but those are not the point. Ignore them. Or, as I do, bask in them. Slick does not always mean most fun.

And I can hear you out there, Whovians of a 6 to 10 rating, muttering darkly.

'What about The Caves of Androzani?'

'*The Android Invasion*?! Ptoooii.'

I don't deny you the right to splutter. That is half the point of the making of lists. Enjoy the indignation.

Mine is a very personal list. I make no concessions to historical importance or script innovation or technical prowess or Who lore: some clever arc back to events on Metebelis 3 or a sacrilegious rewriting of the Time Lords' history.

I included The Android Invasion because . . . well, weird types in space suits whose faces fall off taking over curiously abandoned English village. What fool wouldn't?

Those ten are simply the stories that touched me the most.

Within that list, from season 14 of my Lord Wandsworth beginnings, come numbers 1, 2 and 4 – that's how much they meant to me.

Why The Deadly Assassin?

It feels so utterly stand-alone. The most unique of *Doctor Who* stories. Not just because it is the only one never to feature a companion, but in its style. It's like an episode of *The Prisoner*, only far better. You could actually follow this.

I love surrealism, and The Deadly Assassin is out there. It features the return of the Master, since Pertwee's days and the untimely death of Roger Delgado. How do they bring him back? Not in the guise of Anthony Ainley, which happened later: a lookalike who did a decent job but who could only ever be second best in the eyes of those who had witnessed Delgado. No, they brought him back as this black-cloaked, rotting, animated corpse who lived in a grandfather clock.

The story essentially finds the Doctor trying to escape from an alternate reality, hunted down by a mysterious assassin. Man. The scene in which Baker's brown leather boot is trapped in the train track, as the locomotive thunders towards him, whistling and pumping out steam. The sequence where he is buzzed by the biplane, straight out of Hitchcock.

I could tell that Baker was in his element. No companion. No distractions. I always sensed that he barely put up with certain of his co-stars.

'Now this is me!' he was declaring.

This story had Mary Whitehouse up in arms, for the cliffhanger ending in which the Doctor nearly drowns. Good. Whitehouse stood up to be counted for what she believed in, and nations need people like that, but she was a delusional, ancient killjoy harpy with no sense of what made people under retirement age tick, and we don't need any of those.

Complaining about The Deadly Assassin should have warranted a term in a padded cell.

## Why The Talons of Weng-Chiang?

This story and Horror of Fang Rock (Agatha Christie's *Ten Little Indians*, set in a lighthouse) are the two that I have watched the most, purely because I bought them both on DVD despite already owning the videos.

Think Sherlock Holmes meets Fu Manchu (and indeed there were complaints about the portrayal of Chinese immigrants, as Britain began to consider being PC).

The characters, the storytelling, the delight of the actors in their roles, the blunderbuss, the music hall, Louise Jameson in Victorian underwear, Tom Baker in a deerstalker, the sideburns, the buffoonery, the genius, the mysticism, the gothic horror – all that plus one of the most genuinely scary and one of the most unintentionally duff adversaries ever. The Talons of Weng-Chiang has everything. It rollicks along.

Those adversaries. Mr Sin, the Peking homunculus. Just calling him a homunculus worried me. I had no idea what one was, but it didn't sound friendly. He's a tiny chap with white-painted, leering face in Oriental garb, supposedly a puppet operated by the magician Li H'sen Chang, but by night his eyes flicker open and he wanders the Victorian London streets clutching a stiletto blade. He is so very real.

Far less real is the giant rat mutation that waddles through the sewers. Giant rat? Only a seriously engrossed child of four might be taken in. It looks more like stock doing a runner from Carpet World.

These days, it would be rendered in CGI. Back in February 1977, the computer graphics were nowhere near sophisticated enough. So the designers did the best they could with the resources to hand, and though they failed dismally, that only makes my heart grow fonder.

## Why The Robots of Death?

There's a smack of the *Ten Little Indians* about this one, too. What justifies its rating? The palpable sense of claustrophobia – and those Robots. The designers only occasionally messed up; usually they innovated on a budget of magic beans, and these babies are a triumph.

I bought an actual Robot mask used for this story some years back, from a toy dealer in London. It's in my lounge, on top of the bookshelves, and every now and again I take it down, put it on and look at myself in the mirror. Usually when I am alone.

It's quite heavy but it sits over my head perfectly, as if it were made for me. I can hear and feel my every breath bouncing back off the resin, just as did the actor who wore it, and see myself (T-shirt, jeans, Robot head) through the small holes drilled into its eye sockets. It's strange, but the design is so menacing that it makes me feel slightly unnerved, even though I do realise it's me under there.

Quite apart from their legacy, those masks are beautiful objects, verging on the art deco. Smooth curves, prominent chin, sweeping nose, cheekbones and a sculpted, rather seventies hairdo which might have been modelled on former *University Challenge* quizmaster Bamber Gascoigne's.

In the story, a handful of these Robots have been reprogrammed by a renegade crew member, the deliciously named Taren Capel, to kill all humans on board the spaceship. On such a mission, the effects people made their eyes glow a fizzing red.

Over on the side of good are the Doctor, Leela and another Robot, one of the dim ones, from the dunce division. A true underdog story. I don't want to give too much away, but I never thought I would sob when a robot died.

No, hold on, there was also *The Iron Giant*, when we all thought he was a goner. With a five-year-old Dylan next to me at the cinema, I had to surreptitiously wipe my cheeks so as not to seem un-Dad-like.

\*

So, Leela. The one who supposedly got all the Dads hot under the collar. She was brought in as titillation, all chamois leather skimpies and exposed flesh, primitive and spunky. By then I was old enough to notice, but not so old that my collar didn't remain at room temperature.

To me aged eleven, Leela was far more than a clothes horse for a lack of clothing, who only improved once the producers started giving her chunky jumpers. Louise Jameson somehow inhabited her with such conviction.

Jo Grant was childlike, Sarah Jane Smith was inquisitive. Leela had both those qualities, but would run towards danger rather than from it. It's how every child would like to imagine themselves in the same *Doctor Who* situations.

In my daydreams, I didn't see myself fleeing from the Daleks and the Cybermen, squealing like a tot with a freshly filled nappy. I was there at the Doctor's side, wielding a series of life-size Action Man weapons, gunning the crap out of them.

One last memory from season 14, from The Masque of Mandragora: the way Tom Baker rolled his tongue around the phrase 'Mandragora Helix'. Glorious.


Just as I used to long for Saturday and its tea-times, so I dreaded the corresponding hour on Sundays. *Songs of Praise* was not merely a bunch of Christians with mothballs in their pockets, gathering in unprecedented numbers for television cameras, it signalled the End of the Weekend.

Each successive hymn – well, there was bugger all else on telly at that time on a Sunday – was a further butterfly in my stomach.

Not that school was so bad. I would simply rather have been at home.

Even as I grew older those butterflies never went away, they just became smaller. Meadow Blues as opposed to Red Admirals (for those in the know).

My Dad gave me a brilliant tip one morning, on the drive back to Lord Wandsworth: always think in terms of the day after tomorrow. So, even on a Monday, the day after tomorrow is a Wednesday. Halfway through the week! By Wednesday the day after tomorrow is Friday – so close to home-time. It actually worked.

After Thursday, stop, or your weekend disappears. Saturday, using the same mind-games, would be a positive disaster.

Now I am going to astonish you.

I have a Tardis. And it works. (With limitations.)

I can travel back in time.

I can travel back in time to 1977 and I can relive the events of that year. Up until 7 July, that is, when detailing the minutiae of my existence in my Letts Schoolboys Diary became too much to bear.

**January 1, Saturday**
'Played with Simon. Going with him to Frensham tomorrow.'

A few days later, I was back in the jug again.

**January 10, Monday**
'Went back to school again. Had assembly. First baths.'

**January 11, Tuesday**
'Received dad's book through post. Had bath.'

**January 12, Wednesday**
'Got 30/30 in maths test. Fire alarm at 9.10.'

**January 13, Thursday**
'Had terrific blizzard, got soaked after snowball

fights. Got pencil lead through finger. Went to san.'

**January 14, Friday**
'Rang mum to say it was a half Saturday. Trousers dry. Had bath. Got large plaster on finger.'

Boy, it rolls back the decades.

A few notes: I have no recollection of that obsession with bathing. 'Half Saturday' meant no rugby match so home at lunchtime. The 'san' is the sanatorium, the on-site health centre, where a male doctor will soon feel my testicles while asking me to cough, and ask me to pull back my foreskin, both of which strike me as unnecessary. And was my life really so meaningless that I had to note in a diary when my trousers were dry?

The entries shortly become more detailed, as if I am in the grip of lifestyle masochism. Here are some excerpts:

'Had game of running around' – 17 January

'Got towel exchange' (i.e. exchanged clean towel for dirty one) – 19 January

But the highlight of that first month is this double-header:

'Diary got a bit ripped' – 24 January

'Sellotaped ripped page together' – 25 January

Indeed, that page today remains held together by browned tape, a testament to my ability to eke out tension for 24 hours, and to a blind denial that not everything is newsworthy.

I did manage to maintain a few fruitful interests.

- I was an obsessive fan of Liverpool Football Club, just as small boys these days become fans of the team at the top of the league. (Actually, I'm fairly certain I went for second-placed, make a game of it, at a time when Liverpool were just behind Leeds.) I bagged match reports from the Junior House newspapers and glued them into a scrapbook titled 'Liverpool Rule OK'. My Dad got his work's driver to bring me back pendants and souvenir editions of the *Liverpool Echo* from Merseyside. And my parents bought me bright red Liverpool shorts to wear, though not the official shirt which was over-priced. At school, if we Liverpool supporters – and there were a few of us, from Hampshire – were really lucky, we were allowed to stay up to watch the big European ties on television. Keegan, Toshack, Fairclough, Case, Neal, Clemence . . . As a Spurs fan now, actually close to home, I shouldn't get too misty-eyed.
- The House had a model-making club which I joined. Snobbery was rife. Though I was a member of the Airfix Club, whose President was bizarrely Dick Emery, the comedian who often dressed as ladies on-screen, those in the know bought only Tamiya kits, made in Japan, and spent ages with pins painting pupils in the soldiers' eyes. So I did that too. Loyalty counts for little under peer pressure. Some time around 1995, when I would have been 30, I decided to resurrect my interest in model-making and bought a Dalek kit. My former patience had deserted me and I rather rushed it, painting over bits long before they were dry, though the results were not so haphazard that visiting friends did not pour scorn. Rightly so.
- And, through my love of reading, I had begun to write my own short stories . . .

**March 15, Tuesday**
'Started to write Domain of the Zyclotrant. It is

excellent. Missed bath. I can't understand why though.'

Domain of the Zyclotrant. I wonder what elicited that title?

The tale, fortunately, hasn't survived, as I doubt whether it really was 'excellent'. News of the Cold War had obviously filtered through to me somehow, because all of my early short stories concluded with everyone dying in a nuclear war. No doubt the Zyclotrants ended their days cowering under a kitchen table, covered in sores and pestered by flies.

But there *Doctor Who* is again, inspiring something approaching creativity from a youthful imagination. And here I am today: a career writer. It's kinda beautiful.

If public school life is beginning to sound rather carefree, it was and it wasn't.

Though I was learning to enjoy myself, that old fear of authority still ran through my psyche. I so remember being unable to sleep one night because I thought I had lost my pencil case.

I simply didn't understand the naughty boys. Why would anyone risk bringing wrath and punishment down on themselves for the sake of breaking the rules, showing off to we mere hand-wringers who toed the line?

I found myself mingling with both the middle-ground, the class I was deemed to occupy as someone who played sport, didn't wear glasses and wasn't habitually waving an arm about in class going, 'Sir! Sir! Sir!', and the sidelined nerds, because I could empathise and sympathise. The cool bunch felt out of my league, and anyway it was occupied largely by posers and the occasional bully.

There was one git who shall remain nameless who used to derive vast pleasure from grabbing my ear and twisting it until it really hurt, forcing me to run some petty errand for him. I dreaded bumping into him, knowing that it would lead to pain, which spectating sycophants only encouraged.

I still bear him the tiniest of grudges and wonder whether

one day I might pass him on fire in the street, at a time when my bladder is the only source of dousing liquid. I may have to think twice.

It would take so many years to realise that I wasn't obliged to worry about what every Tom, Dick and Harry thought of me, but that first year at least saw the beginnings of it.

I grew to dislike rugby, very quickly. When I started at Lord Wandsworth, I was among the smaller boys and remained that way, not achieving a height that could offer some confidence until I was nearer 16.

Unfortunately, every rugby team needs a short, suicidal idiot to play hooker.

The hooker is at the very centre of the scrum, with a lunk of a prop under each arm: the so-called 'front row'. The eight forwards 'bind together': a matter of grabbing shirts, shorts, collars, and clinging on as if to flotsam while lost at sea, to pull the scrum tight.

The opposing front rows then bend over and everyone shoves forwards, interlocking the two teams in one mass of primal grunting, often involving the hooker banging his head.

Finally, the scrum-half puts the ball in and the hooker tries get his foot to it first, to flick it backwards among the legs of his own team.

Degree in rocket science not required.

I tried hard basically because I didn't want to get told off.

The fateful day was Wednesday 2 February, 1977:

'Had a rugger practice with Wally. The U12s team was put up. I was picked as Hooker. Found a key. Bought tuck. Got 10 pence out of house bank. Owed 1p.'

Where does one start?

The fact that I referred to rugby as 'rugger' appals me also, but then we all did it.

'Wally' was my maths teacher, Mr Davidson, a Geordie who also coached the juniors. He was my favourite. A few of the teachers had a whiff of institutionalisation about them. He didn't. He was strict but fair and laughed easily.

Sometimes he would let a bunch of us into his room before lights out, to chatter and listen to music. He liked Fleetwood Mac's Rumours and I remember discussing the band with him one evening while the album played, and noting that Lindsey Buckingham was a bit of all right. He had enough decency not to point out that Buckingham was the male lead guitarist.

And it was Wally, I seem to recall, who gave me my first nickname: Rover. Because he said I looked like a dog. He meant it nicely though I'm finding it hard to reason how at this very moment.

So he has picked me for his team. My reaction? 'Found a key.'

And that 'Owed 1p'. Anyone who imagines all public schoolboys to be wading through cash, think again.


We played in all weathers, even when there was snow on the ground.

Some bright spark advised that you could warm your hands by putting them inside your shorts, as the willy area retains some heat. Scant consolation when you're eleven.

Deep Heat was the embrocation of choice, massaged into the thighs for warmth. The changing room soon reeked of it, and I quickly grew to associate its cloying, acrid stench with my own trepidation.

Saturdays were match days. We would run out on to the pitch at the back of Junior House, metal studs rapping on concrete like small, demented drummers with no sense of timing. Schoolmates, forced to spectate, would line the field, cheering half-heartedly or sulking.

Our XV would eye up their XV. I wasn't looking for possible strengths and weaknesses in their line-up, I was assessing my chances of survival. And some of those kids were enormous. Genetic mutations. A couple of the fuckers had beards!

Worst was when the opposition kicked off the first half. We would adopt a position on the field which related to where we stood in the scrum – which placed me right where the ball was likely to land.

Everyone at the start of a game of rugby (besides me) is fired up. They want to assert their machismo, smash into tiny pieces the first poor bugger with his hands on the ball. I'm desperate not to catch the kicker's eye, in case he spots me and thinks, 'Right, he'll do'. Of course, he usually does, alerted by the pungent scent of my fear.

He kicks. The ball flies into the air. I follow its arc. Sweet Jesus, it's heading for me. All hope is lost. I catch the ball. (Actually, that didn't always happen. Sometimes I fumble it and it bounces all over the place while people who actually care tut into their mufflers.) I turn my back to the opposition, whose halitosis is within nose-shot, offering the ball with outstretched arms to team-mates. Any team-mate. Just take it! But I know it is too late.

Whumph! A massed series of meatheads has piled into my rear, removing vital air from my lungs, distorting my spinal column until it resembles an interesting hatstand, and sending my kidneys into shock.

After that, things can only get easier.

Away games were the same, only we all climbed into a minibus first and had to drive to somewhere glamorous like Reading. Though we often won our matches, it was rarely down to me.

★

I came 6th in class at the end of that first Spring Term, according to the diary. Respectably above-average, no cigar. Academically, I would remain that way for the entire seven years at Lord Wandsworth. Parents appeased, job done, without any great billows of stogy smoke.

At least I had settled in.

### June 6, Monday (Spring Holiday)

'I saw the Queen light the beacon. I reckon it was already lit from the inside. Also saw the firework display.'

Another diary entry full of emotion, for the Queen's Silver Jubilee celebrations – 25 years since Elizabeth II had ascended to the throne.

Funny that phrase, isn't it? Ascended to the throne. I've seen photographs of the Coronation, and it's only a few mouldy old steps.

The British seem less impressed by royalty these days. Back in 1977, there was a national sense of jubilation. Wartime spirit clearly still lingered. There were street parties all over the news, cute girls clutching flowers, regal walkabouts and anyone caught not waving a Union Jack was stoned to death by Pearly Kings and Queens.

I remember watching the Queen light that first beacon on television, after which others were lit all around Britain's coast. Sadly I don't recall the ensuing firework display, which is strange because I'm a sucker for a well-packed rocket.

Though my diary entry is noticeably cynical regarding Her Majesty's beacon-lighting prowess, I was definitely taken in by the fervour – although we had, it must be noted, been bribed. Every child in the country had received a free Silver Jubilee mug, made of glass and with a golden crest and inscription. Mine met its Waterloo on the kitchen floor after only a couple of weeks.

(The only other time I received a free commemorative

glass was at the end of the Guinness Marathon in summer 1986. My student friend Martin had invited me along to the event – a charity walk of 26 miles, from the outskirts of London inwards, setting off at 6 a.m. – with the lure of free Guinness along the way. Free booze! It was only a shame that I discovered I didn't like Guinness and that 26 miles is a bloody long way, even walked.)

### June 7, Tuesday (Jubilee Holiday)
'I went into Alton. While walking down the street I saw a sale in a sweet shop. Then saw procession. Got lost in fair. Went into torch procession. Got lift back.'

Though the words fail to capture it, that torchlit procession up Alton's High Street was pretty magical. I can still picture my torch: thick cardboard tube, blue stripe spiralling up its length, with a solid honey-coloured candle jammed in the top and a circular guard to stop dripping wax falling on to the bearer's hand.

Other than on market days, when biddies with an eye for a bargain thronged the square, Alton delivered little sense of community spirit. Not that evening. There must have been hundreds of us, walking up that hill – in the middle of the road, mind – clustered together under the bruising sky, flames held aloft, a collective sense of wonder.

Then I got a lift back.

We were definitely a family of royalists. On the precious few occasions when I shared the lounge with my Dad as the BBC shut down for the night, he would stand up when the Corporation played God Save the Queen. I always thought it was rather odd.

Enos Norman Griffiths – known as 'Norman', being the best of a dodgy job – was born a long, long time ago and never knew his father, who survived the trenches of World War I but died of pneumonia in Abbeville, France, in 1917. Wow. Writing that brought tears to my eyes. The tendrils of a family tree are powerful indeed.

His parents had been dairy farmers in the Black Country of the Midlands and his widowed mother moved with son to Croydon, where she would marry a copper and Dad would meet my Mum, Lilian Naylor (one of seven children). He was working as an apprentice toolmaker; she turned up one day as a trainee inspector.

At this point in the tale, I have some problems. Dad tells me that he was known as a bit of a hard nut back then.

My Dad? Hard? That generous soul with his soothing voice and gentle manner, who shrinks slightly with each passing day? I started to tower over him when I was 17! I reckon by the time he's 100, I shall be able to fit him in my pocket.

But I trust his assertion is true.

The story goes that a workmate spotted Lilian, a looker by all accounts and only 15, during a tea-break, and declared, 'I'm going to ask her out!'

'No you're not,' says my Dad. 'I am.'

And he did.

My Mum didn't turn up to their first date. Her mother, a fearsome type, had told her she was too young to 'go with boys'. Neither did she turn up for work the following day, so Dad went round and knocked on the Naylors' door. Mum shoos him away and Ma Naylor sends brother Les after him, have a word in his ear.

Les and Dad fail to come to blows and instead get on like a house on fire. The rest, as they say, is history.

I pressed my Dad further. He isn't one for romantic declarations. Though my parents send quiet cards to each other on birthdays and at Christmas, filled with sentiment, I don't recall one public embrace. We know it, and we know each other knows it, but we aren't a family who shows it. There's a definite sense of abashment. But I pressed him further and he said: 'In women's papers, it's called "love at first sight". At that point, I knew my destiny lay there.'

And against all the odds, Dad added, they got married. Why against all the odds? 'Well, her mother didn't like me.' Soon, Norman and Lilian will have been married for 70 years.

Tortoises have dated for less time.

Appallingly, it is only during my research for this book that I have ever asked my parents for the full story of their meeting. There have been snippets, and if you catch my Dad in his armchair after Mum has inevitably gone to bed, having drifted off in front of her latest favourite programme, chin on chest, he will volunteer stories of the olden days. I always enjoy any mention of his boyhood friend, 'Niggles' Kemp. I wonder whether the chap is still alive? Imagine if those two could be reunited. What a meeting that would be.

'Norm.'

'Niggles.'

It seems I don't hold the Griffiths family dearly enough, and my lack of knowledge of family history may come back to bite me. Because I was born long after my brothers – four children in six years – and have never lived in their vicinity, there is also a subconscious distance between us. All of them are old enough to be my father. These days, they're old enough to be my great grandfather.

But there is definitely a bond. When my water tank burst, my brother Gordon drove all the way to London from the Kent coast and spent an arduous afternoon fitting a new one, though I had neither seen nor spoken to him in perhaps a decade. The kindness was not lost on me. But I have not paid enough attention, I am beginning to realise.

Everyone is a time machine. The stories they can tell.

The thing is, when my Dad starts, there is often no stopping him. But here's one from the time of World War Two, when Mum and Dad were living in Mitcham, Surrey, and he was an engineer, supervising the toolmaking on Spitfires.

It was lunch break and Dad had wandered to the nearby pig farm for a change of scene. The farmer was up to his ankles in mud in the sty, castrating the little pigs. As Dad tells it, he would grab each one, hold it up by a leg, snip off the testicles and they would drop into a bucket. Brush of tar on the wound, on to the next one. Once finished, the farmer hopped out of the sty. He leaned back in, poured the contents of the bucket into the feeding trough, and the pigs fell over each other to eat their own bollocks.

'I wouldn't have minded,' concluded my Dad, 'but I was eating a sandwich.'

No, I haven't paid enough attention.

Towards the end of 1977, long after I had tired of diary-keeping, I took my first trip abroad. By minibus and ferry to Brussels, with the under-13s rugby team.

In the under-13s you got to wear the coveted wasps shirt: thick red, yellow and black horizontal stripes. I wasn't that keen because the fabric was a bit rough.

We were met at the British School, Brussels, by the opposition and parents, and each of us was allocated guardians for the three-day trip. I can't remember the name of my family, sadly, or their affable son, but they were incredibly good to me, which I repaid by nipping upstairs on arrival and weeing in their bidet.

According to a local newspaper clipping my mother has kept, we beat the ex-pats, then two French sides, and our A team ended up playing our B team in the final of a sevens (seven-a-side) tournament.

I distinctly remember playing the French lot. They were enormous! Under-13? Some of them barely looked under 30.

One opposing hooker, who persistently and purposefully scraped his unshaven chin against my baby-bottom version in the scrum, did actually reek of garlic. I remember being quietly amused by that whilst wishing I knew the French for, 'Please will you stop rubbing your French chin all over my face?'

To my amazement, I was voted Most Improved Player over the tour. Although, thinking about it now, when you're that reluctant to play the game, the only way is up.

In the time off, my guardian family took me to see the Atomium, the Grand Place, the Manikin Pis (as it sounds, a fountain involving a small boy peeing) – and *Star Wars*. What a treat. The movie was yet to open in the UK but I had seen billboard advertisements and it did indeed look out of this world.

We drove into the city centre as dusk developed and bought chips in a cone of paper, crispy and lavished in salt, from a stall outdoors, and ate them as we walked along. They were the best chips I had ever tasted.

Then the movie. Incredible. *Doctor Who* special effects were always going to look a bit ropey after that.

I was given pride of place in the front seat on the drive home, when I started to get stomach cramps. Wind. Dreadful wind. And it only got worse.

'What did you think of the film, Nick?'

'Who was your favourite character?'

I'm sitting there, barely able to speak, focusing on failing to let rip, thinking, 'Please! Just get us home! I've already wee'd in your bidet!'

That journey took forever. When we finally arrived back,

I excused myself, dashed upstairs, locked the bathroom door behind me and farted for a decade.

*Coming up: I reach senior school and become a teenager, no one notices; Doctor Who hits its 100th story milestone, featuring Mary Tamm as Baker's companion, who will one day send me a signed photograph; forced into the Combined Cadet Force, I am handed the itchiest shirt known to man; finally, I discover drink and girls, both treat me poorly . . .*

## Chapter Four

*Age 13–18*

# Trying to Be a Teenager While Wearing Tweed

'*Let's try this pub!*'
The Doctor, The Android Invasion

The eagle-eyed will have spotted that I haven't been sharing my enthusiasm for *Doctor Who* with a clamouring host of friends. Even the mole-eyed would have some inkling. It isn't easy.

You certainly don't introduce yourself as a *Doctor Who* fan to anyone, or they are likely to start jogging to Latvia.

You can always drop it into conversation, if your acquaintance looks to be a likely candidate. (Unfashionable is a fair start.) But when is ever a good time?

None of my Alton friends were particularly keen on the show, and neither did I find an ally at Lord Wandsworth. I never got to swap any of my excess Weetabix *Doctor Who* 'exciting stand-up figures', simply because no one I knew wanted them, which is why I had to eat so much bloody cereal.

It's not even that there weren't any nailed-on nerds around – I managed to find people to share games of Dungeons & Dragons, for heaven's sake.

So if Tom Baker's episodes were being watched regularly by more than 10 million Brits, where the hell were all these people?

I'll tell you where: hiding in their rooms.

I know I was.

The Doctor Who Appreciation Society was formed in 1976. I didn't hear about it. The first *Doctor Who* convention took place a year later. I didn't hear about that either.

Would I have joined the Society? Almost certainly, provided you received some sort of membership card/badge/sticker. At that age, I would probably have naïvely braved wearing it, even.

Would I have attended the convention? No sense wondering. I would not have been allowed to. My parents were banning me from heading for 'dangerous' London, to watch Pink Floyd play, as late as 1981.

After I rediscovered *Doctor Who* with a vengeance in the late eighties, I tried to entrap a succession of girlfriends in my web of glee. It's a brave move in any relationship with a woman – 'Would you like to watch Image of the Fendahl with me?' – particularly when you slip in the request during the early days. It was a calculated risk: they are far less likely to say 'No' at a time when politeness still lingers.

I would talk up the story beforehand, attempt to inveigle them in my enthusiasm. I would draw the curtains, dim the lights and offer them some alcohol. As the theme music started, I would nudge them and grin. 'You're going to enjoy this. Just you wait.' And I would count on the fingers of Captain Hook's bad hand the number of minutes before they started to fidget, and wonder whether Wee Jimmy Krankie wouldn't make better husband material.

It is a shattering moment in any *Doctor Who* fan's life when his loved one yawns and offers to make some tea, just as Romana falls off a cliff in The Stones of Blood.

How could anybody care so little?

I could not sum up my lack of success at finding people to enjoy sharing the *Doctor Who* experience with me, any better than with this email from my friend D (Debbie). Her husband, Steve, one of my closest friends, had just emigrated to America – as many of my closest friends tended to do – and she was killing time before following him out there.

Sensing an opportunity, I took her to the *Doctor Who* exhibition at the Museum of the Moving Image on London's South Bank. This would have been around spring 1995. Take it away, D . . .

'The highlight of the exhibition was a Dalek that you could climb inside and look at yourself in a mirror while you waved the little arm things around (whatever the hell they were). It was right at the end, and we waited around for about 20 minutes until all the kids and their parents had cleared so you could have a go without feeling like a dork! There was much giggling, but I could tell secretly you were thrilled.'

I have no memory of that at all. Obviously flushed it.

It's funny (more odd than ha-ha) being at public school while punk is going off. I vaguely remember the headlines, the sense of national disgust. And I definitely recall thinking of the Sex Pistols, 'Gosh. Those are *really* naughty boys.'

I was into Pink Floyd – the very prog-rock band that Johnny Rotten targeted with his scrawled-on 'I hate' Pink Floyd T-shirt. I would have been appalled, had I seen a tabloid photograph of the vandalised garment. I didn't. But current affairs were starting to seep into my subconscious.

I once went downstairs in my pyjamas after bedtime at home and put my head around the lounge door, just as archive newsreel footage was shown on television of an Asian soldier putting a pistol to a kneeling man's head and firing. From Pol Pot's sacking of Phnom Penh, I now suspect. The victim toppled immediately and blood pooled around him with alarming speed.

I had never seen a dead person. I had certainly never seen someone murdered in cold blood, in real life. The killer was so unmoved, so matter-of-fact; his victim . . . What could have been going through that poor man's head, knowing he would die in seconds? That ultimate power of mortality which one man held over another. New to me. What gave the one with the gun the right? I didn't understand.

Sickened, I ran upstairs to bed.

In a small way, I held my parents complicit. How could they have watched that without expressing disgust?

What I didn't realise was that they were used to witnessing such inhumanity on the television. I had unwittingly taken a glimpse into the adult world. Suddenly the future did not seem as rosy as my childish mind had imagined.

There was another time, which I can picture with such clarity.

It was a Sunday and I was sitting at the end of the breakfast bar, listening to Pink Floyd's Animals on Dad's crappy Dictaphone tape recorder. It had just one button, which you pushed up to play and right or left to forward and rewind. The sound was indescribably tinny.

On the front cover of the newspaper before me was a large black-and-white photograph of a massacre. It gave me the same feeling in my gut as I had when I saw that execution.

The headline told of missionaries murdered in South Africa. The picture showed bodies strewn around the bush.

There is something about the way that corpses lie. That sense of the unnatural. Ungainly. So lifeless are they that their dignity has been taken away. Those people were dead. Yet I could animate them in my mind, imagine what they might have looked like before the slaughter.

I believe the story concerned the Elim Mission massacre of June 23, 1978. Google it. Terrorists from Robert Mugabe's Zimbabwe National Liberation Army killed eight British missionaries and four children that night, including a three-week-old baby. I always found it difficult to listen to Animals after that Sunday. I can never escape the association.

I need a tea-break.

Without a doubt, the worst aspect of my Lord Wandsworth life was its compulsory Combined Cadet Force. What a pathetic, anachronistic idea – even back in the late seventies – dressing up a bunch of knock-kneed public schoolboys as soldiers and air force men, and getting them to parade around a quadrangle clutching rifles by the butt.

'Heft! 'Ight! Heft! 'Ight! . . . Griffiths! Lift that arm!'

Sod off! (I never said that. I lifted my arm.)

I just checked the school's website. What a different beast it is these days. There are women teachers. There are female students in all years! Thanks for thinking of that one afterwards. And, naturally: 'All pupils may opt to join the CCF from the 4th form upwards.'

Opt. Gits.

I despised the CCF. From the ideology down to the uniform. Mainly the latter.

We were allowed to choose which branch of the 'forces' we joined. I remember being excited at the prospect. Army or Air Force? Army. Looks more fun. Let's face it, the RAF boys are never going to get to fly a plane.

As it was, we Army boys never got to fight a war. Didn't make my choice right.

Dark-blue beret with badge (over left eye); surprisingly comfortable combat trousers; big black boots, with toecaps that had to be polished mirror-style; gaiters(!), horrendously rough, itchy strips of material which you wrapped around your ankle in a special way, to stop water getting into your boots; army-green shirt, made from a similar material to the gaiter; tight jumper, which constricted that shirt right into your very soul; belt.

We were the Royal Engineers.

Were we bollocks. We were naïve, mollycoddled youths playing soldiers and when we were actually trained by real Royal Engineers, I felt ashamed and embarrassed. What must they have thought of us? It was a credit to those genuine servicemen that they treated us with fairness. The fun they could have had.

'Eat that toad!'

## Some Things . . . That Have Embarrassed Me

- Reading Festival 1983 – I went because Big Country were playing, but I also liked that Friday's headliners, The Stranglers. I'm standing there, singing along, and Hugh Cornwell reaches the line in Who Wants the World, 'Tasted man, tasted flea, couldn't tell the difference.' I get the words wrong and sing, 'Tasted man, tasted woman . . .', as if I am some sort of cunnilingus expert. The couple in front of me hear this, turn around, spot the 17-year-old virgin, and burst out laughing. It still floors me. Twenty-three years later.
- The best-man speech – One of my housemates from university days, Karl, asked me to be his best man, when we were both around our mid-twenties. Though he assured me he didn't want all the formal palaver, I felt way out of my depth. I do functions like Nelson did ship-spotting. I had one joke prepared for the speech, got drunk the night before and told it to everyone. Bear in mind that lubricated wedding guests will wet themselves

at the sight of a courgette; I tell my crap joke (concerning ghosts and Karl's unhealthy pallor) . . . Nothing. It was lonely up there that day.

- I spent most of those university days single.

- Sorry, that wasn't the end of the story. In the First Year, there was this red-haired girl called Suzanne who I fancied. I cornered her at a party in a pub one night and drunkenly asked her out. She declined the offer so I persisted. Shouting over the music, I made my killer play: 'But I love you!' – just as the song ended, so my desperate declaration reverberated around the bar. I departed in tatters.

- Non-relationships again – The year after I left college, still single, a Brazilian woman started talking to me at Julian Cope gig in London. I went back to a party at hers and left, cursing myself that I had been too timid to make any improper advances, but with plans to return to her flat for a Blues Brothers-themed party. So the following weekend I get dolled up in big suit, sunglasses and trilby and take the tube to Bayswater where I nervously ring her doorbell. A flatmate answers, looks me up and down and goes, deadpan, 'The party's next weekend'.

- The man-talk – One summer in Alton, when I was in my mid-teens, my Dad, reclining on a sun lounger in the garden, suddenly blurted out, 'Do you want to be circumcised?' It's no wonder we never discuss personal matters.

- The New York plumbing problem – I don't fly well. Besides being petrified by the slightest turbulence, it messes up my digestive system, particularly long-haul. So I flew to New York with my friend Jeremy for a holiday. A few days later, I managed to go to the loo back at the hotel. Put it this way, their U-bend refused to cope. I flushed; the water rose and rose while I watched, and stopped a millimetre before the rim. Jeremy had to ring reception; I was too mortified. We left $10 on top of the cistern with a note that read 'Sorry' and scarpered.

That's the last scatological story, I promise. Probably.

I turned teenager in August 1978. It was during the summer holidays and besides my parents, I was the only one to notice.

I don't remember feeling any more grown-up. I hadn't kissed a girl. I hadn't even spoken to one in two years. My Mum still cut my hair (short back and sides, sometimes effected with a TV-advertised razor-comb which might have doubled as a natty instrument of torture), my parents still chose the clothes I wore (no problem, since I had zero concept of fashion), and recently I had fronted a group of schoolmates who had written to *Jim'll Fix It*, asking if we could go up in a hot-air balloon and drop bags of flour on people.

Jim declined to fix that one, for some reason.

I moved up to big school at Lord Wandsworth, to become sited slap-bang in the centre of the educational action at School House, one of the four senior houses. We slept in dormitories still, but lights-out time edged slightly later and, because I now mingled with boys aged 13 to 18, suddenly everyone was much taller.

It used to disconcert me even to walk down the sixth-form corridor, where the lower and upper sixth-formers had their 'cubes' (individual bedrooms). Those boys seemed giants to me, and exuded power. It's strange, but when I reached the same dizzy heights, I felt neither giant nor powerful, just Nick but older.

Late that November of 1978, *Doctor Who* reached its own milestone: the 100th Story, Tom Baker's The Stones of Blood. It would be Baker's 25th story, which was no disgrace in itself.

*The Stones of Blood, for the unfamiliar: The Doctor and*

*companion Romana become entangled in Druidic sacrifice at a stone circle. It all ends in space, somehow, where the Doctor's quick wits find the baddie petrified.*

This one appealed to me not for its place in television history, but because of that stone circle. As a child with burgeoning knowledge and inquisitiveness, you cannot help but wonder about Stonehenge and its brethren. Hairy blokes in animal skins hefted those obscenely weighted blocks of rock around the country, then made it even more difficult for themselves by deciding to stack one on top of the other. Those places have an aura.

Add a chanting circle of faceless men in cloaks and give one a sacrificial dagger and, this being *Doctor Who*, get the stones themselves to move – admittedly while seeming rather lighter than they should have done – and kill people . . . Well, it was 'sav' (savage), as we used to say at school.

Halfway through, the action jarringly moved into a spaceship, ruining the Druidic atmosphere. Baker dons a judge's wig and starts bantering with a couple of dancing lights with poncey voices.

I remember finding it all a bit silly, which was perhaps the first onset of maturity, or maybe I was just becoming my mother.

Mary Tamm, who played Romana, kindly sent me a signed photograph ('To Nick – Thanks for the interview') of her in a red sparkly dress, after I had spoken to her for the *Radio Times*.

She only stayed for the one season and was the Time Lord's most overtly glamorous companion, an all-woman type with hair and lips, though I fancied her successor more: Lalla Ward, as Romana II, who was cute as opposed to sensual, and who giggled attractively.

That actress went on to marry Baker himself, after her

stint on the show, and – when that love-match ended rather abruptly – wed Professor Richard Dawkins, the noted intellectual who wrote *The Selfish Gene*.

I tried to interview Dawkins for a *New Woman* magazine feature. Someone had furnished me with his home telephone number, and when I called I was thinking, 'I wonder whether Lalla Ward will pick up the phone?'

If she did, what would I say? 'Hello, this is Nick Griffiths from *New Woman* magazine. I need to talk to your husband about the differences between men and women'? Perhaps fortunately, Dawkins himself answered, however my line of questioning was so inane that he told me, 'I'm going to put the phone down', and then did so. At least he had softened the blow.

I don't think I would have stood much chance with Lalla Ward.

All this talking about fancying women sits uneasily, looking back. I didn't even have any sisters. I was home alone.

As a newly fledged teenager, my only contact with the opposite sex involved my mother, who was almost into her sixties, the mothers of my Alton friends, Mrs Jansen and Mrs Axtell, and Simon's two elder sisters, who teased gently but wisely avoided chatting at length with younger boys who ripped up farming magazines for fun.

I had no idea.

The only women on the Lord Wandsworth estate were the kitchen staff, who were known back then, ungraciously, as 'The Troggs', on account of their not being regarded as supermodels. Maybe it was a school ploy, I don't know.

One boy who joined us in senior school was celebrated for bringing in pornographic magazines swiped from his brother's legendarily vast collection, and we would gather round, gawping, wondering what various bits were for, as if a naked woman came flat-packed from Ikea.

The clitoris? I could barely have pointed out the head.

Here's a little glimpse into the future:

My first real contact with women came in the lower sixth form, when we were allowed to attend the school's sixth-form discos.

You can imagine what events these must have been. Hormone-ravaged boys of 16, 17, 18, several of whom have not had a meaningful conversation with a girl, let alone touched one in earnest, let loose in a room with cider on tap and boy/girl eighties music, into which girls from neighbouring schools – some of those, single-sex – in make-up and hairspray have been bussed.

I'll tell you how clueless I was. I went to one disco at our Sixth Form Centre wearing a shortened blue flannel-ette dressing gown over T-shirt and jeans, on the back of which my Mum had embroidered the Rush logo from the Hemispheres album.

Think about it: I must have looked in the mirror before heading down and thought to myself, 'Yup. You'll do.'

Actually, incredibly, I 'got a snog' that night, as the parlance went. Even the girls couldn't afford to be choosy.

My first ever kiss had happened at one such disco, away from home, at a neighbouring school, in Farnborough, I seem to recall.

I don't remember the details leading up to the event, but usually I could be found on the periphery nursing a cider, wishing I were anywhere less pressurised, hoping that a song I liked would arrive so that I could lose myself in that. And by some miracle I ended up kissing this dark-haired girl. She was very sweet – well, she must have been – and we talked and snogged and talked and snogged and at the end, when the music stopped and the lights came up, I asked her, 'Do you want to come camping with me?'

I didn't even have a camping trip planned! I hate camping!

What on earth was I thinking? I suppose I had just wanted a reason to be able to see her again.

Life is all about learning from mistakes, it's just that I was making mine at a later stage than most boys of my age. The off-the-cuff tent-trip idea had been a disaster – looking bewildered, she had declined – I would just have to rethink next time.

If indeed there were a next time.

Shock interlude: I have just been down to the local Londis to pick up the new *Radio Times*, my usual copy of the *Mirror* and, far less usually, a *Daily Star*. My Billie Piper exclusive has been picked up by a tabloid!

I should warn you now that this isn't the classiest of exclusives, but it is pretty funny. I have spent the past few weeks interviewing cast and crew for the *Radio Times'* coverage of the new *Doctor Who*, series two, as well as writing this book. Time Lord-wise, it's been hectic.

This week's issue is the major 16-page fold-out-cover special, celebrating the show's return at the weekend. The David Tennant reader Q&A is there, as is my lengthy interview with the ever accommodating, fast-talking and jovial ringleader Russell T Davies, plus my reader Q&A with Billie. That was supposed to take place face-to-face but time proved too valuable during Who filming, so we talked over the phone instead.

I had already interviewed Billie once for the Christmas Invasion episode, so had an idea what to expect. She is as bubbly and enthusiastic as Rose can be in *Doctor Who*, but way more introspective and thoughtful.

There is a depth to her replies, to questions that many actors would brush aside with something glib, which suggests there is more to her than meets the eye. It may explain why Chris Evans bought her a Ferrari before she had even passed her test.

For instance, one reader asked her what scared her in real

life, and it wasn't spiders, heights or dreams of Daleks; it was the thought of becoming depressed. Billie Piper has read up on the bipolar condition.

As with David Tennant, she is easy-going, natural, funny, and I am professionally smitten. All right, when Sinead and I have a minor barney, I occasionally flounce about and announce, 'Right, that's it, I'm leaving you for Piper!' She could at least have the decency to look concerned.

I should also note the fantastic job she has done playing Rose. It's easy to laud Christopher Eccleston's performance, and how it helped to bring the show back from the dead, but Piper's Rose was the rock upon which it was founded. The ballsy, tender, determined, sexy action heroine truly captured the nation's hearts. If the male lead roles had all be taken in the playground, I'd have happily considered donning a blonde wig.

Anyway, this exclusive. One reader asked how Billie and David passed the time between takes and after her reply I added, 'Do you have nicknames for each other?'

I knew that actors in long-running series sometimes did, through familiarity and to alleviate the boredom of waiting around. And she admitted, after a pause, acknowledging that letting this slip might 'cause havoc', that she called David Tennant 'David Ten-inch' – for no reason other than finding it funny, it must be stressed.

How we laughed. (He calls her 'Carlos Carlos', because the name makes her laugh, so they use it twice. Which is perfectly reasonable.)

Every journalist hopes to be told little secrets. Some, more highbrow, prefer to discover whether prime ministers knew about the absence of Weapons of Mass Destruction. Others of us have lower ideals. It was just good of her to let me in on that one.

The *Daily Star*'s headline? Inch-high letters on page three: 'DR WHO'S WILLY IS JUST LIKE A TARDIS . . . it's bigger than you think!'

Ho-hum. *Radio Times* gets a healthy plug, as does the new series, and no harm done. It'll soon blow over. As it were.

May 1979 saw the start of my new obsession: music. I caught Tubeway Army on *Top of the Pops* in the School House common room – where I would later see Boy George sing Do You Really Want to Hurt Me, and in common with the rest of the nation, wonder whether he was a girl – and their synth-based Number One hooked me.

Again, Mum was dispatched to pick up the single, and again felt less comfortable than a badger. It's so insistent, so robotic, yet so yearning. And Gary Numan, the singer: bleached hair, kohl, black shirt (if memory serves). So un-me.

Are Friends Electric remains one of *the* great singles, no matter how many times Numan crashes his plane or votes Tory.

That year's Christmas Number One was the decidedly unfestive Another Brick in the Wall (Part 2) by Pink Floyd.

Though I wasn't that taken with it – as far as I could tell, the one thing those kids really did need was an education – the present I desperately craved for Christmas 1979 was its mother album, The Wall.

Santa duly obliged with the thick, weighty double-LP, white with grey grouting lines and a floppy plastic 'Pink Floyd The Wall' Gerald Scarfe logo which I could have stuck to a window, but was too anal to, in case I lost it.

Inside the gatefold are Scarfe's grotesque illustrated characters plucked from the songs – Mother, the Judge (a big arse, basically), Teacher and little Pink – and the credits. My Mum's scanning through these and finds, top of the list of Other Engineers, one 'Nick Griffiths'.

'Oooh, do you think they put that there for you?' she asks.

Bless.

Later I had to ask her what 'defecate' meant (from the lyrics to The Trial) and she wrinkled her nose and wouldn't tell me.

Another Pink Floyd/parent memory: Whenever I played Dark Side of the Moon over the hi-fi, I had to find a reason to turn the sound down every time David Gilmour sang of not wanting to be given that 'goody-goody-goody bullshit', for fear of causing offence.

I doubt there are many albums I have listened to more than The Wall. While my parents were in the lounge watching Jim Davidson or someone on the telly, I would be in the kitchen, alone at the breakfast bar, playing my taped version over and over and over again. I could still quote you any song lyric from beginning to end. (As my Dad would put it, 'If they could put your exam revision to songs, you'd get straight A's'.)

Anyone who knows the album will be aware that it is no package holiday to Marbella, where the cocktails are cheap and you've remembered to pack the condoms. 'Alienation' is oft-used to sum up its theme. I loved the sound effects, the approaching helicopter rotor blades, the dropped bomb, the 'You! Yes you! Stand still laddie!'

I can't pretend that the bleakness of Roger Waters' vision did not strike me. I do remember sitting out there some-times, feeling pretty miserable for unformed, adolescent reasons. Those words could get under your skin.

But it's weird: I enjoy that. To me, all the most beautiful music is bleak. Minor chords, poetic, oblique lyrics, aching sentiment, actual depth. None of your compelled-to-bop, 'Isn't life just so uncomplicated!'

Some fine examples:

- Baby Bird – Fireflies
- Godspeed You Black Emperor! – The Dead Flag Blues
- Low – Monkey
- Galaxie 500 – Strange

- REM – The Wrong Child
- Laika – Breather
- Sufjan Stevens – John Wayne Gacy Jr
- The Teardrop Explodes – Suffocate
- Boards of Canada – Kaini Industries
- Bright Eyes – Gold Mine Gutted
- Jacques Brel – Ne Me Quitte Pas
- David Bowie – My Death
- Tarwater – The Watersample
- American Music Club – I'm In Heaven Now
- Tom McRae – You Cut Her Hair
- Xiu Xiu – Clowne Towne
- Interpol – everything they have ever done

Sad songs feed the soul. Far from finding them depressing, I consider them immensely uplifting. My wife fails to share this stance, which causes problems when we compile party-mix CDs. Everyone else sides with Sinead.

Overtly upbeat music can actually distress me.

Rock Around the Clock? No thanks, I'd rather stop in.

Boogie Wonderland? Bogie Shitland.

I Just Called to Say I Love You. Wrong number, mate.

But before I could define my tastes, there was discovery – and mistakes – to be made.

After Pink Floyd, I got into Rush.

Previously, I could not stand the band. Geddy Lee's screeching lady-vocals, like Kate Bush with an Adam's apple, and all the early lyrical swords and sorcery guff. But School House classmate Dave Goves kept playing their Moving Pictures album in the dormitory, just to annoy me, and one day they seeped into my brain and refused to budge. My attitude flip-flopped.

I already had a couple of UFO albums, recommended by my denim-clad mate Bill Radford, and some Fleetwood Mac. Santa gave me The Story of the Who. Barclay James Harvest.

You didn't see that.

I started getting my Dad to buy me *Sounds* every week – I don't think Mum could have coped – and began stacking the back issues in my former toy cupboard. (*Sounds*, for those not old enough to remember it, was one of the three music weeklies, tabloid sized, alongside the *NME* and *Melody Maker*. It was the uncoolest of the trio, which is no doubt why I plonked for it.)

I remember Wendy O Williams of The Plasmatics pictured on one *Sounds* cover, sitting on a tank, with a white or pink or probably both shock-hairdo – and she was topless with just black tape criss-crossed over her nipples! On the cover! Gobsmacked. (And slightly titillated.)

I remember seeing a photograph of The Cure, taken from their Pornography album sessions: three dark blurs with forests of black hair and white, almost featureless masks. It genuinely disconcerted me. It would be five years before I could steel myself to buy the album.

Clearly, against my body's better judgement, my head had decided I should start growing up. And it wouldn't bode well for *Doctor Who*. (Don't worry: I later tried desperately to regress to childhood and the obsession would return still more ridiculous than before.)

For me, the departure of Tom Baker was the beginning of the end for Doctor Who. Actually, I can be more specific than that: the arrival of Adric was the beginning of the end for Doctor Who.

### Adric, for the unfamiliar: Little twat.

I do have memories of watching the final season of Baker stories, back when they originally aired in late 1980, early '81. Wonder how they will emerge?

## The Leisure Hive

Silly costumes. Men in bouffant wigs. Green shiny faces? Yellow cloaks?

## Meglos

Baker with cool cactus spikes all over his face. Sand everywhere?

## Full Circle

Adric appears! This mealy-mouthed know-it-all boy with his bowl haircut and chubby cheeks. He looks about 13! He dares to joust intellectually with the Doctor!

I enjoyed this one, possibly because it ripped off a Pertwee story for its monster action. A silver building next to a swamp. Marsh men emerge from the gloopy waters, just as the Sea Devils did in 1972.

## State of Decay

Admittedly, State of Decay is my 12th favourite Doctor Who story, but it does take a few episodes before you realise you would like to sit Adric on top of the Tardis and push downwards. This one had vampires, I suspect for the first time in the series, lost spacemen and a gothic rocket, possibly powered by blood – it's a cracker.

## Warriors' Gate

Blokes with lion heads. Romana II stays behind, leaving the Doctor to his travels. A shame.

## The Keeper of Traken

Large statue in garden, concrete-looking with pleasing/sinister curvaceous design. Its eyes glow red, its head swivels and it kills. Sarah Sutton joins as new companion, at least diluting the Adric effect. My schoolfriend Richard later tells me she lives near him; he has seen her out and about in the village. I am impressed.

## Logopolis

It's odd, given that this is Tom Baker's final story, but I don't remember watching Logopolis first time around – although I did buy the video when it came out in 1992 and (cough) snivelled at the end, when Baker regenerates into Peter Davison. Well, it had been the end of an era, for both myself and the best of Time Lords.

Did Tom Baker have any lasting influence on me, I wonder? We all secretly hope to emulate our heroes in some tiny way. It's possible. I had lapped up his performances for seven growing years, after all.

I admire any natural English eccentric (anyone who has to try to exude an air of eccentricity is doomed to naffness).

- George Melly. He does not give a monkey's. There's the classic anecdote of Melly bumping into Mick Jagger at a party and querying the Rolling Stone's wrinkles. 'They're not wrinkles. They're laughter lines,' demurs Jagger, to which Melly replies, 'Surely nothing could be that funny.'
- The sadly departed Jennifer Paterson of the Two Fat Ladies. Motorbike with sidecar, big specs, fag, tipple and mention of distant cousins who cooked with aspic. Deliciously barking. She reminded me of Withnail.
- The character of Withnail (not the actor Richard E Grant, who appeared in Argos adverts wearing a fright-wig).

Now there is someone who really was an influence. So much so that he will be afforded an appropriate tribute come 1986 and the year of *Withnail & I*'s release.

- Paul O'Grady. The funniest man I have ever interviewed. I asked him what sort of people watched *Blankety Blank*, which he was about to host as Lily Savage, and he suggested: the same sort of people who would say, 'Oooh, let's watch the witch burn'. His travel shows, after he removed the Lily drag, were a work of genius. Spiteful, cynical, but with a heart and played for laughs. To be cherished.

And Baker? Doesn't the whole of Britain love him? He seemed to disappear for ages after *Doctor Who*, though you could occasionally recognise those mellifluous tones voicing over a TV advert; now look at his triumphant return: on *Little Britain* and as the original voice of BT's talking text messages. The man's a national treasure.

As for any influence . . . The way he drifts off on tangents during interviews and in conversation, which only a confident, practised eccentric could match. I have a video of him interviewing himself, and looking surprised at some of the questions.

His keenness to make the Who scripts as joke-laden as possible (Douglas Adams, creator of *Hitchhiker's Guide to the Galaxy*, was a script editor during his reign) – that craving the laugh might have had some effect on me during those formative years of mine.

Any time I am drawn into a pub debate, I hear myself interjecting only with glib quips which no one laughs at, which fails to deter me, and joining the politics only when I have had several too many.

I'm just glad that he was around.

It's telling to remember, but the same year that Baker was hanging up his hat as the Doctor, Jon Pertwee was hanging up his straw head as popular children's scarecrow Worzel Gummidge.

That series really had tested my loyalty. It was on ITV, for a start. It was for actual kids. And it co-starred Una Stubbs.

As Tom Baker departed my consciousness, Pertwee did also.

It really was time to move on.

What did I move on to? The Duke of Edinburgh's Award Scheme. Yes, that really should get the girls into a frenzy, learning about the police force, cutting hedges in an old lady's garden, trudging up Welsh mountains while moaning, and fly fishing.

I took both the Bronze and Gold Awards, having left out Silver to concentrate on my O-levels. Why? Largely to please my parents. A duty to repay them for the financial sacrifices they were making, to send me to public school, underpinned my time at Lord Wandsworth. They hadn't had much money when my brothers were at school. I offered them the chance to make amends.

My Dad retired late, purely so that they could afford it, which I was reminded of more than once. As a parent, I would do the same in times of concern; it's just a weight of expectation. And the thing is, I was such a square for such swathes of my schooldays that I was always going to swot like the bespectacled.

Whatever my parents did – apart from the time my Dad slapped me just for eating the entire family-sized Milky Bar – they did with the best of intentions, with my potential future at heart.

The age gap didn't help. Dad initially suggested I consider becoming an engineer, since he had made good as the same, though the industry was in patent decline.

The rows we had over my wanting to buy a pair of white

cords. Cords! My parents thought they were 'punk'! Had they ever seen Sid Vicious? (No.) I got the cords eventually, and they liked them so much that I was bought a second pair. Oh, the irony.

I spent one year, aged 14, wearing a pair of parent-purchased jeans that were unusually tight around the crotch region and which frustratingly didn't have pockets. Only some years later did it click that I had been wearing girls' jeans.

In the 1977 diary I spotted an entry which surprised me.

### June 16, Thursday

'Had auditions yesterday [for the Junior School musical, Joseph & His Amazing Technicolour Dreamcoat]. I only had a part as a soldier and a citizen. I was very disappointed. Don't want Mum and Dad to see.'

Little did I know then, but I was destined always to play soldier and citizen in any school play, and that I would be very grateful to skulk in the background clutching a wooden sword or wearing a tea-towel on my head. Nowadays, I would rather construct a stage from the hardened earwax of ladies over 75 than have to stand at the front of one.

Anyway, I did well in my O-levels, passing a ludicrous 13 of the things, including Latin, geology and engineering drawing. All have come in incredibly handy since, rest assured.

I also did Computer Science and remember first sitting down in front of the school's brand new BBC Micro computer and typing in, 'Who is going to win the football today?'

I actually got better grades in the Arts subjects than the

Sciences, but enjoyed both (History and Biology notwithstanding).

Which reminds me of our sex education in Biology class. Diagrams of the internal workings of the male and female genitalia and stuff we knew already through gossip, but had had no chance to try out. I seem to recall being handed a condom to pass around and not even finding it funny.

Which A-levels to take? I had not the faintest idea of what career I wanted to pursue – the very idea of leaving the sanctity of education felt bewildering and petrified me; I remember worrying about how one signed up for a gas bill – but, given my love of writing and reading, was veering towards English.

Dad was convinced that the Arts subjects were worthless in the job market and that I should study the classic Maths, Physics, Chemistry. So I did.

People laugh in disbelief when I tell them I have a degree in Electrical & Electronic Engineering. So do I.

I discovered a run of diaries in my old tan-leather school briefcase which lives in the loft, alongside the mementoes and love letters of yesteryear – red, blue, yellow and green envelopes, the odd one still clutching the faintest whiff of perfume – which I am too sentimental to throw out.

Besides the 1977 diary, the only one kept with any determination is the diary from 1982. In the Monthly Planner at the front, I have written in my birthday, my parents' birthdays, my girlfriend Vicki's birthday and the birthdays of each member of Pink Floyd and Barclay James Harvest. That year, I only got bored and stopped writing entries on 14 December. Could I really not have lasted the final two weeks?

It's a sign of the mild ennui that would occasionally grip me. (Sample diary entry, from 23 March 1982: 'V boring day wrt [with respect to, in boffin-speak] lessons. Am beginning to miss Vicki; feeling generally pissed off. Listened to Bob Dylan for the first time ever.')

I think I was beginning to realise that there was more to life. Something lay outside those austere school gates. But what was it?

At least girls and alcohol had entered my world. At last. In a fledgling manner.

The Sixth Form Centre had a bar which also held the discos, and which I would visit on weeknights when funds allowed (not often), usually with my pal Richard Buchanan, who shared my Maths/Physics/Chemistry route. Besides David Coppin, he is the only Lord Wandsworth friend with whom I remain in regular contact.

He would readily admit that he was not one of the cool kids. In fact, the cool kids used to try to take the mickey out of him; what impressed me was that he didn't seem remotely bothered. He had a strength of character that would see him become an inspector in the Hong Kong Police after university, while I flogged Terence Trent D'Arby albums in Our Price, Wood Green.

Never play him at any racquet sport. He is the flukiest individual I have ever known. If he skies a tennis shot, it will land in a tree, be carried down by an irate squirrel, dropped on to the back of a passing tortoise and be deposited perfectly on the base line over the course of half an hour.

And he was rubbish at drinking. Half a cider and he'd be reeling around, singing loudly. And I'm convinced he's tone deaf. You don't want to hear someone singing Phil Collins' You Can't Hurry Love at the best of times. When he does it, alley cats start throwing things.

There's a diary entry to prove it. Wednesday 10 March 1982: 'Recorded Buchey [as he was then known] singing. He admitted it was terrible.'

Richard had his revenge for me constantly deriding his drinking ability in April 1982, though my record fails adequately to cover it:

### April 23, Friday

'Up at 6am. In France by 12am. Had large lunch, bought Foreigner 4. Was sick on boat. Home about 10pm. Lost crown. Did not phone Vicki.'

I would have been 16⅔. It was the first time that booze really bit back. It went like this.

A couple of teachers had arranged a sixth-form trip to France. Calais, I think it was, by ferry. Take in the culture, sample the cuisine, try to speak the lingo. Let's be honest: I can't even remember where we went.

Me, Richard and Adam Clarke took off on our own, found a nice restaurant and settled to a steak meal with wine. I'm not sure I had drunk red before. This was a rich, fruity concoction that smothered your face in fumes and was wonderfully quaffable. So we shared a second bottle. Feeling suitably woozy, we went to the supermarket and bought some more wine, white this time, and beer. So cheap!

While we were drinking those on a grass verge some others from our school group passed by and offered us a swig of advocaat. It's yellow but it's booze. Why not? By now, heads were starting to do the butterfly stroke, so Richard sourced a bottle of calvados, an apple brandy which he heartily recommended. We swigged that, too.

Hauling ourselves back on to the ferry, I sat down. Then the world went weird.

I had dressed myself that morning in peach shirt, brown tie and my mid-brown, blouson-style, leather-look jacket, of which I was very proud. It was plastic really and, given its colour, people with very little fashion sense referred to it as my 'shit jacket'. I can't remember what trousers I matched with that classy ensemble. Something in brown, probably. Anyway, I vomited over all of them.

I was totally incapacitated. Nothing worked.

'Nick to arms! Nick to head! Nick to anything! Come in! Urgent!'

[Sound effects: whistling wind, distant church bell.]

I could only stare, head lolling, at the remnants of my dinner and alcohol consumption, soaking into the fabrics (though handily sliding off the jacket).

Richard, one of the world's worst drinkers, remember, and Adam were standing over me, pointing and laughing. Others from our party joined them, to mock and take photographs.

'Help me,' I managed to mumble.

Click, flash, click, flash. Hahahahaha.

Eventually, a decent human being or two hoisted me up and dragged me below decks to clean up. That ferry had a stupidly high step at its toilet door. I tripped over, fell flat on my face and my crowned front tooth flew out, to remain lost forever.

I was deposited in a toilet cubicle and left to rot.

I remember staring at the door, that terrible swirling sensation going on in my head, which refused to stop, wondering whether this was actual hell on earth. At least the person/people who had helped me had removed my brown tie and flushed it.

I slept for the entire journey until Richard came to fetch me, shaking me drunkenly, causing my head to bounce repeatedly off the back wall, which I could hear but not feel. Still I couldn't walk. And someone had stolen my passport from my inside pocket while I was comatose.

Fortunately, my head had cleared sufficiently for me to take in the staggering embarrassment of being carried through customs with a teacher under each arm, with one of them going, 'He's lost his passport'.

We were wisely waved through.

On the minibus trip back to school, no one wanted to sit near me. It would be 16 long years before I could face touching wine again.

But the worst thing? Despite all that palaver, I somehow managed to keep hold of my Foreigner album. A little poodle-topped AOR – that's just what I needed.

Tell you what, I haven't played that record in decades. I'm going to stick it on right now. Quick dose of marred nostalgia.

Ready? Altogether now (bar Richard): 'You're as cold as ice . . .'

## Some Things . . . That Made Me Ill

- Those beers in Fleet – This was another early warning on the alcohol front, at a Fleet Country Club rock night. A bunch of us from school went along and drank too much. Somehow, I got talking to a woman and remember discussing Gordon Giltrap (about whom I knew absolutely nothing) before excusing myself, breaking into a run, slapping open the toilet door and projectile vomiting into a sink. My date had disappeared by the time I returned, self-consciously swiping at carrot pieces on my AC/DC T-shirt.

- Offal – It isn't always drink. I've had some terrible food-poisoning (honest). A couple of years ago, Sinead and I travelled around Mexico. Guide books advise against eating anything from roadside sellers, but I am always determined to experiment food-wise. It looked like mince as the cheery vendor grilled it before me. When I sank my teeth into its texture, I realised it was offal. Still it tasted great and the jalapeno chillies disguised any heinous crimes. That night, the stomach cramps started and we spent a day at the Mexican seaside holed up in a hotel room, watching television so poor that my wife almost developed the runs in sympathy.

- Curry – This one was even worse. I won't say where the curry was from, but I took the unprecedented step of informing Health & Safety. The stomach cramps started when I was in Kent, visiting my parents, and appeared at such clockwork intervals, and with such violence, that I wondered whether I was having a baby. (Actual mothers should freely rubbish the exaggeration.)

- All the 'fun' of the fair – Visiting a university mate in Poole, Dorset, he suggested hitting a fair that had pitched up locally. I don't even like fairs. It was a pokey outfit and, given the paucity of entertainment on offer, I decided to have a go on the Waltzer. Round and round it went, while a bloke span the car itself, so my head and stomach were spinning on two axes. I started to feel sick. There was no one waiting for a ride, so we got a second, free, tagged on to the first. Then a third. The nausea was stunning. When I was finally able to stagger away, I vomited in front of some small children clutching candy-floss, who pointed and giggled. Never again.

- The Games Day – But sometimes it is drink. Though one does learn, occasionally enthusiasm overtakes common sense. My university pal Andy and I are keen pub-quizzers. Our usual quizmaster, Steve King, also ran Games Days: rotating games such as cribbage, pinball, pool, etc, played in a pub. This one started at noon and continued until early evening. It's hard to keep a tab on your alcohol intake when you are focusing on beating someone at Jenga. My stomach hit the alert button just after the Victoria Line tube left Kings Cross for Highbury & Islington – handily, one of the underground system's longest trips. The concentration that took. As the doors opened I was ready to bolt, but the volcano had already started erupting. As I ran, spraying like a fireman's hose, I heard a woman on the platform gasp,

'Oh my god!' I really shouldn't find it amusing in retrospect.

- Rock Night II – Having said that one does learn, only a few months back I was visiting the same Andy in Stour- bridge when we hit a local club for some late-night action. Unfortunately, it was Rock Night. The music sounded like people in hell holding a Best Distressed Caveman Impression competition. However, we have this little psychological trick to turn a bad time good: simply tell yourself you are going to enjoy. This involved spotting the rainbow-hued test-tubes behind the bar – lurid shoo- ters – and sampling colours at random. Then we head- banged to the Led Zeppelin tribute band, grinning to each other at our hilarious irony, pulling devil's-horn hand shapes, and ate a large pizza each. The following morning, the joke was on me.

Interlude: Sinead and I did a pub quiz last night and the Table Round was on . . . *Doctor Who*! Sixteen names of companions, but which were genuine and which were made up? We hid our mouths to snigger. 'Sharron McReady'? Pfffft. I got 32 out of 32 and the bloke who marked the paper told Sinead, 'Someone on your team knows too much about *Doctor Who*'. Sometimes it comes in handy, mate.

Interlude 2: Of late, I have been wearing my red Converse trainers, which had lain forlorn in the clothes rack for several years, purely because David Tennant's Doctor wears Converses (white) with his suit. Nick Griffiths is 40 years old.

And the trainers make his little toes sore, but that won't stop him.

Series two of the new series debuted last weekend, while I was down in Cornwall visiting the in-laws. (Blimey, I never thought I would use that phrase.) New Earth: the one where the Doctor and Rose travel 5 billion or so years into the future and the Cat Nuns are breeding humans as disease carriers. (Never thought I'd use that phrase either.)

We sat in the lounge, three generations of Hanks's, a family friend and myself, the baked potato chef, watching as one. It was a riot. The pace was unrelenting, Tennant's new Doctor had everything and Rose showed off some cleavage.

Afterwards, we all retired to the Fowey Hotel for a snifter and gave the episode marks out of ten. The returns were tightly grouped, from 6.5 (the matriarch, Mrs Hanks) to 7.5 (12-year-old Jack, my sister-in-law's son). I gave it 7, anticipating the tales to come, and with high hopes.

### January 25, Monday (1982)
'Worked all afternoon. 35 mins trying to phone Vicky. Engaged (the phone, not Vicky!)'

Developing a sharp wit already, you will notice.

### January 28, Thursday
'Might go to Wispers [Vicky's school] tomorrow. I love Vicky.'

I didn't go to Wispers. What was I planning to do, make a break for it on a stolen tractor? And I had only met the girl once.

### February 1, Monday
'Two letters today. One from Vicki. [Teacher] Lonnon reckons I'm going to do my Physics essay again, 'cos I didn't do it in ink, some hope! Spent 35p and 45 mins phoning Vicki. In the end I had little to say! She can't make it to the disco.'

★

I did rewrite the essay.

Ah, Vicki (who spelt her name with a 'i'). I didn't call her that night of the French trip, if you recall.

We had hooked up at a sixth form disco the previous Christmas. She was wearing a tartan skirt, had mid-length brown hair, went to Wispers School in Surrey, and I really fancied her. I may well have been wearing my David Bowie Scary Monsters T-shirt with light grey jacket, sleeves rolled up. It definitely wasn't the Rush dressing gown. And when I say 'hooked up', I meant snogged each other's faces off while slow-dancing to Tainted Love.

It's a heady experience.

I never once went to a sixth-form disco expecting to 'get off with' anyone. Just being in the same room as girls while music played and hormones fought in corners was a treat. To actually talk to one of them and for them to like you enough to let you touch their breasts . . . Nirvana.

I made that sound too glib. Really, for someone deprived of female company, it made you feel wanted, attractive, amazed, elated, male, young, grateful, sexual, freed. All of those things.

When the visiting girls were packed back on to their bus once Soft Cell had faded out, the lucky ones stood and waved mournfully, as if their womenfolk were off to join the Land Army, while the unlucky ones skulked back to their rooms muttering. You buzzed afterwards, not just from the three halves of cider.

The next morning, when you woke up and the first thoughts poked at your grey matter, you couldn't believe it had happened.

I immediately assumed that Vicki was my girlfriend. It was a bit of a blow when she wrote me a letter and stated categorically, 'Nick, I am not your girlfriend'.

But I am not one to go down without a fight. That 1982

diary is filled with sullen snapshots of me standing in the school's single telephone shed, clutching change, queuing in a howling wind, often vainly trying to track her down at Wispers and bemoaning the wasted pennies.

Happily, the persistence paid off.

Vicki came to a few Lord Wandsworth discos during that year, and even stayed over at Princess Drive. I dared to ask my parents whether we could share a bed. Their reply was more predictable than a two-horse race in which the second horse is a disguised goat.

(Diary entry: 'Vicki came into my bedroom at 8.30 [a.m.] looking v nice in just a shirt.')

I can picture so vividly us sneaking back to my cube under cover of darkness, during one summer disco: up the path past the dining hall, beside the lawn where the teachers played croquet of a lunchtime, hearts pumping for several reasons, past the silent classroom block and into School House, removing our shoes to tread like randy panthers up the polished stone staircase, staring in fear at the door to the housemaster's room which overlooked it, along the sixth-form corridor to safety and amateur night.

When we left, I would feel less worried about getting caught.

But it was hard to maintain a relationship when you lived 14 miles apart, were yet to pass a driving test, barely had the money for a phone call, let alone a train fare, weren't generally allowed to go out anyway, your girlfriend flew to Singapore most school holidays, and you had no idea what the opposite sex had in mind.

I wonder where Vicki is now, almost a quarter of a century later? Probably married with children.

All those former complete strangers we share segments of our lives with, who then drift back into the populace.

I looked Vicki up on friendsreunited.com but she's not registered. Probably for the best – such reunions are rarely the desired hoot. You start off with the 'So, what are you up to these days?', reminisce with decreasing enthusiasm and end up flailing through the pros and cons of assorted mortgage packages.

'Gosh, yes, please do take up another hour of my life enthusing over the fiscal advantages of your base-rate tracker. I'll get the beers in.' But I wish her well. To be the object of someone's first love is a great responsibility, though you fail to realise it at the time.

It's impossible to do justice to the emotions in words. Good chemicals start racing, everything becomes slightly surreal, an ache appears somewhere you cannot place; you sense that if you took a running jump, you might float off into the atmosphere. But with the highs come the lows, as any student of Newton will tell you.

Missing someone is a joyless experience. The ache turns bad, the longing hurts and distraction inhabits your brain. Worst, I find, is the utter inability to do anything about it. I missed one girlfriend so much that I got on a plane to Guatemala, just so that I could be with her and cease the cursed yearning.

Those months with (and without) Vicki were crucial to my development. There was the outside world, and it had lady-bits. It was kind and funny and sexy and it liked me back.

I met Vicki off trains, standing there, waiting, for my girlfriend; I called her up to wish her Happy Birthday (diary entry: 'It's not her birthday, how embarrassing. Why do I always get dates wrong?'), we went to pubs together ('Vicki had 2 G&Ts'), we worked stuff out, and inevitably we drifted apart.

The relationship didn't end, it just ceased to be.

One day afterwards, I bleached my hair. Some of the cooler kids had already done so, and no one had shot them at dawn. David Coppin had a bottle of hydrogen peroxide which he used to treat cuts. I sloshed it on my hair and my hair went orangey.

When I looked in the mirror, I was horrified. Guilt at my temerity, fear of reprisal, secret self-satisfaction.

Luckily the dazzle mellowed quickly and I loved the new barnet. My previously mousy flop, which I had disastrously middle-parted in the past, lathered in adolescent grease, suddenly looked pretty good. Not only was I was finally aware of my own appearance, but I was kicking (or at least tapping) against the system.

Naturally, I shat myself when I went home that weekend. Would they notice? Would they kill me? They hadn't and so they didn't.

Then, Monday morning, as I was ready to return to school, Mum asked, 'Have you done something to your hair?'

There was nothing for it but to come clean. I was way too old for 'No!' and 'I didn't do it!'.

'I like it,' she said.

Gobsmacked. For folks of their era, they can be remarkably enlightened. It takes a while, but they usually get there. My Dad once told me that their having me at such a late age kept them young.

Mind you, it is hardly hip when your parents approve of your rebellious statement.

I hated cross-country and recall a collective sense of disgust among my School House peers that we sixth-formers were obliged to compete in the annual school run, through beastly mud and oomska, and chilled puddles the size of Lincolnshire. With myself among the ringleaders, a delegation went to the housemaster, Mr Dames (aka 'Smooth', on account of his manner), and demanded/asked to be excused.

He declined. So we made 'Ban the Run' notices, pinned them to our shirts, hit the Start line to protest, were told to run and did so.

Those who dawdled were made to do it again.

Another time, Dames failed to make me a house prefect. To put this into perspective, only two of us weren't and the other guy was no angel.

I guess I was too middle-of-the-road, too mild-mannered, too lacking in authority, but still it smarted. Prefects got to eat dinner after the melee of everyone else, in their own special dining room, at regular intervals. A decent privilege.

A few months later, I was called into Dames' room and offered the job.

Surprised at my own pride and nerve, I told him, 'No thanks'. (Sod 'em – if I hadn't been deemed worthy before, I didn't want it as a half-baked gesture later.)

He said it would look bad on my report. I said I'd think about it. I accepted.

It was a start.

I lost touch with *Doctor Who* around that time. It didn't help that the schedulers had moved the series from its traditional Saturday teatime slot to Monday and Tuesday evenings, while we were enduring prep (homework – no telly, no talking).

That wasn't the only barrier.

As anyone of the era will tell you, Peter Davison made his name in *All Creatures Great and Small*. Christopher Timothy was James Herriot, Robert Hardy was Siegfried, the man who employed him, and Davison was Tristan, Siegfried's bumbling brother. And they were all vets. Loveable, family-viewing vets, in the rolling Yorkshire Dales, arms up cow's bums and a dog named Tricky-Woo.

We Griffiths lapped it up. I just never expected to see Tristan Farnon in the Tardis. He was so instantly recognisable, even in cricket gear, with a celery stick in his lapel. And what was all that about?

Every Doctor had their trademark: Hartnell the irascible

grandfather, Troughton the cosmic hobo, Pertwee the dandy, Baker with his hat and scarf . . . Now Peter Davison – the cricketer with a fetish for European biennials? Talk about tagged on.

But Davison had a far worse albatross than his costume. He had inherited Adric.

I don't know whether my mind is playing tricks on me, but I feel sure I managed to watch the episode in which the puffy-cheeked git received his just desserts. It was also a Cyberman story, the first since Baker's Revenge of the Cybermen, seven years earlier, which might have come to my attention.

*Earthshock, for the unfamiliar: On 26th-century Earth, palaeontologists are going missing. Amazingly, people notice and care. It's the Cybermen's fault. Adric helps to save the day but dies with the Cyber Army in an explosion that also explained away the extinction of the dinosaurs. (Don't ask. Just be grateful.)*

By this stage, Davison had become some sort of crèche leader.

He had three companions: Nyssa (the aforementioned Sarah Sutton, all perm and concern), Tegan (spunky Australian) and Adric (whale's penis). It was probably just me getting older, but they seemed so young, as if the Doctor might have to help them do some colouring-in and then toss pancakes while they clapped delightedly.

Little Adric was only the second companion in *Doctor Who* history to be killed off. (Good.) Why he was so annoying? Where would you like me to start?

He was a mathematician. A child prodigy. A know-it-all swot. His voice was the sound of a precocious teenager showing off his abacus collection on *Blue Peter*. Or the sound of polystyrene being scraped down a blackboard while the cast of *Hi-De-Hi* chatted in the background.

When that spaceship exploded, while Adric clutched his

dead brother's belt, my heart burst with it. They actually played out the episode with no theme tune, in total silence, as if a nation were sitting in its armchair, stunned or weeping. The neighbours probably heard me whooping.

Of course, *Doctor Who* later employed Bonnie Langford as a companion, wearing a polka-dot pink shirt, hair in ginger ringlets, which would make Adric seem like Han Solo.

No one has a crystal ball.

I never got to meet Matthew Waterhouse, who played the character, and though I hold nothing against him as an actor – he was in the wrong place at the wrong time – I am hardly gutted.

I did, however, manage to pick up two genuine props from Earthshock, at a memorabilia exhibition at the Birmingham NEC, which are among the pride of my *Doctor Who* collection. That would have been around the late nineties, and the car park was so sprawling I couldn't find my Peugeot 205 afterwards.

One is a trooper's helmet, custom-made in fibreglass and charcoal grey, a bit like a motorbike helmet with ostentatious cheek-pieces. Inset into the those are two torches, one either side, which were used to light the way in the 'caves'. I also have the trooper's rifle, which is a real boy's-own piece of kit. It seems to be an air pistol attached to a mini vacuum cleaner attached to telescope attached to a rifle butt, very impressively. In silver and grey. It exudes the fun the designer had making it. Sometimes I clutch it to my shoulder, peer down its sight and imagine I am picking off Adric.

Adric: 'Hey! You just shot me!'
Nick: 'And?'
Adric: 'I'm on your side!'
Nick: 'Sorry, I thought you were a Cyberman.'
Adric: 'I look nothing like a Cyberman!'
Nick sprays Adric silver.

There is a sense of pride at actually owning a piece of Who history. Like the Robot of Death mask and my Hand of Fear (more later), you can't help but wear it or pretend to fire it (the trigger doesn't actually work), trying to imagine what the actor experienced, while feeling a little foolish.

I remember nothing Davison-wise after Earthshock, until the Twentieth Anniversary Special, The Five Doctors, of late 1983.

A new hero had overtaken my life: David Bowie.

Keith Robbins introduced me to his music. Keith was in my class but seemed more mature, a bit more switched on.

I drove round to his house in Basingstoke one weekend in 1982, after I had passed my driving test, and he played me the Space Oddity LP. It's among Bowie's earliest and a strange place to start when you're living in the early eighties, but I remember being captivated by God Knows I'm Good, a strummed tale of a female shoplifter caught pinching some stewing steak by store security. No, it doesn't sound that hip on paper. But Bowie gave it such emotion.

The joy of getting into his work relatively late was that I had a whole back catalogue to mine – and what a back catalogue. Every new album was a revelation. Each reinvention of musical persona and style a window on to something magical and adult.

Off the top of my head, some songs that sunk in deep: Five Years. Life on Mars. Station to Station. Word on a Wing. Future Legend. Sweet Thing. Candidate. Sweet Thing (Reprise). 1984. Aladdin Sane. Drive-In Saturday (my parents had a version on one of those crass hot-panted-lady *Top of the Pops* compilations from the seventies and I already adored the song, but never realised it was Bowie's). Sound and Vision. Joe the Lion. Sons of the Silent Age. Look Back in Anger. Warsawa. Kooks. Quicksand. Andy Warhol. The

Bewlay Brothers. Karma Man. Fashion. Ashes to Ashes. Up the Hill Backwards. Teenage Wildlife.

God, I had the lyrics to Teenage Wildlife pinned to my lower-sixth cube wall – alongside a large black-gloss 'Pink Floyd The Wall' and intricately painted Barclay James Harvest logo – a written testament to my adolescent angst. There are precious few Bowie songs I could not recite to you right now.

Imagine taking just those listed above and cramming them into the brain of a teenager who thought Rush were the business. It was mind-blowing.

Then there was his look. Theatrical, provocative, imaginative, sexual, downright bonkers. What had I been doing wearing girl's jeans and a dressing gown?

Bowie inspired me to try harder. He was another glimpse into that outside world. I read of his killing off Ziggy at the Rainbow Theatre in London and wished I could have been there. (I would have been seven, so it wasn't about blaming my parents.)

When news came of his first release since Scary Monsters, I was stupidly excited. Capital Radio announced that they would play the first single off the album exclusively one teatime, and I was there, at the Amstrad in my cube, straining to hear through the fuzz, and Let's Dance came on and I thought, 'What the hell?'

Fear not, I soon got into it, it was just a bit of a change of direction.

The Let's Dance album isn't one of Bowie's greatest triumphs, created back when he started to worry about innovating, but he looks incredible in the videos for Let's Dance and, particularly, China Girl.

When he's stood there in his overcoat, bleached hair, tanned, defiant, gorgeous, clutching the bowl of rice which he tosses into the air and the grains rain down before him. I wanted to be that man. So I redid my hair. Shorter, blonder, more hairspray.

As I just mentioned, I had passed my driving test. Talk about freedom.

You start off on a scooter, then the kid's bike, boy's bike (a fairly nerdy Puch Pavemaster, which I nevertheless coveted), racer (Carlton Cobra). Actually, I went via pogo stick back there somewhere.

Ten gears! Come on! The trouble is, no matter how fit you are – and I was in the 1st XV rugby (unfortunately) in my final year at school – a teenager's bicycle can only travel so far, bearing in mind the same distance home.

I once cycled all the way to West Meon, to try to track down Vicki who was staying there with a relative. It was a 12-mile round-trip. I had no address but hoped I might just bump into her.

I cycled around, peering over people's hedges, then cycled home again.

So it was momentous when I was given the use of Mum's old Silver Mini Metro (KJB 317W), and celebrated by driving to the pub to join some school friends.

I didn't drink, I just soaked up the potential. And when I arrived back in Alton just after midnight, my concerned parents had called the police.

We rowed, a few weeks later they chilled out. As I said, they usually got their heads around things.

It would have been easier to assert my independence, had I done well in my A-levels.

But I hadn't.

The marauding butterflies on results morning, waiting for the postman; the fear as the footfalls came and the envelope thwacked on to the doormat; the genuine belief that my future lay mapped out within; the sliceable tension as Mum ripped open the top; the sudden death of all the butterflies and their sinking into my gut when the slip read: C, E, O.

(The O was a particular travesty since I already had an O-level in Chemistry, and who needed two?)

Mum called Dad at work. The shit hit the fan.

What would that future have been, had I made the grades to read my chosen course? Accountancy in Leeds.

Accountancy. My Dad's idea, when I had none of my own. Fair enough. It was all about earning a living. But I look back and I consider turning to Catholicism, just so I can praise a higher being.

Right now, I might have been living in suburbia, new-build mansion in a topiaried close, wife and two kids, her in jewellery, them precocious, competing with my neighbour for nattiest hosepipe and fattest 4 × 4, obsessed with figures on bank statements (not just my own, which is even scarier), drinks every Friday night with the boys from work, wearing slacks and Gucci, discussing golfing aspirations and office chairs, slagging off the missus while imagining we could pull the barmaid, share portfolio, pension fund, pot belly, long socks, gimp mask in the wardrobe, history of affairs, dependency on Prozac.

I might have painted that a little bleakly towards the end, but that's how it feels. Like I inadvertently escaped from Alcatraz.

*Coming up: While retaking my A-levels I am amazed to meet a second girl who likes me, she buys me a Duran Duran single and I fall in love; a* Doctor Who *companion compares me to a pop-star David, sadly not Bowie; moving to London for university, I buy some red shoes but am incapable of dancing the blues; Live Aid happens;* Withnail & I *is released;* Doctor Who *loses the plot . . .*

## Chapter Five
### *Age 19–22*

# Bright Lights, Big City (Via Farnborough)

*'Yours is indeed a towering intelligence!'*
Bloodaxe, The Time Warrior

I have met royalty. And royalty asked me a question. It's just that I couldn't work out what it was.

I have let my parents down on countless occasions. It's the offspring's occupational hazard. You mess up; they shout; things change very slightly; repeat the process over a long period of time until you mould each other into faintly compatible, mutually appreciative human beings; then move as far away from each other as possible and play ostrich. Foolproof, down the ages.

But I have never actively tried to disappoint them, like some septic-nosed body-art enthusiast with a chip on their shoulder. I have no chips. Even now, at 40, I try to make them happy (and they are over the moon about this book). So it's great when a plan comes off.

Remember that Duke of Edinburgh Award? All that mooching over Welsh hills – we got disorientated and had to climb up Pen Y Fan (South Wales' highest mountain) bloody twice – clipping of old ladies' hedges and keeping of a fly-fishing log book actually paid off.

I passed my 'Gold D of E', as we streetwise veterans know it, which after my A-level failure was a recompense of sorts. It meant a trip to Buckingham Palace. If not to see the Queen, at least her foot-in-mouth husband.

My parents debated who should accompany me and Mum won.

I put on a suit that wasn't too itchy and we walked through those Palace gates, where other similarly over-decked, flushed types were gathered, and were ushered into a very large hall with a very high ceiling and wall-to-wall red carpet.

I didn't know anyone else there, though my friends Richard and David had also passed. I might have chatted awkwardly to people my own age, I don't recall; more likely, I clung to my mother, who clung to her handbag. Parent and child were separated by a flunky and I was shown to a place in a sweeping semicircle of nervous nerds, far left if you were facing us.

Then the Duke of Edinburgh appeared. I remember thinking that he was smaller than he looked on television.

He started at the opposite end of our group, asked a question which I couldn't hear because he was facing away from me and mumbles a bit, then slowly walked around, counter-clockwise, asking subsequently, 'And you? And you? . . .'

I'm thinking, 'God, I hope he doesn't ask me. At least I'm at the end here, and behind someone else.'

And he looks me in the eye from ten feet and goes, 'And you?'

And I go, denuded of etiquette, 'I'm sorry, what was the question?'

I couldn't tell you even now what it was. It's gone.

Alright, it's hardly Oliver Cromwell, and I certainly meant no offence, but Mum and I had a laugh about it afterwards.

Though I realised I had done good, it's only since I became a parent myself that I realise that trip's true significance.

When he was ten, Dylan made it into his school's swimming team and his mother, Aileen, and I attended a gala.

He was there in his swimming cap, bright red with self-consciousness, in a queue of boys waiting to line up for their event, and I was so proud that tears escaped my eyes and I had to wipe them away, now battling my son for Most Self-conscious Person at Gala.

I'm happy if he spells 'necessary' correctly or adds 23, 35 and 76 in his head.

My Mum, a British citizen of the war years, got to step inside Buckingham Palace and watch her son fail to understand Prince Philip. It feels good to have paid something back.

Interlude: Here's a coincidence. In this morning's *Mirror*, celebrating Elizabeth II's 80th birthday, Prince Andrew is quoted as saying how he and Edward would skate around the state rooms as kids, then settle to watch *Doctor Who* with Mum (your actual Queen). The royals are fans of the show! Andrew even mentioned that he used to hide behind a sofa! No mention of Prince Philip, you will notice.

So I had left public school. Summer 1983. And I must say that I largely enjoyed the seven years. I made good friends, lived in a lush part of the country, never took a bus to school, to be been beaten up by bigger boys with spots and sneers for my lunch money. I became fitter than I have ever been since, received a decent education which hadn't seen me through my A-levels as expected, I'd travelled abroad with the school (not always returning with dignity, agreed), and had been skiing also. I scored my first ever match-day rugby try, during my final year, in the 1st XV, and was so stunned that I had to confirm with a team-mate that it had actually been me. I had co-run the Science Society with Richard and our video screenings of *Horizon* documentaries had been a roaring success (evening entertainment opportunities being limited). I had sneaked through hedges to the pub at night-time, concerned about capture but enlivened by my daring, and had been dragged around a field by a dog named Henry at 7 a.m. as a punishment. I had vowed never again to eat a curry after the sultana-rife mess that served for one in the dining hall, and I had emerged after all that with minimal psychological scarring.

Naturally, there were inherent setbacks. I remained too subservient to the idea of authority for someone of my age. I wasn't exactly frightened of my own shadow, but I might have been were it bigger than me, or wore an official-looking badge. It would take me far too long to suss that not everyone in a position of power is right.

I was no social butterfly. Which is an understatement. Neither was I Casanova – more Vauxhall Nova, when it came to girls.

But I had entered Lord Wandsworth at the age of 11 and left at 18: an entire adolescence.

I would just have to play catch-up.

It was only after leaving that I realised the stigma that can attach itself to public schoolboys. The number of times I have had to defend myself.

# Some Things . . . People Imagine I Am, Given My Public School Education

- Born with a silver spoon in my mouth – Amniotic fluid and the occasional thumb.
- Gay – Just because I lived exclusively with boys and we went through puberty and hormonal crises together, and shared dormitories, changing rooms and showers, and didn't meet girls until the sixth-form . . . Blimey, the circumstantial evidence mounts, doesn't it!
- Cocky – This one is a favourite of my wife's (who went to Oxford). To say that public school made me over-confident is like saying that Nookie Bear made Roger de Courcey over-famous.
- Well-mannered – That's mainly my Mum, being wishful.
- Well-dressed – Mum again.
- Well-groomed – Every time I go home, she pleads to comb my hair.
- Poshly spoken – Hailing from Hampshire, I can do the partial plums, but I've lived in London for more than 20 years and am more often Mockney these days. I can't help it. Maybe it's a subliminal desperation to fit in: I've had a few fishing trips, staying with a friend in Scotland, and heard myself going 'Aye'.
- A sucker for a big black-tie do – I think we've covered this one.
- A rugby lover – Ditto.
- Overly defensive – Balderdash.

The eighties had begun in earnest, a decade I was happy to inhabit, with all its frippery and unashamedly letting the good times roll.

Of course, it wasn't all good. Around the time I was leaving school, the Soviets were shooting down a Korean commercial airliner that had entered their airspace, killing all 269 on board. Thirty-eight prisoners were escaping from Northern Ireland's notorious Maze Prison. And the president of Grenada and Philippine opposition leader Benigno Aquino were both assassinated. At least Donna Griffiths (no relation) had finally stopped sneezing, having done so continually for 978 days.

What a mixed-up place. Meanwhile, out in Britain's streets, boys had started wearing blusher, eye-liner and shirts that billowed.

I utterly loved Duran Duran. Pop had entered my soul. I remember cycling to Basingstoke, one afternoon off school, and wilfully purchasing their Rio album, knowing full well that it was not a chap thing to do, but caring not a jot. Almost enjoying the alleged perversity.

Independence of spirit had been creeping in. Vicki, the car, David Bowie, 'Ban the Run', the prefect palaver . . . It had all been adding up.

I was still naïve, of course, just more lime than green.

I'm a sucker for eighties music still, particularly the synthesised end of the spectrum: Ultravox, Depeche Mode, a-ha, Blancmange – spare a spade? I reckon I can dig myself a deeper hole – Howard Jones, Nik Kershaw . . .

Pick of my crop, though, were the Eurythmics. A song titled Here Comes the Rain Again was always going to appeal to me, or Never Gonna Cry Again, with the suspicion that you were. Annie Lennox's voice was pure, crystalline woman; Dave Stewart, a gifted tunesmith.

Come the We Too Are One tour, a girlfriend and I collared their mini bass player, Chucho, outside the Edinburgh Playhouse and the lovely man gave us backstage passes to the night's gig. Afterwards, we sat next to Billie Mackenzie, singer of The Associates, who would one day take his own life, too awed to talk to him, and still later waited patiently outside the venue for Lennox and Stewart's autographs.

I have a huge admiration for the pair, it's just . . .

I attended the Panopticon *Doctor Who* convention in 1996. On behalf of *Radio Times*, as we have previously concurred.

Oh all right, it was fabulous: my first ever convention, 20 years after they had begun, and I had the perfect excuse. 'I'm here on business.'

Was I bollocks.

Anne, the commissioning editor at the *Radio Times* responsible for its *Doctor Who* coverage – and my consequent brushes with Time Lords – had been talking to the Doctor Who Appreciation Society (DWAS) as research for the magazine's 16-page TV Movie special, heralding the one-off arrival of Paul McGann's Eighth Doctor. Thus was she invited to their Panopticon and took along *RT*'s art editor, Paul, another fan, and myself, the writer. Who had nothing to write about.

We could not possibly cover the event, since it had no TV-show hook, which the magazine always requires. They knew it, we knew it. We all kept quiet.

Walking into Coventry's Leofric Hotel, I had some idea of what to expect. Stalls selling merchandise, of no interest whatsoever to the normal people shopping outside – check. Whovians in home-made costume, of variable quality and shamelessness – check. Talks and film shows, which I would have to avoid for fear of guilt by association – check. Actual actors from the show – yeek.

I admit that I was trying to appear mildly aloof, while less mildly buzzing inside. What would I witness next? Could I afford that Jon Pertwee jigsaw? Was that guy geekier than me? Of course he was! The old comparisons on the unwritten Nerd Scale would trouble me all afternoon.

Luckily, as VIPs, we were allowed backstage, where I could hide, stop worrying, and where the stars were hanging out.

I can tell you exactly who was there at the time because I dashed back to the merchandise stalls, picked up a classic black-and-white photograph of a Dalek on Westminster Bridge, and, practically trailing wee with excitement, returned, disguising my out-of-breath panic, to get it signed.

*To Nick, Hi! Sylvester McCoy*
(The Seventh Doctor.)

*To Nick, love Sophie Aldred*
(His companion, Ace.)

*To Nick, Love Wendy Padbury x*
(Troughton companion Zoë.)

*'Hello, Fraser Hines*
('Hello'? Where's the love? Troughton's Jamie.)

*To Nick, Lots of love Mark Strickson xx*
(But that's too much love. Davison's Turlough.)

*For Nick, love Caroline John xxx*
(Pertwee's Liz Shaw. Yes, I know I didn't rate the character.)

*To Nick, from Nicholas Courtney*
(UNIT's Brigadier.)

*To Nick, John Nathan-Turner*
(Doctor Who producer from Tom Baker's last season until the end.)

Luckily, they passed it around among themselves, so I didn't have to go up to each one, at the age of 31, supposedly working for the nation's most respected television listings magazine, and whimper, 'Would you sign this for me, please. It's for Nick . . . No, he's not my son/friend's son/nephew.'

What it meant, though, was that I was standing there like a ninny while that happened, with nothing to do bar make conversation. What on earth do you say to these people?

It can only be embarrassing. I could hardly start recounting favourite storylines, or gush over performances, or ask after most memorable scenes, or ply gossip about what Tom Baker was really like, or which breakfast cereal he preferred, or whether I could have someone's hat. They had heard it all before, and I certainly didn't plan to hit 9 or 10 on their own unwritten Nerd Scales.

It was Fraser Hines (also *Emmerdale*'s Joe Sugden) who broke the ice. I reminded him of someone, he said.

It was an awkward moment, standing there, surrounded by *Doctor Who* alumni, each appraising me for likely celebrity look-alike, as if I were something from Madame Tussaud's.

Suddenly Hines declares, 'Dave Stewart!'

Dave bloody Stewart!

As I said, I admire the man enormously, but he wore sunglasses indoors. I have a chin. And I'm taller than him. My face is much squarer. I don't have a gingery beard. I LOOK ABSOLUTELY NOTHING LIKE DAVE STEWART.

I protested; everyone laughed.

I considered finding them less companionable.


There was a consolation prize. The DWAS hierarchy showed me an actual Tardis prop that had been used in the series and when I asked, 'Can I go inside?', they said, 'Yes'.

The experience wasn't quite as awesome as I had expected.

The Tardis is one of television's great icons, despite being a telephone box. The blue panelling, the Police notice on the door, the light on top, the 'Vwooorp-vwooorp!' sound effect.

Obviously it isn't really bigger on the inside than the

outside, and though I realised that, it was a palpable let-down when I stepped through the fabled door to find just a battered, unpainted wooden box inside. Kind of, 'Oh' with a slight echo. It was a bit like looking over a house and trying out a walk-in wardrobe.

There really was nothing to look at, so I passed the time imagining the parade of actors before me who had done precisely the same.

I'm not sure which era this particular Tardis was from, as several were made during the classic show's 26-year run, but feasibly Jon Pertwee and Katy Manning, or Tom Baker and Elisabeth Sladen, had dashed into that very same space, pursued by Daleks, and had stood there panting, twiddling their thumbs, perhaps playing a quick round of Scissors, Paper, Stone, waiting for the director to shout 'Cut!'

Poor old Peter Davison: he had three companions at one stage. Four bodies in there would have been a right squeeze – and one of them was Adric's. I wonder whether the Doctor, Tegan and Nyssa were ever tempted to lay into the pouting bachelor's baby during such moments in the Tardis, and emerge as a trio, whistling?

'Adric? No, haven't seen him. Didn't go in there with us.'

I interviewed Bruno Langley, formerly of *Coronation Street*, who played Adam Mitchell, the young chap Rose and Christopher Eccleston's Doctor meet in the very first Dalek episode of the new series, who joins them in the Tardis for the following story (Simon Pegg with bright white hair, giant slug monster dripping from ceiling).

He confirmed that the weirdest part of his brief tenure was arriving on set, first day, leaping into the Tardis with Piper and Eccleston and them standing in there, cramped, staring at each other.

If you ever get a chance to do the same, to step inside the Police Box, but would prefer to keep the *Doctor Who* illusion alive, step back, raise a hand and just say 'No'.

The last time I sat down to watch a full episode of the classic series was 25 November 1983, near the end of Davison's run. It was the 20th Anniversary Special, The Five Doctors, and I would have just started at Farnborough Tech, on my maths and chemistry A-level retakes.

I had already notched the C in physics up to a B, having revised some more and taken the train to London comfortably alone, to sit in a strange exam hall, and treated myself to Ultravox's Quartet album afterwards, from the Virgin Megastore on Oxford Street, back then a cornucopia of delicious vinyl.

There have been a few of these multiple-Time Lord stories: The Three Doctors, The Five Doctors, The Two Doctors. You see a pattern emerging.

The Two Doctors, a Colin Baker story, I caught on video some years after its original airing in 1985. Despite bringing back Patrick Troughton, Fraser Hines as Jamie, and a classic monster, the Sontarans (baked potato lives in a spacesuit, scarier than that sounds), and being set in actual Spain (a rare treat for actors usually confined to quarries), it was such unadulterated, plotless tosh that it doesn't even warrant a précis.

The other two do, mind . . .

*The Three Doctors, for the unfamiliar: Giant orange bubble-wrap creatures are after Jon Pertwee's Doctor. Jo Grant isn't much use so he calls on the Time Lords, who send his previous incarnations to help. Somewhere in a black hole, renegade Time Lord Omega is wearing robes and a lengthy frightmask, intent on power. Omega touches the Second Doctor's recorder and dies because it wasn't antimatter.*

This Tenth Anniversary celebration debuted on the cusp of 1972/73 and caused great excitement in my head because it meant that I could find out what William Hartnell and Patrick Troughton were really like. Though the companion *Radio Times* was yet to come out, with pictures and all, I was aware of their existence – and there they were suddenly, on my telly, reprising their roles.

Unfortunately, Hartnell was not well and was confined to a box.

He barked orders in an old-person's voice and looked rather fragile. I didn't take to him.

Pertwee and Troughton jousted verbally with one other, and I felt rather protective of the former, he being 'my Doctor', yet Troughton was such a slight fellow, like a pixie with his recorder and his prancing.

I have watched the story since; there is plenty of proprietorial 'I'm the Doctor!', 'No, I'm the Doctor!' banter, and I wonder whether there was any small basis in reality. Whenever Pertwee appeared at any Who convention he would raise his arms and cry, 'I am the Doctor!' (also the title of his biography, in case we had missed it). What other Doctors present thought, one can only imagine.

To me, at the age of eight, The Three Doctors felt like a once-in-a-lifetime chance to be able to glimpse the past and treasures I had missed on account of being unborn.

And if that were a treat, imagine if they could have done the same, but with more Doctors.

*The Five Doctors, for the unfamiliar: With Peter Davison's Doctor at the helm, his previous incarnations – bar one, and including a cheat – plus assorted companions are whisked by an unseen bloke into the Death Zone on the Time Lords' home planet, Gallifrey. There, they face a dazzling array of old foes, climb the Dark Tower and meet the previously unseen bloke. It's one of their own, who wants immortality. Greed. Tsk.*

I remember this one so distinctly. Despite having lost interest in the series, the prospect of gathering together so many elements from my past in a single Twentieth Anniversary story was too compelling to let slip.

I was back home at Princess Drive. With my parents disinterested, I settled into my 'playroom' upstairs with milk, snacks and the spare telly.

I had been looking forward to The Five Doctors all afternoon, even though I felt too old to be watching. Well, no one need know.

'Wuh-duddly-do wuh-duddly-do wuh-duddly-do wuh-duddly-do . . . Wuh-ooooooooo-ooh!'

It was trashy but glorious, the only letdown being the non-attendance of Tom Baker, trapped punting with Romana II in Cambridge (actually having declined to appear, since he had only lately quit).

There was no William Hartnell either, the actor having died, and his First Doctor role was taken by lookalike Richard Hurndall.

That's what you didn't get.

Here is what you did get:

Doctors: Troughton, Pertwee and Davison.
Nemesis: The Master (Anthony Ainley version).
Companions: Susan, Jamie, Zoë, Brigadier, Captain Yates, Liz, Sarah Jane, K-9, Tegan, Turlough.
Monsters: Dalek, Cybermen (several), Yeti, Raston Warrior Robot.
Vehicles: Bessie.

Now that's a ten-gallon tank of nostalgia to bathe in, by anyone's reckoning.

The appearance of the Yeti was a boon. I had seen plenty of photographs, but never one moving. And there it was, looking like a giant, filthy Womble whose nose had been brutally sliced off, roaring like the same, waddling through caves in pursuit of the Brigadier and Troughton.

Also great was the new monster, the Raston Warrior.

This was a nimble bloke in a silver catsuit with a very shiny, smooth helmet that covered his entire head. He shot metal spears from his arm and disappeared in an instant, only to reappear behind pursuing Cybermen, to karate chop one's head off. It was simple cut and paste editing, wise old Nick could tell, but that didn't stop his eyes widening.

And there was Jon Pertwee – in Bessie! Same cloak, silver curls further akimbo since his swansong nine and a half years earlier, accompanied by Sarah Jane. Really, my heart fluttered.

I remembered them. They brought back all the cosiness of childhood.

Admittedly, there were some naff bits.

There's a scene where Sarah Jane falls down a bank, supposedly so steep that Pertwee has to use Bessie's winch to pull her free. In truth, two small children aged three and five, one with a liquorice bootlace, the other with some tadpoles in a jar, could have done the same job. It failed to matter.

So I had been let loose into the big wide world, or at least the bit of it named Farnborough.

I remember being neither elated nor fazed. Leaving Lord Wandsworth has left nothing on my subconscious. I was probably nervous but there was still work to do, and as I have realised since, I can be incredibly pragmatic.

Those A-level grades needed upping, considerably. I believed that my future prospects rested there. If I messed up again, I genuinely foresaw a life under bridges with bag of glue.

Sometimes I drove to Tech, other times Dad dropped me off at Winchfield Station on the way to work, and I'd stand there on the platform smoking a Silk Cut (I'm afraid to say), feeling the free spirit.

I made two good friends there, one so good that I lost my virginity to her. Martin and Tammy. You work it out.

Tammy, if you're reading this, I know I said I'd done it before but I hadn't.

Mum and Dad, I assume you will be reading this. Please: never talk to me about it.

Dylan . . . Oh, you know.

At lunchtimes I drove Martin and Tammy to the pub, or took us record shopping in Aldershot, other times . . . it's weird but my memories of that Farnborough year are more vague than any other, I guess because I had fallen in love. It consumed me. (That and my studies, Mum and Dad.)

Tammy was a petite girl with a trimmed mop of raven hair who rolled her Rs slightly, had dark, lively eyes and sometimes wore a mauve jumper. Perfume drifted off her, the make of which I forget, and I fancied her like mad.

I don't even remember the lead-up to us going out, but I can picture a walk in woodland in vivid sunshine, no one else around, holding her hand, and this sense of bonding that I had not experienced with Vicki. This was my new best friend – and she was a girl. All new.

It was that overwhelming ache again, but this time requited. No queues in phone boxes, no waiting for the disco bus.

I started giving Tammy a lift into Tech in the mornings. One time she had an unexpected gift for me. Duran Duran's new seven-inch single, The Reflex (B-side: a cover of Steve Harley's Come Up and See Me (Make Me Smile)).

I was stunned. A girl had never given me a present before. Honestly, I had no idea that they even did.

I would drive to meet her at home in Fleet of an evening and we'd go to the pub, me drinking softs, then sit in her lounge afterwards, after her parents had gone to bed, and talk for hours.

I'd get home well into the early morning, having been

given a key to the front door. That drive at night in the Mini Metro, no one else on the roads, window open, heater on, lost in a swirling delirium.

My parents, to their credit, knew when to cut some slack.

I watched *Casablanca* with Tammy one Sunday afternoon on her lounge floor. The movie I watched before that might well have been Sylvester Stallone in *Cobra*, with Martin, because I remember us quoting his line, shortly before the hoods threaten to blow up the store: 'Dat's OK, I don't shop here'.

She changed my reading habits entirely. From Ray Bradbury and Sven Hassel, I switched overnight to L. P. Hartley (*The Go-Between*; *The Hireling*) and Ian McEwan (*The Cement Garden*; *First Love, Last Rites*).

When she wasn't around, I pined at home to records or walked into Alton town centre and checked out the slithery covered hardbacks in the local library, to return home with an armful of new paged feelings. I even read Daphne Du Maurier's *Rebecca*.

Tammy introduced me to a woman's world and I was smitten.

The first night I ever stayed out, I had told my parents that Tammy's folks had OK'd me staying over. They weren't fully convinced, but to my relief they let it pass.

Of course, her parents were away and I drove us to a party in a woods, where friends of hers had lit a fire after nightfall, amid a largely destroyed fortification, and were sitting around supping from cans, just chatting. I had recently turned 19 and it was incredible. Young people did that sort of thing!

When everyone dispersed, we sat in the Metro, I kept the engine running and the heater on, we put both seats back and tried to sleep. But it was too uncomfortable and the chill crept in through the gaps. So I drove us to glamorous Fleet

Services on the M3 at about 5.30 am, hoping something might be open.

The first thing that hits you at that time of the morning is the bird-interrupted silence and the sleep-deprived sense of surrealism. The second thing that hit us was that only other person in the car park was one of the world's least convincing transvestites, tottering across the tarmac in high heels and wig, looking like a bloke who lost a bet after bingeing on tequila.

It only added to the sense of being grown-up..

All my memories of Tammy and that Farnborough year come washed in sunshine. If it ever rained, I don't remember it.

First love. You might come close but you can never get it back.


Brilliantly, the band that always recalled those times for me was blinking Rush again. Those three long-haired blokes from Canada who had made me wear a dressing gown in the evening.

Their Grace Under Pressure LP had been released and I was playing it in the lounge, one summer's day. Dad was away at work, Mum was in the garden and the track Afterimage came on.

It's a song about vanished friendships which starts with such a heady swirl of sound. When Geddy Lee sang of how 'We ran by the water on the wet summer lawn', I looked outside to our own slabs of vibrant green and suddenly everything fell into place. The emotions, the excitement, the newness of all that had happened converged on my brain, as if focused by some looming H. G. Wells contraption, sparking me alive. A moment of pure revelation.

It was such a high.

Of course, Newton would be waiting for his payback.


Despite the distractions, I swapped my E and O in maths

and chemistry for two As. It had been easy. Maybe it was the extra year, maybe the teaching made more sense, probably both.

I could go wherever I wanted and I had chosen London. King's College on The Strand.

Originally, I had picked Leeds University because I imagined one should flee as far from one's parents as possible. With hindsight, I realised that London was quite far enough. Also Tammy was going there, to neighbouring University College, as would be my old Lord Wandsworth friend Richard.

What was I planning to study? Having discarded Accountancy as the profit of fools, I'd chosen Electrical & Electronic Engineering. Why? This is the God's honest truth. Having spent so long in pubs with car, so unable to drink, I had grown rather fond of the fruit machines. I reasoned that if I took electronics, I would be able to build my own one.

Honestly.

## Some Things . . . I Decided to Do Which Weren't Necessarily Well Thought Through

- The proposal – It's disorientating, at the age of 40, deciding to get engaged for the first time. I took Sinead for a surprise weekend in the Highlands, but worried that if I thought the proposal through too much, I might trip over the script. So I left it to chance. Stupidly nervous, I downed three pints in half an hour and, around midnight, asked her join me beneath Britain's oldest hanging tree (a marvellously historic, gnarled structure, leaning, like a giant's hand emerging from the soil). The inept romanticism worked wonders until my gob got carried away and observed, 'Imagine how many hanged blokes must have wee'd themselves here'.

- Speaking of which – Ever started out a journey and thought, 'I could do with a wee, but I reckon I can last'? I once drove from Alton to London like that. By the time I reached Euston, my right foot had pushed the accelerator through the floor of the car and my bladder was clawing at the driver's-side window, whimpering.
- Parascending – After a traumatic relationship split, I was offered a press trip to the Swiss Alps during summer and leapt at the chance to escape the country. They took us to the top of a mountain and asked if we would like to strap ourselves to a bloke wearing a large kite, and jump off. Despite my fear of heights, I went for it. When the bloke said, 'Run!', I did, but I was so terrified he was forced to point out, 'You're meant to run off the mountain, not back up it.'
- Bravado – Back in London, around that same time, I found myself walking through Camden in the early hours of a morning. Two hoodie types walked past and one asked for a cigarette. 'Sorry, don't smoke,' I said, and carried on. 'Poof,' one spat. Instead of letting it go, nursing a minor death wish, I turned round and called out, 'What did you say?' What on earth was I thinking? I have crossed the road to avoid mothers with dangerous looking prams. As they marched back towards me, I was wondering whether police people had seen us on CCTV and were already rushing to my aid. Incredibly, I brazened it out. Never again.
- The museum trip – One Sunday, Dylan suggested we visit the London Museum. Great idea. No need to check the map, I decided, I know where that is. When we got there Dylan felt obliged to point out, 'Dad, this is the British Museum'. We ended up climbing the Monument instead. I get us lost all the time. My only hope is that it instils in him the spirit of spontaneity.
- Harry Shearer – I once interviewed Matt Groening and various *Simpsons* cast members, including Harry Shearer

(the voices of Mr Burns and Smithers, among others), who was also bass player Derek Smalls in one of my favourite films, *This is Spinal Tap*. As he walked away afterwards, I just couldn't help myself. I called after him, 'Harry!' He turned around and I went, 'Stone'enge'. He didn't laugh.

London. Dancing girls couldn't drag me away, though the offer of a salt-blown, shuttered house overlooking the sea and a pet dog that bounces might.

I chose an intercollegiate hall, housing students from all London universities, hoping that it would mean a broader range of potential mates.

Hughes Parry Hall is on Cartwright Gardens, south of Euston Road near King's Cross. It's a tall block and I was allocated room 501, on the fifth floor. I point it out to Sinead and Dylan every time we drive past and they are always enthralled.

It wasn't much of a room – window, bed, storage – but I stepped in, dropped my luggage and sighed. I had left home, and though it felt like cheating because I wasn't working and remained institutionalised, the fact stood: I was out of Alton and into the city.

I sparked up a fag and hung out of the window, watching people playing tennis opposite, letting it sink in. It wouldn't. Everything felt unreal.

So I got out, wandered into Covent Garden, savouring the succulent smog, and browsed in Flip, which sold second-hand clothes with an American vibe and attracted cod-tourists like me.

I didn't belong – yet. But just to walk around that churning metropolis, knowing that there was no bell about to ring, no one structuring my bedtime, no one to tell me what to wear or what not to drink, and realising that Flip was not the zenith of the opportunities; that Camden, Portobello, Wardour Street, Chinatown, Soho and pubs and clubs and gigs and people (and study) awaited me . . . I knew it was the start of something big.

That night started on the smaller side, with a meet-and-greet in the Hughes Parry bar.

It had been advertised in the lifts and I was dreading it. Introductions to strangers, the same old questions that no one really desired answers to, small talk. And the bar area was pretty soulless.

The first person I got talking to was Steve, from Redcar, who was doing Chemistry at King's. No doubt he told me what A-levels he had taken and which school he had been to, but I forget.

Actually, the first thing he asked me was, 'Have you ever done it in the back of a Mini Metro?' It struck me as a bit forward. I could only imagine that he had, or it was one hell of a shot in the dark.

My first new friend.

Unfortunately, it didn't get much further than that. No conversations stuck. People continually swapped places and I drank lager for the sake of it, liquid bravery for the social melée.

That Monday I walked down Southampton Row to King's College with Steve, to register for the course and to sort out my grant cheque. Oh, lovely cash. More money than had ever inhabited my bank account, and I would have to make it last . . . unless I spent it all, in which case I could always beg off Dad. I think the option was always in the back of my mind.

The Fresher's Fair that day offered an assortment of societies that I felt obliged to join, which I did, and then never attended any of their meetings. I did spot an attractive unkempt-red-haired girl there, tall with cheeks, ears and a grin, at the Anarchist Society stall, whom I had noticed the previous night in Hughes Parry, and nearly went to talk to her. Instead I wandered around alone like Billy No-Mates, wondering what an actual student would do next, and made a mental note to try later.

King's College itself was pretty disappointing. I remember consciously avoiding universities with campuses, because it all sounded too cordoned off, a never-shifting community – like public school. Now I wished King's had one.

There was a bar, the Nelson Mandela Bar – no doubt he would have approved ('Oh yes, how lovely, you have named a shit bar after me') – almost as soulless as Hughes Parry's, and another floor for concerts and discos; entertainment-wise, that was about it. I heard tell of a badminton court somewhere, which I never tracked down in three years, and I wonder now whether it was the King's College version of the Golden Fleece.

Lectures were held around a labyrinth of lecture rooms. Those university-student scenes I occasionally saw on telly, where the students sat in tiered rows, all grown-up, looking down on a lecturer with a desk and whiteboard – it was like that.

I just checked the King's website. Their Department of Engineering was set up in 1838, it boasts. It is 'arguably' the oldest engineering school in England. You do wonder who might bother to argue with them.

My fellow electronics students were largely Asian, some shyer than others, who tended to keep to themselves, all more talented in and dedicated to the subject than I would ever be.

There was one Brazilian, one Greek and the British contingent, a motley crew, most of whom were staying in a King's hall of residence south of the river, and who would later share the same flat without me.

The eldest, a likeable bloke called Kev, had tattoos and used to be a merchant seaman. He had joined the course to better himself and was worryingly determined. I had joined to make a fruit machine. I could see some commitment issues on the horizon.

There were three or four girls out of 30-odd. At least that needn't have concerned me, not with Tammy living just around the corner.

Who dumped me after six months.

Which was a blow.

To start my post-parent life in the heart of the capital, with my girlfriend beside me, was beyond dreams. I'd go round to hers, she'd come round to mine; if the other wasn't in we would leave little notes for each other. It was a proper, settled relationship.

Hold on a moment, I spotted a couple of those notes before, when I was snuffling around in that old tan-leather briefcase, among the letters, Friends of Barclay James Harvest newsletters, Liverpool pennants and pair of Free-with-Shreddies 3D glasses.

. . . It's taking a while, sorry. Invites to 'Jazz and Cock-tails' and the 'Hughes Parry Summer Ball' (which I didn't attend, having no partner), *Melody Maker* calendar 1984, 'All Night Film Show' flyer, theatre-ticket stubs – I'd forgotten, Tammy cajoled me to the theatre, even *Swan Lake* in Covent Garden – a two-sided A4 letter I hand-wrote to someone complaining about student loans, but obviously never sent, and Michael Duggan's business card. He was a *Financial Times* journalist I got talking to down the Nell Gwynne pub off The Strand, and drunkenly asked for advice on getting into the business – which he actually followed up. Cheers, Michael.

Oh my days (as Dylan would say), I just came across *Tool*, the King's College Engineering Society Mag, Feb 85, Issue 3, Vol 1. *Tool* – how apt. No wonder I never went to any society meetings.

Another thing I had forgotten: there's a letter from the staff at the Market Hotel in Alton, where I had worked as a barman, the summer before coming to London, which jokes about my living on Hughes Parry's 5th floor: 'All the girls are out shopping at the moment for crampons and scaling hooks.' Bless.

So: Tammy's notes. Can't find them for nostalgic detritus, I'm afraid. And I have been rooting around in there for at least an hour, enjoying myself as people do in attics.

I did discover a 'Sorry' postcard from Vicki, apologising for not letting me know what her plans were, 'or even phoning', which ends, 'Well see ya around', which sums up the end of that one. And I've pulled out another few bits, which I may save for later, appropriate moments.

Anyway, Tammy and I hit the college parties and discos together (as well as the theatre and one ballet). I remember discovering cocktails before one of those University College All Night Film Parties and swiftly depositing my spaghetti meal outside their Student Union, and being amused to discover it still there, dried, like swirly punk artwork, some days later. We never got to see the films.

I don't think I was sophisticated enough for Tammy.

She was studying Geography & Anthropology. I didn't even know what anthropology was. My Dad definitely wouldn't have reckoned it would get her a job.

Tammy's room was decorated with postcards of gallery paintings and photographs of friends and family. Mine was accumulating a stack of *Sun* newspapers and had pictures of David Bowie, torn from calendars, covering its walls.

Ever sartorially eccentric, while trying unsuccessfully to get a grip on fashion, I had lived in a favourite pair of red shoes, purchased from Shelly's, given David's advice in Let's Dance to 'Put on your red shoes and dance the blues'. Sadly, I danced the blues like a record-breakingly large American might dance the can-can.

Tammy had tried her best with me – I knew my L. P. Hartley from my J. R. Hartley – but it wasn't right.

She ended up with a bloke from her hall of residence

whom, I discovered, she later married and had children with.

Although I had fallen in love with the woman, surprisingly the effect of the split wasn't as debilitating as I might have expected. Yes, I spent a weekend in Basingstoke immediately afterwards, and if that's an improvement on your situation, things must be bad, but there simply wasn't the time to mope.

The second year was looming, when we would have to find and share our own digs, and I had neglected making many other friends.

Actually, sick to death of male company, after seven years of skateboards, spots squeezed in mirrors, unsightly bottoms in showers, conversations about engine oils and all the sensitivity of a gnome community out of pile cream, I had switched my chattering allegiance to women.

Whether the unkempt-red-haired girl from the Anarchist Society stall came up and spoke to me, or vice versa – I think we can guess – her name was Jane and she had a friend called Tracey – it really wasn't Oxford – and I spent most late nights in their rooms (since mine was full of *Sun*s and Bowie snaps) talking.

It was such a dose of fresh air.

Jane introduced me to the indie music I had been too naff to absorb. The Smiths, Billy Bragg, The Wedding Present, Aztec Camera, Cherry Red Records and Postcard. I didn't like the more twee stuff, and The Smiths' Queen is Dead stance made me a little uneasy (I'd have had to find an excuse to turn down the entire song if I had played it at home), but this was a whole new musical life.

Jane and Tracey both loved Siouxsie and the Banshees and Tracey told of going to one of the gigs wearing yellow, which wasn't black so everyone stared at her. My kind of person. They laughed a lot and we made tea; conversations came and went easily; there was no posturing or mentioning anyone's penis.

Girls, I realised, were far more interesting and fun than boys, even platonically – but that didn't help my impending accommodation dilemma. 'Would you mind if I lived with you?' might have seemed forward.

Interlude: I interviewed Mathew Graham yesterday for the *Radio Times*. He's the writer of Fear Her, episode 11 of the second series of new Who, the one set during the 2012 London Olympics.

We talked about the differences between Doctors Nine and Ten, Eccleston and Tennant, and he seemed to prefer the latest incarnation.

I would concur.

Obviously, it isn't an acting-prowess thing. Eccleston could effortlessly act his way out of a decently guarded fortress – and his cachet did the series all sorts of favours – but for me he felt like a square peg that had been deftly sanded to fit a round hole.

No doubt that weighty CV, laced with grit, had hung over my mind. *Cracker, Clocking Off, Our Friends in the North* . . .

I did love the way they brushed aside Eccleston's Salford twang:

Rose: 'If you're an alien then why do you have a Northern accent?'

Doctor: 'Lots of planets have a North.'

But for a fan shuffling horrified into middle age, who had mostly lapped up the toothy bamboozling of Baker T, he exuded a presence that failed to chime with men trundling around in Dalek casings. When he went 'Fantastic!' with that stiff-necked beam, I felt oddly unconvinced.

Of course, kids – the prime audience – didn't, having none of my ancient baggage: proof that Eccleston did a formidable job. I just fancied something lighter.

So when David Tennant was announced as his successor, my hopes performed a crap tango.

I'd only caught him in one series previously, *Blackpool*, where he played a detective who shags his prime suspect's wife while miming to the likes of These Boots Are Made For Walking – I avoided *Casanova*, in which he played the title role, since any show about men who appeal to women makes me jealous – and he exuded such boyish charm despite being 33 at the time.

As it is panning out, his Tenth Doctor is indeed this viewer's round peg (so to speak).

Why? Dapper with a hint of louche, quiff, urgency, humour, sex appeal, cheesy grin, still impressed by stuff he's seen a thousand times, chemistry with Rose, heart (two of them), excitement, danger, shoes. The lot. All right, I might tone him down slightly on occasions, but let's not quibble.

I hope he stays three seasons. Then lets Robbie Williams have a go.

(Kidding.)


Interlude 2: We're now three episodes and a Christmas Special into Tennant's run. The latest instalment was The One for the Dads: School Reunion. The one where they brought back Sarah Jane and K-9.

How would the new boy cope with an old girl plus tin mutt? Don't underestimate that. It was a major test for all.

If Sarah Jane had jarred with the new cast, the producers' plan would have backfired, alienating rather than endearing the ageing diehards. And if Tennant hadn't managed to pull off the emotional déjà vu, his Doctor would have been found wanting.

Nothing of the sort happened. When Time Lord and ex-companion fell into each other's arms, I turned to fall into Sinead's, only to find her reading a magazine.

It peeled away the years, seeing those two dashing down corridors, as if David Tennant really were Tom Baker, thirty years on. New meets old. Sold to the gentleman currently staring outraged at the liver spot on his right hand.

The bonus, allegedly, was the appearance of K-9, battered yet functioning, and though I enjoyed the nostalgia, I can't pretend that I was ever a major fan.

He had debuted during the embers of 1977, in The Invisible Enemy, when I would have been trying hard but failing to come over all teenaged. The annoying nasal voice, the machine superiority, the lame name pun, the trundling around wonkily, looking as if its progress might become impeded by a passing beetle in its path.

Nope, K-9 felt too much like a toy in a series I wanted to take seriously. (Ironically, aged 30-odd, I went out and bought an actual K-9 toy, which spoke in that annoying nasal voice.)

Still the mutt did offer the aforementioned nostalgia, as well as comedic opportunity. Witness Rose's on-off beau Mickey realising his place in the scheme of things.

'I'm the tin dog!'

Indeed you are, Michael.


The floors in Hughes Parry ran alternate male/female.

My fifth floor was occupied by a bunch of lads who hung out together and who nodded 'Hello', but that was about it. I had hardly made the effort while Tammy was around. Neither would you have done.

After we split, I brazenly walked into Quinch's room – I'll come to that shortly – where they were gathered, apologised and effectively asked if I could be their friend.

There were five of them: Andy, Andy, Andy, Karl and Ralf. A bit like Duran Duran with its Taylors. Only girls were less likely to scream at this lot.

Karl was a teetotaller from Wales who was heavily into comics, studying Pharmacy. He named the Andy who did Material Science 'Quinch', since he vaguely resembled the character of that name from 2000AD comic. Ralf was German. I really don't remember what he was studying.

Then there was Andy Computer-Science-at-Imperial-College, who became Bruce, because he thought he could do kung fu (Bruce Lee – geddit?). He used to adopt a kung fu position of stability on the tube and we would push him over.

Finally, Andy from Stourbridge, also reading Computer Science. He was 'Funk', because he liked that sort of music and Level 42 in particular. Tosh, in other words. He had an outrageous, flappy flick of hair and tucked his jumpers into his trousers.

And now we were all mates!

Quinch had a girlfriend at Hughes Parry, Karl had a girlfriend back in Wales (whom he married, when I was asked to be best man and my speech was rubbish); the other three and myself were single. It would remain that way.

So we filled the time maturely, buying water pistols and chasing each other around the corridors and floors of the hall.

I have a photo of me, wearing my straw trilby with red band, Duran T-shirt, combat trousers, cardigan and flip-flops, back to the wall, water-machine-gun in hands, clenched teeth, pulling a 'You'll never take me alive!' pose. That's what we did. Yes, I know.

Girls used to complain about the disturbance during exam weeks and one time Ralf, I believe it was, broke a toilet seat while hiding during a water fight, and we were ordered to report to the hall bursar. It was like we had never left school. (Rather embarrassing.)

When the first academic year ended, we agreed to meet up for the start of 1985/86, to find a place to live, where we could throw parties that no one would come to.

Though I had found the lectures increasingly dull, and had skived off as many as possible, depending upon the authoritarian air of the lecturer, I had conscientiously swotted for the year-end exams and did reasonably well.

That summer holiday was one of my most memorable.

I stayed in London and managed to find a flatshare on Camden Road, courtesy of a frizzy-haired girl whose parents owned the place, and who was a friend of a friend. She charged rent. I needed a job.

I found one in Ponti's wine bar on The Strand, having walked in off the street and asked on the off-chance, which was unusually daring.

The manager was a friendly Italian named Marco, and most of the staff were his fellow countrymen. Downstairs in the kitchen was a South African chef with a Musketeer beard who loved telling a story and who was regularly exasperated. I didn't blame him – there were no windows down there, amid that heat.

I worked the sandwich bar, making fresh sandwiches – 'white or brown for you?' – wrapped and bagged. Lunchtimes were incredibly busy.

The start time was hideous. I seem to recall setting my alarm clock for 7a.m. – I was a student, remember – putting on my white shirt, black trousers, black shoes and sleepwalking to the tube.

I could choose anything off the menu for my lunch, always blagging a cake, and often sat with the ex-flustered chef. I don't think the Italians believed his stories.

One time, a staff member came in wearing a straw hat; Chef took it off him, examined it, acting all travel-expert, declared it a genuine Panama hat, and the bloke took it back, looked at the label and went, 'It says "Made in Taiwan" here.'

There was one problem: the Italians were quick. Quicker than me at making sandwiches. Marco chivvied me along and I did try, but I could never quite understand what difference it would make to the customer if they got their sandwich ten seconds later.

After a couple of weeks, Marco told me it wasn't working out.

But I had been really enjoying myself! The banter, the cakes, the pay, the sunshine outside, the customer who tipped German youngster Boris Becker to win Wimbledon, and I didn't bet, and Becker won.

I was crushed. I had been sacked. I just couldn't halt the tears.

It was excruciating. I could barely speak for holding off more serious waterworks, clenching my jaw, cursing my childishness.

I could see in his eyes that he felt bad, but not enough to relent.

No matter. After a couple of interviews via the Labour Exchange, I went to work in a pub in Tufnell Park.

I loved that, too. It involved vacuuming the place before the doors opened and returning for the evening shift, but the locals were chatty.

A middle-aged blonde lady came in one late-morning and started talking. She was a brassy sort, possibly loaded, and invited me to her lunchtime drinks party. Save a trip back to Camden, I thought.

'What do you drink?' she asked.

'Fosters,' I replied, and took the address.

When I turned up, it was just me and her.

I looked around for more party-goers, in vain. There were no knocks on the door, no 'Hellooooo! Brought some vino!'

God knows what we talked about but I remember the discomfort. She was attractive enough, if several years beyond my bag. (Actually, I'm not sure I even qualified for a bag, back then.)

I excused myself to go to the loo and stood there, pissing distractedly, head swirling, not from the Fosters, and when I came out, she was waiting in ambush.

'I'm known for seducing young men,' she told me.

Perhaps in practice for a career in journalism, I made my excuses and left.

I was 'headhunted' from the pub by the boss of a small building firm who needed a van driver/labourer. My first student summer holidays and already on my third job! And this one was brilliant.

My van was a white VW Transporter. When I sat in it, compared with the Mini Metro, the only other vehicle I had driven, it was like sitting on a hill overlooking minions. My boss, Phil, demonstrated the various knobs and levers, told me to go fetch some sand, hopped out and into his sports car.

And I was left there, sitting in this . . . tank, petrified.

Ten minutes later, having not escaped second gear, I was confronted with a double-parked Jag.

'Go on, you can get through there,' urged its owner.

I bet I bloody can't, I thought.

I protested, he demurred. So I went for it. And scraped right down the right rear wing of his lovely, expensive car. I heard onlookers gasping.

Amazingly, after I had reversed, no damage was visible.

It was really hard to spot traffic behind you and to your left in that van. Or maybe I hadn't set the side-view mirror correctly.

A couple of days later, under the A40, I was in the wrong lane and had to pull out, or end up in Oxford. There was nothing for it but to spin the wheel and pray.

'Whump!'

It was like bumper cars, only without the fairground.

The driver whose car I had hit pulled ahead, actually beamed, gave me a thumbs-up and sped off! Either he had nicked it or he wasn't one for pride in vehicles.

There's a bigger prang to come, but that's right at the end.

Van driving/labouring is one of the best jobs I have ever had. If the writing thing fell apart I'd be back like a shot.

I had to be on site by 8 a.m., which was the only downside.

There were three sites, all posh flats being gutted and renovated: in Fulham, Golders Green and Highgate. Places I had never even seen before. And there were builder's merchants all over the place. Sand, cement, radiators, plumber's piping, taps, concrete lintels, unwieldy lengths of wood, bricks – I hefted the lot. On day one, I could barely lift a single sandbag; by the end, I had one on each shoulder.

It took about a week to get the hang of the van, after which I was James Hunt (not Nigel Mansell), swinging it around corners (one time hitting an iron bollard and grooving the rear wheel arch – which Phil blamed on his brother, while I stood there sweating; sorry, Phil's brother), whipping it up through the gears, elbow hanging out of the window, carefree.

Forget your Leonardo di sodding Caprio – up there in that seat, *I* was king of the world.

And, despite the fact that I was a public schoolboy who had not substantially long ago barely kissed a girl, I got on well with the builders. Alright, they dubbed me 'Hampshire', and played wind-ups – they hadn't really met Sam Fox in that pub – but I ended up sleeping on a couple of their sofas after nights out and was offered occasional weekend work, cash in hand.

Actually, it was all cash in hand – and I was on 40 quid a day. As a student. Not that I admitted as much, as it would let on that my employment there would have to be finite.

Every Friday, Phil came round and I was handed £200 in notes. I had never even seen a £50 note. One time, I held four of those babies.

Every Saturday, I'd hit Camden Market's record stalls and pick up Bowie rarities and bootlegs.

A week before the start of my second year at King's, I told Phil I had to go back to Alton. I had run out of money, or something.

On my final day, with the foreman in the passenger seat, I turned into the road of the Highgate site and was confronted by a dustbin lorry.

Quick check in (broken) wing mirror, into reverse, foot down, 'Crash!' followed by 'Tinkle'.

We sat in stunned silence. What had I done? (No, don't spell it out.)

The pensioner other-driver finally came to my window. I grovelled.

We inspected the damage. The front of his Metro was crumpled in. In the back seat, two old ladies sat mute and perturbed.

I tried to pull away. But our bumpers had overlapped and I ended up dragging the Metro and dual biddies with me. I felt awful.

I ran up the road for help and a couple of builders returned with me to the crash scene, wielding pickaxes. Only with one soiled lunk jumping up and down on their bonnet like a demented monkey, while I edged forwards, were we finally able to free the vehicles.

If there was a positive side, it was that the Transporter was barely damaged.

As Phil pointed out: 'If you weren't leaving, I'd have fired you.'

Otherwise, what a summer! It was more than just earnings, time in London uneducated and Bowie buys. If anything gave me confidence, it was that glorious season.

I discovered that, contrary to my own suspicions, I could get along with anyone: any class, race, colour, age. I had social skills! And earning a living wasn't difficult. I could do it. I could do adult life.

★

I'm not going to relive the routine of years two and three.

Suffice to say that I grew utterly disillusioned with Electrical & Electronic Engineering shortly into the second year so spent much of it down the Nell Gwynne with my coursemate Malcolm, or playing Centaur pinball in the King's bar, which I became very good at. My end-of-year course notes comprised an awful lot of photocopies made from friends' own versions, and I scraped through with a majority of Cs.

Decision time: did I stick it out, just to get the degree, or hitch the camper-van to India, sporting backpack and bumfluff, flicking V-signs at my parents (the squares) through the rear window? The former, naturally. I wasn't that cool and hard.

I graduated with a 2:2, somehow with Honours, having been nervously more conscientious in the final year, while understanding increasingly little.

Students around me were soldering components to boards, drawing circuit diagrams and solving equations that were literally Greek. I had not a clue, and I failed to care. There was no way I was going into electronics as a career, which was handy since no one would have had me.

The fruit machine never got made. I can wire a plug and spot a capacitor, and that's about the extent of it.

Two events stand out from those years in higher education. You will notice that neither of them involves intimacy with a lady.

### Live Aid – 13 July 1985

Jane got the tickets and four of us camped outside Wembley Stadium the night before, unconcerned with sleep, quaffing a minimum of cans, chatting to groups of similarly excitable individuals, about where they had travelled from and music, music, music. Not *Doctor Who*.

I was there for Bowie, of course, but the line-up held

several attractions: Kershaw, Jones, U2 (who we had seen play Brixton Academy, from the front, me in my overcoat almost dying of dehydration), Ultravox, The Who.

I didn't like Elvis Costello and I couldn't stand Queen, and I made sure everyone knew it. I was becoming forthright in my views. It was fun to flip off the fence and trample, ranting, over one side of an opinion. I no longer 'didn't mind' – I either 'hated' or 'loved' something. It has served me well as a television critic.

Anyway, as the morning dawned we started to queue. Everyone wanted to get to the front. There was jostling, tension and much evil-eyeing of anyone who dared try to 'talk to friends' up ahead, but no violence. It was a charity event.

When the doors opened, we ran. We were right at the back of the stadium, and I could see those giant video screens and Africa/guitar Live Aid logos as I sprinted for the stage, over tarpaulin that had been laid across the entire pitch.

I lost all my friends but was only five squashed bodies from the front. As bands came and went, shoulders shifted, some gave in to the heat and by the time tiresome smoothies Spandau Ballet were boring the world with True, I had reached my goal: the very front, right up against the barrier. Behind me, a bloke was waving a rubber chicken on a stick.

This was history, son.

It was a hot day. Security guards lobbed bottles of water into the crowd and sprayed our faces. Last night's hairspray stung my eyes and red dye off my hat ran down my face.

The only problem with being in such a privileged position was that the stage was so high, I could only see the artists if they practically leaned out over the front. Drummers were well off limits, as was anyone playing the piano. And when Bono dropped down into the crowd, frustratingly it was at the other end of the stage.

Bowie came on. TVC15, Rebel Rebel, Modern Love,

Heroes. Not a set-list I would have chosen – try Station to Station, 1984, Ricochet, Joe the Lion, if we're sticking to similar eras – but it was him, at Live Aid.

When he left the stage, I pulled back from the barrier, knackered and gasping for liquid. At least I hadn't needed a wee.

I found some space, perhaps 20 yards back and watched the video of those African children. Around me, people wept. You could actually hear them. The entertainment had sucked us in, now Geldof reminded us why we were there.

A friend had bought me a programme, as pre-arranged, which they presented to me when, incredibly, we spotted one another while The Who played.

'What's this?' I asked, looking at its red-stained, bowed pages with lumps.

'Someone puked over it,' they explained.

Postscript: If you look closely, bottom left of screen in the Live Aid DVD, guess who you can see waving his arms and singing along, wearing a straw trilby with red band, while Elvis Costello sings All You Need is Love, and later 'rocking' noticeably to Queen's Radio Ga Ga?

### Withnail & I screening – June or July 1987

I don't remember what drew me to this minor British film, which spent just one month in cinemas during 1987, because I was no movie-goer. I can picture myself wandering alone into the Odeon Haymarket one afternoon, and passing a vast poster for the film as I headed down the stairs to the screening room.

I can only have lapped it up because every time I visited a video shop afterwards, I always looked for *Withnail & I*.

Withnail & I, *for the unfamiliar: Withnail and Marwood are*

*actors and flatmates in a Camden grot-hole. Their dealer, Danny,
spikes their rats. They escape to the Cumbrian countryside, 'to
rejuvenate'. It doesn't work. Withnail's Uncle Monty, a rotund
homosexual, pesters Marwood for sex and the two actors return
to London. Marwood heads for a starring role in rep, leaving
Withnail behind, quoting Shakespeare to the wolves of Regent's
Park.*

It is a girdle-breaking work of staggering genius. Every one
of writer/director Bruce Robinson's lines is a gem. I could
watch it 40 times and still find some new detail, still laugh
at the same nuances in speech, the same way with swear-
words, the same casually dropped one-liners. So that is what
I have done.

Robinson's love of the English language courses through
its script like booze through its hero's veins.

Withnail. No first name. A failed Thespian and product of
private education who props up his time with stimulants.
Now that's romance. That's England.

He isn't supposed to be likeable, yet ask any Withnail fan:
they adore the man.

An outsized, faux-gilt-framed photograph of Withnail,
bewildered with fag, sozzle-eyed, hangs over my marital
bed. It is tempting to suggest that he guards over Sinead and
I, but I doubt he even realises we are there.

Marwood. Demolition ball crashes into building, toppling
its London-diseased brick. Hendrix kicks in. Cut to Marwood in driving seat of crap Jag, fag dangling from lips. He
looks out, flips sunglasses down over Lennon specs, pulls
away.

Paul McGann looks so exceptionally cool in that scene
that it made me want to buy my own crap Jag, to recreate
the moment, but a policeman might pull me over, check my
credentials, inspect the car, tick me off.

(I have been pulled over, just the once, shortly after I had
passed my driving test, on a dual carriageway near Farnham.

He followed me quite blatantly and I spent more time looking in my mirrors than forwards at the road, with butt cheeks clenched. When he turned on the blue lights, though my life was cleaner than the average cancer-research lab, I foresaw a future of buggery by the criminal and burly.

(When I wound down the windscreen, I squealed. It sounded like the Second Policeman from *Withnail & I*.

('NickGriffiths6PrincessDriveAltonHants!' I had done nothing wrong, I just looked young. He waved me onwards. An hour later my butt cheeks relaxed.)

Uncle Monty. Richard Griffiths (no relation, unfortunately) is a god. I interviewed him briefly on-set one strangely silent Sunday in the City, for a television drama called *In the Red*, about murdered bank managers. According to imdb.com, it would have been 1998.

It was unmistakably him: the same man who quoted Baudelaire wading through grasses and enlightened Marwood on the mystery of carrots. Enormous of girth and delightful of nature.

At the end of our work words, I could not help but mention my love of *Withnail & I*. It had been hammering at the rear of my incisors throughout the interview.

Rather than backing away, warding me off with holy water and cross – Withnail fans can be an obsessive bunch – he recreated, just for me, the 'garlic, rosemary and salt' scene, using a flustered young member of the crew as Marwood.

Had I played Marwood in that film, I might have considered relenting to Monty's advances.

*Withnail & I* is one of the reasons I wanted to become a writer. Bruce Robinson took mere words and arranged them into a script that makes grown men – and some women, but mainly men – revert to giggling, tiresome asses. And we love it.

Only a couple of weeks ago, a barman at a pub quiz spotted my *Withnail & I* T-shirt and we spent the rest of the night, him sober, me increasingly plastered, wheedling lines into conversation. Anyone who knows that script off by heart is a friend of mine.

My former *Radio Times* colleague, Christian, is as disturbingly addicted as I. We set out on a pilgrimage, to the film's locations. A delightful weekend in the country.

(That was a line from the film, by the way. I'd do it to new girlfriends – 'How should I possibly know what we should do? What should we do?' – who had no idea what I was talking about, and they would look perplexed, considering me uncouth.)

We stayed overnight in Shap, Cumbria, having played the Withnail soundtrack on repeat in the car – not a Jaguar, though Christian did try to blag one for the weekend – until even we grew tired of it.

And we tracked down, with cameras:

- The phonebox from which Withnail calls his agent.
- The farmer's gate that Withnail fails to close on the bull.
- The river stretch Withnail wades through to shoot at fish (Christian slipped backwards off a rock and fell in; I could barely photograph straight).
- Ma Parkin's farmhouse (it's up a narrow road, miles from anywhere, leading only to that farmhouse, yet the farmer who spotted us on his quad-bike registered not a blink, such must be the fan-traffic down the ages).
- The rock overlooking the lake atop which Withnail spreads his arms and declares, 'I'm going to be a star!' (we did that too, at the dead of night, revelling in the echoes).
- Crow Crag Farm itself. (Then a weather-pustuled, abandoned stone hutch, which was boarded up, but someone had already broken in so we did the same and sat upstairs, with French cheeses and a vintage bottle of

Chateau Margaux – with which Withnail had attempted to delay Marwood's departure back to London – which Christian had saved for such an occasion, and which we used to toast a weekend of misted eyes and unrepentant juvenilia.)

I have also met Richard E Grant, who occupied Withnail with such passion. Inevitably the man is a hero of mine (Argos ads notwithstanding).

It's a privilege to be able to step into the aura of someone who means so much to you, for whatever pitiful reason, and I know it.

Some people's heroes are politicians and rebel leaders: those they consider to be making a difference. Others choose adventurers, scientists, inventors, architects, artists, designers.

Mine are a movie/TV actor, a singer and two telly stars: E Grant, Bowie, Thaw, Baker T.

Amazingly, I have been able to meet them all. What was it like? Was it all it's cracked up to be?

I'll tell you.

## Richard E Grant/Withnail

Of course, I was hoping that he would be just like Withnail. He's not. He's an actor who is tall.

He was out in the Czech Republic filming the first series of BBC1's *The Scarlet Pimpernel* and I was dispatched there by a kindly *Radio Times* commissioner who knew of my sad fixation, to seek him out.

You really do have to keep the fandom under wraps in such situations. If I had gone bounding in there, tongue lolling among my meagre chest hairs: 'Richard! Richard!

Over here! It's me! Nick! From *Radio Times*! I love you!',
they would have sent me straight back to England.

I was able to watch him playing various scenes, from
behind the camera, in a series of dusty chateaux, but he was
often too busy for an interview. Occasionally, I caught his
eye and looked away self-consciously. Occasionally, I stared
at him while he was walking around gathering his thoughts,
or chatting to other actors, or eating his lunch. I used a
disposable camera to snap the odd covert photograph of him
when he definitely couldn't see me, so most are of his back.

Eventually, I spoke to him twice. One time, seated before a
rusted-out blue van in a courtyard. The *RT* photographer
snapped us without my knowledge and a friend on the
picture desk had the photo gratuitously enlarged and framed
as a gift. He, in full dashing garb, looks vaguely intent on my
line of questioning; I, overly Sun-In'd, look as if I am trying to
disguise the jitters.

The second time was out in the grounds of the latest
chateau and at the end I produced the *Withnail & I* video
sleeve I had carefully packed, which he signed for me: 'To
Nick, Chin chin! Richard E Grant'.

He was gracious but he wasn't actually Withnail.


## David Bowie

You can imagine how exciting this one was.

I was working for *Select*. David Bowie was recording a
session for Mark Goodier in Radio 1's Maida Vale studios,
with his awful Tin Machine side project. I volunteered to go
along, suppressing desperation.

Two PR men were there to oversee my efforts, and
informed me bluntly that there was no way I would get to
interview The Man. No way was that going to stop me.

I sat in the gallery overlooking the studio with DJ

Goodier, who was tinkering at an ancient turntable. He beckoned me across for a chat and as I knelt beside him, I jogged the record.

'Careful,' he whispered. 'That's going out live.'

I couldn't believe how rubbish Radio 1's equipment was.

Mark Goodier was cagey but I got the feeling he didn't think much of Tin Machine either. It was of no consequence. Bowie was a genius. He reinvented himself – and music – with every new seventies release.

He is untouchable. If David Bowie released an album of himself repeatedly asking Iman whether she wanted tea or coffee, until she became exasperated, I could forgive him.

And he agreed to talk to me, after much pestering of everyone anywhere in the studio, provided I spoke to the rest of the band also.

In terms of insight, my interview was cock. It was a short series of fan questions with the shrouded suggestion that maybe Tin Machine weren't that great. Like he gave a monkey's tink.

David Bowie stood there before me, in a garish shirt, outrageously tanned, making Mockney quips and being remarkably friendly for a man who is a legend.

When I asked him to sign my Tin Machine poster – which I have since lost, or had stolen, which guts me – this slipped out: 'I've got records of yours you didn't even know you had made.'

He had heard it all before. 'Please, don't,' he said, though kindly.

But the best was yet to come. Maida Vale studios are a lengthy maze of corridors, and guess who, by pure chance, was walking out at the same time as me?

Yes! Sod interviewing a hero. I chatted to him (obviously about Bowie albums – he suggested I listen to Lodger again, so I did) for a good couple of minutes, before he spotted the waiting fans and said cheerily that he had to zip ahead.

I danced up that road afterwards. And then I called my Mum from the nearest phonebox.


# John Thaw

Why? Because he starred in *The Sweeney*, that show from the landing of Princess Drive, and *Inspector Morse*, another adorable series, and though I don't like getting all luvvy about actors – it appeals to their egos – he was bloody good in both. Frankly, he was bloody good in anything he did.

The man is a national treasure. When he passed away, I was more saddened than I should have been about a complete stranger.

But I was lucky enough to spend 15 minutes with him, again for *Radio Times*, seated in the cafeteria of a London television company. He, white-haired and radiating a presence he didn't seem comfortable with.

A colleague had forewarned me that Thaw didn't enjoy being interviewed and might be difficult. Nothing could have been further from the truth. Sure, he didn't emote or guffaw; he was softly spoken and came across more like a favourite uncle.

Naturally, I was desperate to ask him about those cop shows, but some actors are sensitive about their television pasts, at pains to be seen to be moving on.

I wouldn't rush to ask Martin Shaw about his time in *The Professionals*, for instance. So when I put the first *Sweeney* question to Thaw, it was with reservations. Not a problem. Same for *Inspector Morse*. None of those answers ended up in the piece, but I was happy.

I very rarely ask *Radio Times* interviewees for autographs (contrary to how it may seem) for professional reasons, but again heart ruled head.

He signed my *Kavanagh QC* press pack afterwards: 'To Nick, All The Best, John Thaw'. I still have that.

## Tom Baker

Ah, Tom. Wonderful, expressive, eccentric Tom. He over Pertwee because I was older then, able to appreciate his performances with a more critical air, pestered by teenage exuberance.

It was a Longleat *Doctor Who* celebration, a summer, of either 1996 or 1997, I can't be certain. Don't imagine that I'm looking forward to remembering a wedding anniversary.

Producer John Nathan Turner was there, as was Nicholas Courtney (Brigadier) and a host of amateur types dressed as Cybermen, with plans to stage a Cyber-battle in the grounds. Plus Tom, cajoled out for just one more performance for his adoring fans. (Not me, obviously, since I was there for *Radio Times*.)

The plan was to contribute to a trilogy of features on television-show fan conventions. *The Prisoner* was to be another one. Sadly, it never came off. I never even transcribed the tape, so when I play it back now, it will be the first time I have listened in almost a decade. At least I can picture the scene perfectly, given the series of transparencies before me, which the RT photographer took of the interview.

Too much Sun-In again, with roots, my favourite Paul Smith flag shirt (obviously I was trying to make an impression, though the garment is so colourful that Baker's might well have been, 'What a tit'), clutching notepad and tape recorder, with pouting cheeks and flushed face, suggesting a desperately suppressed glee. Baker, taller than me, jowls of a face that might be melting, silver mop of hair, jacket slung casually over shoulder, suppression of glee not required. In the final shot of the three, he looks distracted, staring off to my left, perhaps wondering what's for tea.

How had it really gone? Time for a listen . . .

. . . It's often excruciating, listening back to one's interviewing technique. Your voice sounds silly, occasionally you drop a howler. That Harry Shearer interview I mentioned previously: what I didn't mention was that an announcement was made over the venue's PA during our chat, which distracted me and I completely lost my thread, so we stood staring at each other for interminable seconds during which I went, 'Em . . . Er . . .' and grinned foolishly.

Baker is a joy. The consummate raconteur.

He talks about his rare convention appearances and suggests that the organisers caught him at the right moment. I ask him what that right moment might be and he replies that if he knew, he wouldn't be talking to me, he'd be writing a book called *The Right Moment*, published at £17.45.

And playfully, when I ask after memories of the original Longleat Doctor Who Celebration, 'Twenty Years of a Time Lord', from 1983 – no surprises, I have a Commemorative Programme, though I wasn't among the 50,000 who attended – he recalls being pulled by a woman who informed him that there were two types of people in the world: the spankers and the spankees.

It's a typical, delightfully bizarre Tom Baker tangential anecdote. He just loves entertaining.

Another national treasure. It was a privilege to be entertained by him.

I should mention the Cybermen of the Cyber-battle. I interviewed them also, and at one stage was surrounded by three of the things.

At my age, you could spot the costume. The cricket

gloves painted silver, the flaking, aged body suit – yet the design is so clever, of the helmet in particular, that when I stared at one who was answering my queries in a distinctly human voice, I became quite rattled. Take away the surroundings, focus on that head, and you lose sense of perspective; suddenly, it becomes purely malevolent.

Think about it rationally, and the idea of dressing up to play aliens is potentially suspect. And one of the buggers had actually freaked me.

Dylan had accompanied me to the event, aged perhaps two – too young to understand how teeth-clenchingly exciting it all was – with his mother, Aileen.

At least he was also too young to consider me a nerd.

His mother wasn't.


I caught no *Doctor Who* during that time at King's, and omitted to mention my affection for the programme, for obvious reasons.

I did, however, read in the *Sun* that Bonnie Langford would be joining Colin Baker's Doctor (for his penultimate tale, it would transpire) as his new companion, Melanie Bush.

Just as Peter Davison would always be chirpy vet Tristan Farnon to me, so Langford would always be that excruciatingly annoying child star who kept bloody winning *Opportunity Knocks*, the oxymoronic 'talent show'. She sang, she danced, she was the voice of a thousand nails scraped down blackboards, while cats shagged in the background and camels licked your face.

For me, it was a final nail in the coffin. *Doctor Who* had truly lost its way.


Finally, from these university years, I found an invitation to a party, amid the old tan-leather briefcase, from my Hughes Parry friend Tracey. It goes like this:

It's all really informal. You'll probably hate everyone there, and the place, and you're such a shithead I really don't know why I'm inviting you.

But if you really have to spoil my evening by coming, invite anyone else you want, and I'll see you soon.

Lots of love, Tracey

She was, of course, joking, and I was incredibly popular.

*Coming up: Discovering that bootleg tapes of old* Doctor Who *stories exist, I find myself a dealer and the whole thing begins again, only worse; I start collecting all the old merchandise that a childhood of austerity denied me; I move in with a woman, she later moves out; I become a music journalist, my dream job; a new girlfriend becomes pregnant, how much of a hash can I make of that one?*

## Chapter Six

*Age 23–27*

# Loving the Alien – Again

*'There's no point in being a grown-up if you can't be childish sometimes.'*
The Doctor, Robot

You may recall my fear and loathing of dentists. I maintain there's a good reason.

After King's and a final year in a flat above a fruiterers in Wood Green, I kept in regular contact with 'Funk', the Andy who somehow liked Level 42. We shared a student penchant for rubbish nightclubs, pointless drinking and Kentucky Fried Chicken.

We were on first-name terms with the staff at the local KFC branch, posted regular suggestion cards to Mrs Huggett of customer services, prizing her replies, and so voracious was our appetite for the tender pieces that Funk and Quinch were one day able to build 'Bucket Man': a seven-foot-tall man made entirely of Kentucky Fried Chicken bargain buckets and boxes.

A classy work of art, in anyone's book. I photographed him and sent it off to KFC HQ, suggesting that Bucket Man might make the perfect star of a future advertising campaign.

To ensure that they didn't simply steal this brilliant idea –

think cartoon spin-offs, think merchandising, think million-aires – I sealed a copy of the picture in an envelope and mailed it to myself.

They never replied.

Anyway, I have visited Andy (as he is now known) regularly in Stourbridge ever since, and vice versa. He was down in London only last weekend. It's nice to stay in touch. Someone else you can prove likes you.

During one of my first Black Country weekends, Andy took me to a perfectly rubbish nightclub in his home town. We drank a few and got unlucky. I remember being sick in the toilets – the beers or the music policy, I couldn't say – and feeling much better afterwards.

We left at a small hour and headed to the only open eatery, a kebab caravan. There, a girl started talking to us, about transport or something, all very innocuous. As we headed off, a bloke came running after us.

'Oi,' he snarls. 'My girlfriend wants someone to sleep with tonight.'

I was confused. Why was he telling us? Was he pimping his girlfriend? If the girlfriend wanted to sleep with some-one, why didn't she tell them herself? Why would anyone want to sleep with us, anyway? Why was I eating a kebab? From a caravan?

Then he hit both of us. Bam-bam. Now I was really confused.

'Hey!' I said, slurring righteous indignation. 'Don't do that!'

Always talk down to a nutter like a total public school-boy.

He kicked me in the face and I fell backwards.

Only as we were walking back to Andy's did I notice the blood down my lovely yellow shirt, and counted my two front teeth without getting past 'One'.

Back home (actually, his parents' home), Andy called a friend with the gossip. Ten minutes later, a volunteer vigilante squad had gathered, which we wanted no part of. Cowards seek no revenge, only sympathy. The vigilante squad wanted to kick the crap out of the guy. With persuasion, I was prepared to watch.

So we're out there at heaven knows what hour, trawling the lanes of Stourbridge, and suddenly it dawns on me: I'm at the front!

At least we never found him.

Far worse was to come. Having no money, I was obliged to attend a dental school for emergency treatment.

I should have offered to sharpen the drills for a lifetime elsewhere, anywhere.

The student dentist's diagnosis was heartening: I had a tooth missing.

People of a nervous disposition: skip the rest of this section.

She injects me first in the roof of my mouth. It hurts a lot, someone jabbing a needle there. Then she injects me behind the upper lip. Fine, had those before; no fun but reasonable. Then she injects me in the hole in the middle of the tooth stump where the nerve lives. AAAAAAAAAA-AAAAAAAAAAAAAUGH!

Now I'm scared. The woman is either insane or a needle-based sadist.

She consults with a supervisor. Something is up.

THEY HAVE NO POSTS FOR CROWNS.

What? It's a dental school! Didn't they think they might need some?

The supervisor has a bright idea. Break off a bit of a paperclip and use that! Really. So that's what they did. After 'cleaning out' the cavity, they put some broken stationery in my mouth, and stuck a temporary crown on to that.

A few hours later, the crown fell off – I know, I was

amazed too – and I'm standing there with a paperclip where a tooth should be. It's not a look Brad Pitt would cultivate. Frankly, it's not a look Quasimodo would have cultivated.

A proper dentist fixed me up.

For the next five years or so, I had a recurring abscess where the root hadn't been properly cleaned out: a throbbing ache right beside my nostril.

I was forced to go to another dentist and he offered me a choice, accompanied by a kind of Dracula leer: more injections then slice open the roof of my mouth with a scalpel, or take a course of penicillin tablets.

Hmmmm.

Annually afterwards, in total fear of the dentistry profession, I would end up pleading to pharmacists, friends who had penicillin, anyone with an infection that might lead to them getting penicillin, praying that friends who didn't have infections might get one . . . I became a penicillin junkie.

That's why I don't do dentists.


I started seeing Jane from university days. It seemed pretty obvious; we'd been like brother and sister. Once we had slept together, the brother-and-sister thing necessarily went out of the window.

Confident of our relationship, given its history, we bought a flat together in South Tottenham.

I got into DIY. I knocked down a whole red-brick larder, uncertain that the ceiling wouldn't follow, and plastered over the holes. We painted everywhere. It was fun-ish.


Living with Jane felt perfectly natural. We shared an adoration of *Coronation Street* (visited the Manchester set), REM (had photos taken with the band outside one venue, and each shook Michael Stipe's hand) and tea shops (Tottenham's Empire Tea Rooms, RIP), if not Time Lord adventuring.

I had come some way since Vicki. I could identify different vegetables, had started to cook and even bake – chocolate torte, a speciality – became slightly interested in other people's relationships and started making artworks.

I sketched and inked one psychedelic picture of Jane's mother surrounded by floaty images of Jane's mother's dog, her Chihuahua, Harvey. I'm not sure she liked it.

But there was domestic harmony of sorts; the newness felt enlivening.

And the flat was only broken into twice.

The first time, I was lying awake around 1 a.m. and the bedroom curtain started to move unnaturally. Then a head popped through the window.

I had always imagined that I would hide under the covers in such a situation, but with Jane asleep I did the manly thing, leapt out of bed and went, 'Fllllllllhhh hhn!' ('Fuck off!', in mortal-peril speak; notice that I had stepped up my language since the kebab incident.)

Thinking me insane, he starts panicking and legs it up the garden path.

I shout after him, 'Hn hhhhnll hn hlllllsh!' ('I'm calling the police!')

It's funny, though only in retrospect, how fear literally debilitated my vocal cords.

The other time, after Jane had moved out, a guy threw a brick through the front window in broad daylight, helped himself to my TV and stereo minus speakers, and drove them home. My rare Best of Pylon CD was in the tray at the time.

It was in South Tottenham that I rediscovered *Doctor Who*, shortly after the show had been axed by the BBC.

There was but one official video release on the market: Revenge of the Cybermen, classic Tom Baker. I had spotted it in a video rental shop a few years back and had watched it half a dozen times.

Casually browsing through *Loot*, London's free ads paper, I noticed an advert for *Doctor Who* Videos.

Eh?

Send for list, it said.

What I received offered for sale practically every story ever aired (bar the missing episodes), glorious title after glorious title. I was gobsmacked. How? Surely video-taping technology didn't exist back in Hartnell and Troughton's day? (Little did I know, being too skint to afford satellite television, that *Doctor Who* had been re-running on UK Gold.)

Scanning that list was like popping my clogs and discovering, against my sceptic's judgment, that heaven really did exist. Every Pertwee and Baker T story brought memories flooding back, of home and comfort, of innocence and shorts to school, of adventure and aliens and hiding behind an armchair and therefore Ken Dodd.

I wanted it. I wanted those times back. But I played safe. Still suspicious as to the provenance of such tapes, I made a deal with myself to start with just the one story. The choice was obvious.

The One with the Giant Maggots. The Green Death. Jon Pertwee, 1973.

Every child of the seventies remembers The Green Death.

*The Green Death, for the unfamiliar: Global Chemicals' artificially intelligent computer is trying to take over the world. Already its waste products have caused maggots to mutate into giant versions of themselves, which rear up and hiss. Touch one, you go bright green, not in a crazy partying way. Pertwee sorts it, Jo Grant falls in love with a Welshman and leaves. Byeee!*

It had the environmental message, some way before its

time, it had sooty Welsh miners, but best of all it had Giant Maggots. So disgusting and so very cool.

*Doctor Who* is often at its best when the viewer can relate to the threat. Sea Devils and Zygons look top, but only a five-year-old could imagine one hiding under their bed. That's why they trapped Pertwee on planet Earth for the majority of his Tardis run, and why the new *Doctor Who* has similar ideals.

Think Aliens of London, the Eccleston episode in which a sizeable spaceship takes a chunk out of Big Ben and crash-lands in the Thames, and its follow-up, World War Three – set in Britain. Or that other series one two-parter, The Empty Child/The Doctor Dances, based in London amid the Blitz ('Are you my mummy?' – that creepy kid lived in blinking Blighty).

Boom Town: Aliens plan to nuke Cardiff. Bad Wolf: *Big Brother*, *The Weakest Link* and *What Not To Wear*, turned murderous. Every viewer under 90 in the country is going to recognise those shows. Is that really what might happen in the future, they wonder? (In *Big Brother*'s case, let's hope so.)

Keep that threat close to home.

Anyway, back to The Green Death and 1973, where your writer feels far more comfortable – everyone goes 'Bleugh' at the sight of maggots, fishermen and weirdoes who 'farm' corpses, notwithstanding. Now what if they became a foot long and as wide as a python swallowing a chicken?

They shone translucent colours, like a film of oil. They had a hideous mouth that resembled – there's no better way of putting this – the end of an uncircumcised penis. (Coincidentally, I read somewhere that the creatures were actually stuffed condoms.)

As a kid, those maggots engrossed you and grossed you out. Bingo.

As an adult, the story was a bit dull.

The Green Death was one of those six-parters, rife with padding. Too much chat about damage to the planet, not enough death-by-creepy-crawly.

Jo's leaving was actually dealt with rather poignantly, and there's a lovely scene of Pertwee driving off in Bessie against the horizon, but I had to admit, I was disappointed. The Green Death hadn't lived up to my expectations.

Time for some more!

I could have delved further into the past, see what the earlier Doctors were like, or even sample some late-incarnation action. Be adventurous. But I'm not, so I plumped for five Pertwee and Tom Bakers, and waited, gathering drool.

They never arrived.

I rang the vendor and his mother answered. Apologetic, she said her son had been inundated with requests and would get around to it.

He didn't.

I drove all the way to Croydon from South Tottenham, and tracked down his tower-block, to confront him, and thought, 'What exactly am I going to say to this charlatan whose Mum has to take his calls? What if he finds me threatening?'

Like any true crusader for consumer rights, I felt a bit sorry for the bloke and drove home.

However, my hopes had been raised.

I read *Loot* daily until another advert appeared.

I rang the vendor and, throwing caution into a tornado, offered to buy his entire Hartnell-to-Tom-Baker collection. The lot. I'd have to collect them, he said. From Croydon again. (It's all right, it was definitely a different address.)

That night-time journey by train into the heart of the unknown (Croydon) was unduly creepy. I found myself traipsing around housing estates, A-Z in hand, youths 'hanging out' in shadows, until I eventually located the address, partially freaked. As I knocked, I will admit that I wondered whether he might be a gay rapist, using *Doctor Who* as a honeytrap.

Inside his flat were all the videos – and even with two or three stories to a 240-minute tape, there were a lot – and a Robots of Death Robot mask! You could buy actual props from the series! Woah!

As I left, with this enormous holdall crammed with tapes, two thoughts pestered my mind:

1. Will youths mug me, thinking I'm carrying something valuable?
2. Will youths accost me, discover I'm carrying *Doctor Who* tapes, and beat me up for being a nerd?

Quite honestly, 2 worried me more than 1.

Talk about a feast. I was like Henry VIII confronted with a banquet table of meats and possibly some grapes.

It was hard to know where to start, but I managed.

I couldn't tell you which ones came first, there were so many, but I remember watching certain tales, such as Pertwee's Ambassadors of Death – astronauts taken over by aliens in space – and realising that I had somehow missed it first time around. Cracking space-suited entertainment *and* a homegrown mystery.

Boy, it was a joy.

Jane, fair play, did try to watch a few with me, but you really had to be there first time around to appreciate the nostalgia flow. Classic *Doctor Who* was never meant to be watched in one sitting, hence the cliffhangers, and even the four-part stories showed flab.

She did also accompany me on a summer's trip to Longleat, circa 1989, to catch the *Doctor Who* Exhibition. I have some photos.

Hang about, this is the Student Days album.

Me washing my reeking feet beside Eric the Mini in Paris, while Quinch looks on appalled . . . Me asleep at Le Mans in the midday sun, with my ankles, shortly to go scarlet, clearly exposed . . . Me in straw trilby with red band and Duran T-shirt, Quinch in overcoat despite the ludicrous heat, at Le Mans (I don't even like motor racing) . . . Bowie at Live Aid . . . The Christmas cake I made for us in Tottenham digs, second year . . . Me showing off Smash Hits T-shirt in Cartwright Gardens, opposite Hughes Parry . . . Oh God, me with Angie Bowie (so obsessed was I that I went to see the ex-missus sing, and it was no nightingale moment) . . . Funk and I dancing in the sea near Land's End, him with hair dyed black after I had introduced him to The Cure, who were preferable to Level 42 . . . anyway.

Right, here it is:

- Me leaning on the barrier that stopped people from touching a Tardis console that looks suspiciously fake.
- Me, looking unimpressed, beneath circular photos of Hartnell, Troughton and Pertwee, stuck into (suspiciously fake-looking) Tardis wall.
- Me staring at a Dalek behind a window, bearing the label: 'Remembrance of the Daleks, 1989'.
- Mounted heads (the only good bit): four different Cybermen, two different Davroses, Sontaran helmet, Robot of Death, Silurian, baddie from Castrovalva and others I fail to recognise (from the later era, no doubt).
- Jane outside in grounds, in long red dress, staring at duck.
- Me outside in grounds, in blue stripy shirt, scowling pointedly.

I felt so ripped off. London to Longleat is a long drive, and I was expecting a veritable museum of *Doctor Who* goodies. If memory serves, it was just that one room. And we had been the only ones in it. Gutted.

That's not why we split up: me dragging her across Britain to crap Time Lord exhibitions. Were it only that simple. The freshness of cohabiting having worn off, I was no Mrs Beeton. There were others. We should have stayed just friends.

Jane walked out. Distraught.

At that time I would have been working at Taylor & Francis publishers, copy-editing the *International Journal of Control* and the *International Journal of Systems Science*. Yes, it was as tedious as that sounds. But having finally realised towards the end of my last year at King's that I wanted to write for a living, I somehow had to turn Electrical & Electronic Engineering into Journalism.

Beats Sudoku.

My first job on leaving university, to my parent's delight after the financial sacrifices, was working in Our Price Records.

Mum and Dad kept asking, 'You're not going to do that forever, are you?'

No fear.

I found my appointment letter in the tan-leather brief-case. Dated 7 September 1987, it begins, 'Following your recent interview, I am pleased to advise you that your application to join Our Price Music has been successful.'

Wa-hey!

'I would like to offer you the position of Sales Assistant at the starting salary of £4,888 per annum . . .'

*How much?*

No wonder I never had any money. No, I was not going to work in Our Price forever.

My proudest moment involved played the 12-inch of REM's It's the End of the World as We Know It (And I Feel Fine) so often that someone eventually relented and bought it. Which thrilled me until the manager said I couldn't re-order it, so we were stuck with Terence Trent Bloody D'Arby on the shop turntable.

Another time, I scrawled on Bros's When Will I Be Famous? 'job-bag' (in which the record itself was stored), 'Not very soon, matey'.

Nick Griffiths, pop guru.

## Some Things . . . That are Pet Hates

- Hordes of people coming into your shop and buying rubbish albums, even though you're playing REM at them – Rick Astley flew out of the place. So did anything new by Daniel O'Donnell.
- Fat-faced blokes who grow a very thin beard to show where their jawline used to be.
- Receiving a parcel and the contents are packed in poly-styrene – That squeaky noise makes my teeth implode. I have to wait for someone else to unpack the goodies while I cower in the loft wearing earplugs.
- *My Family* (the alleged comedy) – I preview Thursday and Friday programmes for the *Daily Mail*. *My Family* is always on a Friday. It is the pits, everything that is bad about British sitcom: smug, over-acted, crass, unfunny, unlikely, unlikeable, Middle-England, non-punchlines, characters you would like to punch, quality actors making tits of themselves, pish, tosh, balls. The albatross of my career.
- Justin Lee Collins – My new pet-hate TV presenter. The one with the hair, Bristol accent and no volume control and who thinks he is great (referring to himself as 'The JLC'). I had to watch him present *Bring Back . . . The A Team* last night. He actually went, 'How good is this?!' while standing in a lift. How easily impressed? I'd love to show him one of those moving walkways at airports, and watch him pass out from the excitement. Then I'd tape his

mouth shut and post him to Botswana. (I just Googled him to confirm the origins of that accent, and one of the first links offered runs: 'Justin Lee Collins – A twat?' So it's not just me.)

- Lentils – Why?
- Waiting at a bar, and everyone who arrives after you gets served before you.
- And when, exasperated to distraction, you point out to the latest customer to push in, that actually you were there a good 15 minutes before them, they reply, 'No you weren't' – Even thinking about it is making my blood boil.
- People who drive down the middle lane of motorways – Aaaaaaaaaaaagh!
- I'd better stop there – Time for a calming Earl Grey.

## Some Things . . . That are Pet Loves
## (Because it's Not All Bad)

- Oysters – With a squeeze of lemon and lashings of Tabasco.
- In fact, almost all stupidly spicy food – Especially vindaloo.
- *The Apprentice* – We chortled, we cringed, we were astonished at the misplaced self-belief. Must-see programme of 2006 (alongside the Doctor, natch).
- Programmes involving Gordon Ramsay, Hugh Fearnley-Whittingstall, Rick Stein or Ray Mears – Television isn't all bad.
- Martin Jol and Robbie Keane – Of the Spurs contingent, though I could offer a dozen other honourable mentions. I have drawn a picture of those two from memory which hangs in my heart. (The likenesses aren't great, but that isn't the point.)

- World Cup and Euro Championship summers – Big boys in the pub, camaraderie despite national affiliations, ladies even enjoying the beautiful game, England scoring a goal, the cheers, the backslapping, as if somehow we contributed, the tension until the following game, actual goalposts for goalposts . . . the going out on penalties to Germany or Portugal, the waiting another two years, the relentless hope.
- Fly fishing – I know, I know. You're all right because there aren't many opportunities in London, but stick me in a boat in the middle of a Scottish loch, with my ineptness and solitude and I am at peace. (Until I need a wee.)
- Seafood – Even better when (rarely) you've caught it yourself. Oh for a mackerel barbie at Sinead's Mum's in Cornwall, caught by myself, Dylan and his cousin Jack on a sea-fishing trip, savoured by all, washed down with cider, while the sun departs for a different portion of the globe.
- Shade in the summer – I could burn under an energy-saving lightbulb.
- Jet-skiing – But here's the one thing that draws me to a beach. It was first love, the moment I sat astride one in Greece, whumping over the waves, clinging on for dear life, resolutely full-throttle, salt-spray to the eyeballs, cackling uncontrollably like a witch who enjoys a turnip joke discovering *Blackadder*.
- Speaking of which, *Blackadder*, *Fawlty Towers*, *Some Mothers Do 'Ave 'Em*, *I'm Alan Partridge* (series one), *The Mighty Boosh* (series one), *Dad's Army*, *Cheers*, *Frasier*, *Red Dwarf*, *The Office* . . . – It's funny, I woke this morning feeling rather too Monday, yet compiling this list has turned my mood around.
- In fact, I could continue for ages, and I haven't even properly mentioned loved ones yet – Next time I'm feeling low, I'm going to read this very outpouring.

Why not make one of your own, and keep it in a back pocket?

On 22 October 1989, my big career break came out of the blue.

I had been to see Bowie play with Tin Machine at the Tufnell Park Dome. Sure, the songs would be crap, but it was a chance to see the man at 20 paces rather than 200.

In the end, I couldn't stomach it. The songs were *really* crap, the aural equivalent of wading through tar pursued by poodles, and I left early, so disturbed at my hero's new dirge that I penned a scathing review for *Sounds* the moment I got home.

Naïvely, I thought they might print it and that would be the end of the matter. Instead, I received a letter. That turned up in the briefcase, too:

Dear Nick

Thanks for your letter and trial review. Bit on the long side and weak final few pars but otherwise pretty fine . . .

Please ring me and we'll sort out a few commissions, that is if you're still interested (I've just noticed your letter arrived three months ago).

Shaun Phillips
Sounds Reviews Editor

*If I was still interested*?! I'd read *Sounds* since I was a kid! It was a music bible to tens of thousands. One of the trinity of 'inkies'. They had interviewed Bowie, Bolan, Big Audio Dynamite, Band Aid, Bauhaus, The Beatles, The Beach Boys, The Beat, possibly even Brotherhood of Man. And they were asking me to write for them.

I literally jumped up and down, going 'Yes!' repeatedly, until lack of fitness made me sit down and shut up.

By then, I was working at Pitman Publishing, having quit

Taylor & Francis after six months to write and edit two subscription-only magazines, *Business Education Today* and *Professional Secretary*.

No, it's not *Vogue* and *Tatler*. At least it was magazines – another step closer.

*Sounds* was not only the goal. It was the dream. Now, how to pick up the phone to a complete stranger and not waffle nervous garbage, so turning dream into nightmare?

Phoning Shaun Phillips was nerve-wracking. To me, anyone who worked on *Sounds* was the zenith of cool. I was the nadir of nerdiness.

After some flannel chat during which I lost a stone in perspiration, he asked whether there were any gigs I fancied reviewing.

I had no idea who was playing. Great start. Obligingly, he ran through a list of upcoming concerts and I picked a couple, fearing that if I let the opportunity pass, I might not get another.

- The Shamen: psychedelic light-show Scottish band, whose track Christopher Mayhew Says sampled the Labour MP's ramblings, having taken 400mg of mescaline hydro-chloride for *Panorama* to film his trip. It never aired. The song is a headblast. Unfortunately, little did I know, The Shamen had just gone techno.
- Jesus Jones: Had a hit with Info Freako, sort of indie-dance-in-a-beret, not as good as EMF.

I phoned The Shamen's press officer, trying to sound pro-fessional.

'Hello, it's Nick Griffiths from *Sounds.*' It felt like fraud. I couldn't even believe I was saying it.

She asked me whether I wanted a 'plus one'. I had to admit that I didn't know what one was.

'Do you want to take someone else?'

No I didn't.

Sorted.

And relax.


I started collecting *Doctor Who* memorabilia. (It's OK, I didn't tell *Sounds*.)

Buying a Tom Baker doll at the age of 25, with no intention of doing anything bar storing it in a big box, or a Dalek playsuit ideal for toddlers, must seem ridiculous to an awful lot of people. And they would be right. Collecting is a form of dementia.

People collect for one of three reasons: (1) to sell at a profit; (2) for nostalgic purposes, to hold something that helps them remember their past; or (3) because they are a sad, lonely individual and their collection is their friend.

I don't think I could ever bring myself to do (1), though I sometimes excuse my indulgences by convincing myself otherwise. In my case, (2) is much nearer the mark, admittedly with a hint of (3).

Part of it is the thrill of the hunt, e.g. tracking down the Denys Fisher Giant Robot. If I set myself a goal, I can be stubbornly determined; I hate for something to defeat me. Hence I try not to set myself too many goals.

In the Giant Robot's case, it's usually the asking price that performs the *coup de grace* . . .

The other part is the elation of the find and the subsequent adrenalin swirl of the 'Dare I spend that much?'

I'm not one to waste money. Actually, that's not true. But I don't enjoy blowing large amounts. Actually, that's not true either. There are special moments.

The Cyberman . . . let's call him an 'action figure' rather than a 'doll', cost me £90 at a toy stall in Camden Market, having knocked down the vendor from £110. A significant amount for something that was £2.50 in 1977.

Sure, it would have been satisfying to find the same item in a charity shop, priced 20p, but then you miss out on the internal guilt trip: 'Ninety quid . . . Can't you knock him down any lower? . . . No, I've tried that . . . I suppose £90 is pretty reasonable . . . It is . . . But it is only a doll . . . Action figure . . . Sorry, action figure . . . Do I really need it? . . . Of course you do – you already have K-9, the Tardis, Leela and Tom Baker! . . . Yeah, and how much did that lot cost? . . . Sorry, can't remember . . . But it was a fair amount . . . Depends what you mean by a "fair amount" . . . You're sidestepping the issue, aren't you? . . . Yes, I know, but that's done now, can we move on please? . . . All right, so what do you plan to do about the Cyberman? . . . Let's be honest with myself: it's the only one I've seen and there is no way I'm walking away without it . . . So buy it then! . . . But it's 90 quid! . . . Give the man the money! . . . I daren't! . . . Just do it! . . . I did earn some extra from that Gaz Top interview . . . Right, so you've covered the cost . . . But shouldn't I spend it on food and lighting? . . . *Buy the bastard doll!*'

All that takes place in a millisecond, accompanied by a physical sense that travels from base of spine to cerebral cortex, of horror mixed with elation.

That is the joy of collecting, and the reason I have amassed, among other things: Tardis Play Tent, Zarbi and Venom Gun badge, Patrick Troughton autograph, plastic Sonic Screwdriver, Doctor Who trump cards, way too many trading cards, those Tom Baker bathroom tiles (framed) – and the Hand of Fear.

*The Hand of Fear, for the unfamiliar: Sarah Jane finds an old hand in a quarry. Only it's not any old hand – it's the Hand of Fear, belonging to an alien called Eldrad who blew up in space over Earth. Eldrad's body regenerates at a nearby nuclear power plant and it transpires that he's hell-bent on – anyone? – ruling the world. Hoi, Eldrad, mate, mind you don't trip over that scarf and fall into the . . . Oh.*

I got my Hand of Fear from my toy dealer at Alfie's market

in West London, at the same time that I bought the Robot of Death mask. He told me that he'd got them off a bloke who worked on the show. And they were around 40 quid each. I nearly snapped his own hand off.

Talk about iconic.

It's pretty lightweight, a knobbly thing painted grey, with long fingers and nails shaped like giant cut jewels, with just enough wrist to take a watch. Study the palm for ages and ages while thinking, 'I've got the Hand of Fear', and you can make out certain details of the human hand it was clearly moulded from.

There are but two catches to this tale.

1. I watched The Hand of Fear especially, after I bought the item, and couldn't recognise the features of my own Hand of Fear in there. Presumably they made a few spares, as that thing could break easily. Which I know because . . .

2. Mine broke. I dimly left it on the arm of the sofa and Dylan knocked it off one Sunday afternoon. Two fingers snapped off. It's hollow inside. I superglued one back on, but the other broke into finger plus tiny bits which I couldn't find, so it's stuck in a mug to this day while I try to work out how best to repair it. And believe me, I've tried.

I must mention the non-Time Lord pride of my collecting days.

I own the Crow Crag Farm sign from *Withnail & I*, the original prop, certified by Bruce Robinson.

Christian and I attended a charity screening of the film at the Odeon Leicester Square in 2000, in aid of Richard E Grant's former Waterford-Kamhlaba School in Swaziland.

All the surviving cast attended, it was wonderful to hear Robinson's lines causing live hilarity, and afterwards there was an auction.

A once-in-a-lifetime opportunity, star and director had donated lots, including rare film posters, shooting script, stills, Withnail and Marwood's coats and Robinson's original typewritten script. I demanded to have something.

The early lots went for vast, unreachable sums. Then Lot 9 came along: the Crow Crag Farm sign.

Bidding went slowly. Though I hate making a spectacle of myself, at £300 I stuck my hand up, in the middle of the Odeon, Leicester Square. Heads swivelled.

'Three hundred!' went the auctioneer.

No more bids! I was going to get it!

The auctioneer asked who it was that had bid. I put my hand up.

'Three hundred and fifty!' he declared.

I had outbid myself! And it was a charity auction, so I could hardly protest.

No matter. The cast members passed my sign between themselves and signed it in thick felt tip.

Admittedly, the prop doesn't actually appear in the film, though it does on page 45 of my original screenplay. And Robinson himself mentions the sale of the sign on page 133 of *Smoking in Bed: Conversations with Bruce Robinson* (edited by Alistair Owen), though erroneously quoting a price of £600.

I own a part of that glorious film. Paranoid of house fires and the like, it – and any valuable collector's pieces, including the Cyberman – is in storage, so I rarely get to see them. But I know. Oh yes, I know.

Interlude: What a weekend for new *Doctor Who*. First, The Girl in the Fireplace, best episode of the season so far, from writer Steven Moffat. I was watching it with Dylan on the sofa (while Sinead read a magazine), and was the only one to jump and go 'Whaa!' when the clockwork droid tried to grab Tennant's hand from under young Reinette's bed. Those masks were well scary, the perspex-cased workings beneath them stunning, and Moffat gave the Doctor a whole new sense of melancholy and depth. I didn't cry, no way, but I did feel tears behind my eyeballs as Reinette read that farewell letter in voiceover, referring to the Doctor as her 'lonely angel'.

I had never thought of him as lonely before.

Trying it now: he's 900 years old, give or take a decade, and with the show on air, in total, for 28 years . . . what's he been doing for the unseen 872? Please don't say he's been moping around the Tardis on his own, playing Interpol and solitaire to ease the pain.

Girl in the Fireplace also introduced a genuine look of lust, for Reinette, followed by meaningful snog. How unlucky? He meets her when she is seven or eight, and 40 minutes later she's being carted off in a hearse.

Russell T Davies and team have taken the show to a whole new level, hence part two of the triumphant weekend: the Baftas. The series took Best Drama, as well as the Pioneer Audience Award for Best Programme of 2005, while Davies himself collected (from a kilted David Tennant, with beard) the Dennis Potter Award for outstanding writing for television. The classic series was Bafta-nominated twice, in 1977 and 1978, but disgracefully won neither.

Chin chin to them.

PS. That night, I had a nightmare and woke with a start, clinging to Sinead, when I dreamed that a shadowy figure rang the front doorbell at night and barged past me when I answered. When I fell asleep again, I was involved in the production of 1971's The Claws of Axos, which wasn't going to plan. I've been thinking about this show too solidly, for too long. When this book is finished, I'm going to holiday on a distant isle where the local tongue for 'Doctor Who' sounds suspiciously like, 'Would sir fancy an ice-cold beer?'

Clutching my hand-written Shamen and Jesus Jones reviews – I didn't even own a computer – I took the tube to Blackfriars and headed for the *Sounds* office. I could have faxed them from work, but I wanted to see the place, put faces to names I had read for years, feel a part of the outfit. Needless to say, I was crapping myself.

*Sounds* was based in Ludgate House, along with Express Newspapers. This was actual journalism. I so distinctly remember someone in a pub asking me what I did and saying, for the first time, 'I'm a journalist', wondering whether it could actually be true.

The music paper was on one of the upper floors. Record racks, filled with stiff brown envelopes, labelled for each staff member. Desks, covered in press releases and albums. A turntable playing something unrecognisable. And people. Lots of people beavering at computers.

Someone pointed out Shaun Phillips, who had long black hair, tied back, and eyes, and was friendly without my ever feeling comfortable. He introduced me to Anne Scanlon, the features editor, and Robin Gibson, the deputy editor, I think, amid my fear-haze, and took my reviews off me without reading them, thank goodness.

When *Sounds* came out the following week, I bought it and rushed back to my office at Pitman.

Texas on the cover. Coverline: 'Texas – can white kids play the blues?' (Answer, frankly: No.) Date: December 2, 1989.

There it was, among the Live reviews, three short columns at the foot of page 46: 'THE SHAMEN Charing Cross Road Busby's'; me bemoaning the three-hour acid disco beforehand, uncultured of such things, and generally suggesting the band had no future (hoho). Byline: 'NICK GRIFFITHS'.

The beginning of my career as an actual journalist. I don't think any byline since has touched my sense of euphoria.

I went round every friend in the Pitman office, showing it to them, most nodding politely. And when I sat back down, heart at acid-disco bpm, I remembered Jesus Jones. And there it was, on page 48 – almost an entire half-page, blocked out, headlined ('Men Without Hats') and with photo! I had to do the same office tour all over again, with loo breaks.

After that, I took a pseudonym, because I thought that all music journalists did, and didn't want to feel left out. 'Robyn Smyth'. Oh dear.

I reviewed the likes of Kylie Minogue, Eleventh Dream Day, David Bowie (on his Sound and Vision tour), Adeva, Into Paradise . . . a mixed bag, though I never really felt part of the *Sounds* team.

My non-punk credentials and general low confidence hardly inspired the staff to request my company for beers.

The highlight of my *Sounds* stint was taking a call from Shaun Phillips in Pitman reception, when I was just back from lunch, expecting something to have gone wrong, and he told me, having read one of my freshly filed reviews: 'You're a funny man'. No one has done that since. (Perhaps best not to dwell on why.) He's going in my Acknowledgements section.

As is David Cavanagh.

It could all have ended with a whimper. *Sounds* folded in April 1991, and my writing career might have folded with it, were it not for the genial/laconic Irish writer whose writing I had admired for some years before becoming an actual colleague. He was working on a new, monthly magazine, from the *Sounds* stable: *Select*. And he asked me to contribute.

I had only been working there a few months, having just escaped a degree in Electrical & Electronic Engineering, yet he must have spotted something of worth in my writing. I'd only been bloody headhunted!

There was an incredible couple of weeks in 1990, when *Sounds* wanted me as their News Editor (I would have been rubbish, given that I hate phoning strangers) and *Select* wanted me to write for them, with rivalry meaning that I couldn't do both.

Thank fate I plumped for the latter.

I quit Pitman and went freelance. Back then, risks seemed fun.

With a small team of writers, sub-editors and designers I worked into the night on the launch issue of *Select*, in an office overlooking Blackfriars Road. Forget the conspiratorial sense of fluorescent-lit bonding, the sense of doing something non-nerdy for once was enough.

The editor, Tony Stewart, sent me to Dublin to interview Hothouse Flowers. A feature! A trip abroad! With hotel! For free! To interview the lengthy-locked band who had scored a major hit with Don't Go! About whom I knew very little!

Those were the days. I spoke to The Edge of U2 at the aftershow party and even members of the band's families, including one grandmother, such was my keenness to cover every possible angle for the feature.

I was mixing with real pop stars (badly – you have no idea how long it took me to pluck up the courage to interrupt The Edge's conversation and ask him for a quote), with a laminate Press pass around my neck, drinking booze that a record company was paying for.

Which was all good, but the highpoint was yet to come: my first ever feature, with my byline, in a monthly music magazine that tens of thousands would read.

And there it was, the Hothouse Flowers story, printed full-colour in the launch issue, with Prince on the cover.

Sadly I don't still have my copy, but I do remember the headline, with typo: 'And Granny Came To'.

It went on: The Stone Roses in Finland, Sonic Youth in London, Carter the Unstoppable Sex Machine in Reading (you'll notice it's heading downhill) . . .

Simultaneously, I joined *Deadline*, the comics/music

magazine that published Tank Girl, as contributor and later features editor, and interviewed Julian Cope, Ride, Inspiral Carpets, Curve, Right Said Fred . . .

*Deadline* eventually folded and something wasn't right at *Select*.

They had sussed my nerdiness.

Tony Stewart was offered a Duran Duran interview, for the Liberty album of 1990, and planned to laugh it out of town until I piped up.

Only Simon Le Bon, Nick Rhodes and John Taylor remained of the original line-up by that stage, and John wasn't available for the interview. But it was enough.

I remember sitting at a chair in the photographic studio, waiting for the band, and hearing Le Bon and Rhodes and then turning round and seeing them, and . . . I'd loved that band since Rio. 1982. Tammy had given me The Reflex. Without compunction I will hit any dance floor and groove my ill-timed thing whenever Girls on Film is played.

I actually sat on the floor, the two of them seated, for the interview, like a small, rapt child. I remember telling them that the obscure B-side of Union of the Snake was my favourite song, and asking what it was like on that hot rock at the finale of the Save A Prayer video. It was no incisive interview, which became clear when I filed the piece.

Tony Stewart wasn't happy. He wanted to know about their cocaine exploits. I didn't even know they had taken cocaine.

*Select* was bought out by Emap and Mark Ellen, formerly of TV's *Whistle Test*, became editor. As a fan of the show, I was slightly over-awed to find the presenter standing in the office, now my new employer. I introduced myself, gabbling something about loving *Whistle Test*. He failed to sweep me up into his arms.

Mark Ellen had his favourites and I wasn't one of them.

I was reduced to subbing and picking up reviews of albums by bands only their mothers had heard of. Writing a feature was out of the question. It was pretty demoralising, but it was still work in a career I enjoyed. At least it was only pretty demoralising.

One day I went to the *Select* offices and was stopped by the receptionist as I headed upstairs.

'They've moved,' she said.

I tracked down the new offices and turned up like a sea slug in a rock pool. Sod 'em. Still it was crystal clear: my days as a music journalist were numbered.

All the while, my days as an over-aged *Doctor Who* fanatic were lengthening. There's always an upside.

My ill-completed 1991 and 1992 diaries bear several entries which read 'Dr Who evening' followed by 'No!', as if everyone I invited had cancelled.

Admittedly, I have no memory of such events, although I do recall planning to sit friends down in front of a chosen *Doctor Who* story, so that we could all share the delights of the monster mayhem. Me as philanthropist.

I have emailed every possible participant, asking them to shed light on such nights – and not a thing came back.

I can draw but one conclusion, which seems unfeasible. I sent out the invites. Everyone was otherwise engaged.

There was but one successful event, while I was working at *Radio Times*, around 1996.

I had discovered the *Doctor Who Pattern Book* by Joy Gammon, for some reason in the magazine's research library. Inside were instructions on making a cornucopia of tat, including: K-9 shoulder bag, Tom Baker scarf, Tardis sleeping bag, Romana II's sailor top and – don't start me – Adric's anorak.

I got Mum to knit me a Baker scarf, for which I had to buy the wool. From a ladies' wool shop.

Yes, I know what I stated in the Foreword: '. . . nor do I wear an outsized, multi-coloured scarf'. The fact is, your honour, that I didn't ever wear it, because after Mum had worked her fingers to the bone on its ridiculous length, I realised that I was 31 years old and would look laughable should I ever put it on. Sorry, Mum.

The book gave me another idea: confectionery. Why not hold a *Doctor Who* evening, in which guests each bring a Who-related cake? (It's a rhetorical question.)

Real people turned up. Four or five of them.

Paul, the art editor from *Radio Times*, won with his Dalek made from shaped sponge-cake layered with cream, with half-Maltesers as the base hemispheres and . . . some other ingredients. I forget. It looked impressive.

Anne, the commissioning editor, went for a Green Death-inspired slag heap of cornflakes covered in melted chocolate and peppermint-cream maggots. Which was eternally preferable to my Dalek, which had melted in the room-heat and resembled a puddle of marshmallow and cream into which Smarties were oozing their lurid colours, while three chocolate fingers poked from the mess like one American and one British hand gesture.

We watched Genesis of the Daleks together. Unwisely, a six-part story, during which people drifted into the kitchen.

When I said 'successful', it's all relative.

I wasn't overly devastated when the music journalism fell apart.

At the back of my mind, I knew it would have to end. Like the bands they write about, most music hacks begin to look less hip with age. Also, going to two or three (mercifully free) gigs a week had begun to take its toll on my enthusiasm.

I remember going to see Jane's Addiction, one of my favourite bands, at The Marquee back when it was in Charing Cross Road – and talking throughout to my music-hack mates. I loathe people who talk at gigs. And I was doing it myself. The burning question, though, was: where next?

I'd been reading women's magazines, partly to try to understand the opposite sex. The likes of *Loaded* didn't even exist back then, since some bright spark had decreed that men didn't read magazines.

I had an interview to sub on *Elle*, which led nowhere, and eventually began freelancing regularly on *New Woman*, who asked me to write features from the man's perspective. 'What Makes A Man Grow Up?' (obviously I hadn't shown them my Tardis play-tent), and so on.

And I started writing for *Game Zone*, a now defunct Nintendo magazine which had a stable of funny writers and reminded me of *Smash Hits*.

A woman's magazine, even though I clearly wasn't one, and a publication for computer-games geeks, which felt like regression.

All right, I was making money while writing for a living – but where did the future lie? Where was the career path? Mine was staring to look more like a rockery.

My parents started wondering out loud whether I had ever considered teaching.

I write because I love manipulating words, and I always try to make people laugh. It's about making people happy, hopefully. Of course, with writing you don't know the effect you're having on people, you just hope.

I even manage to cram the odd, occasionally lame joke into my *Daily Mail* copy, and I've sat on the tube more than once, watching someone reading the paper, following every page they turn in my peripheral vision, urging them to read quicker until they hit the television section, because it would make my day to witness a stranger actually reading something I had written, and it would make my year if it raised even the faintest of smiles.

It's been a learning curve.

As a freelance writer, only very rarely does an editor comment on your work. If it's printed, you assume you did OK. If the piece has been heavily rewritten by the subs, you swallow your pride, analyse what stayed in and what was cut, and try to learn from it. (Or you slag off the sub-editor to colleagues as being completely useless, and hope they are similarly bitter.)

Laughter really is the best medicine. Take the logical conclusion: if everyone in the world laughed forever, there would be no violence, no wars (unless the perpetrators were cackling sadists, which some are).

According to www.helpguide.org, laughter can:

- reduce stress
- lower blood pressure
- elevate mood
- boost immune system
- improve brain functioning
- protect the heart

among others.

A nursery school child laughs about 300 times a day. The figure for an adult is nearer 17. How depressing is that? All those woes of daily living have piled up, people. (At least there's an upside: adults don't bawl if they're handed a tomato, and they don't fight proprietorially over a plastic figure in the shape of a duck.)

And you can forget the treadmill. Laughter burns about three calories per minute. Proof, perhaps, that even Bernard Manning doesn't laugh at Bernard Manning's jokes.

Undoubtedly, it was my voracious appetite for books, as a child, that set me on the path to writing.

When I read a sentence now that has been beautifully worded, I read it repeatedly, in awe of the author's prowess. There was one recently, by A A Gill, who I didn't even realise I would like (Gordon Ramsay threw him out of his restaurant once, along with Joan Collins, and I always trust Ramsay's judgement).

It was a *Sunday Times Magazine* feature on Gill's trip to Greenland, and I'm a sucker for any snowbound piece. If you're lucky, it may still be at http://travel.timesonline. co.uk/.

Although his description of the old lady in hot pants pulling faces made me laugh out loud, causing my train-compartment companions to stare at me as if I were giving off wee steam, it was this description that wiped me out:

'. . . the cold pinches and slaps my face and searches like a dog's nose for tiny chinks in my clothes.'

Searches like a dog's nose for tiny chinks in my clothes. It's so perfect, so visual. What thought process got him there? How to develop a similar way of thinking?

## Some Things . . . I Have Really Enjoyed Reading

- *The Wasp Factory* – Iain Banks. Really dark, wonderfully bizarre.
- *The Cement Garden* – Ian McEwan. Ditto.
- *Head On/Repossessed* – The first instalments of Julian Cope's manic, hilarious biography.
- *Diary of a Nobody* – George and Weedon Grossmith. I read it in two days, on a too-hot holiday in Sardinia. Considering it was first published in 1892, it is very, very funny.
- Inspector Morse/Sherlock Holmes/Columbo – Colin

Dexter, Sir Arthur Conan Doyle and William Harrington, respectively. I'm a sucker for a good detective.

- *Atlas Shrugged* – Ayn Rand. Architectural thriller over many pages, read because (cough) the author inspired Rush drummer/lyricist Neil Peart.
- *Rats* – Robert Sullivan. *New Yorker* journalist's true tale of the city's rodents. Somehow compelling, with great trivia. (Did you know that, despite their size, a rat can squeeze through a hole three-quarters of an inch wide, by contracting its skeleton?)
- *Into Thin Air* – Jon Krakauer. True account of a doomed Everest expedition. Beats any fictional thriller. I gave a copy to a friend as a birthday present. He enjoyed it so much that, despite people's noses falling off in the book, it inspired him to take up mountaineering. He's since climbed Mont Blanc. The idiot.
- *Without Feathers* – Woody Allen. A comedy masterclass.
- *Breakfast of Champions* – Kurt Vonnegut. A writing masterclass.
- *New York Trilogy* – Paul Auster. Another guy who knows how to spin a sentence.
- *All Played Out* – Pete Davies. England's 1990 World Cup journey.
- *Catcher in the Rye* – J D Salinger. Anyone else heard of it? Or is it just me?

Another chapter in my disastrous love-life opened, and this one didn't pan out any better.

I met Aileen, an East-Scottish émigré, necessarily flame-haired, slightly spiky, with a smile that could floor entire townships, who wore polka-dot leggings and rode a motorbike. She was cute. And I found her via the Lonely Hearts in *Time Out*. Hey, London's a big city.

Our first date was in an Islington pub which she chose, she told me during the date, because it had a ladies' loo window you could climb out of. Obviously, that was after she had decided she wouldn't need to, and we got on surprisingly well. She was a journalist too, on contract magazines, *Beauty Counter* and *Your Pharmacy* (to which I would shortly contribute, while knowing nothing about beauty or pharmacies).

It took some wooing – pub quizzes, grovelling, that sort of thing – but we started going out.

From a one-bed flat in Islington (where I actually caught a burglar climbing up my wall, one night; 'Oi!' I called out from my window, 'Sorry, mate,' he replied, before shimmying down to mingle with the city's less nice people), I moved into her place in Clapton.

One Sunday, she came back from a morning stroll with details of a three-bedroomed maisonette in Chardmore Road, Stamford Hill, south of Tottenham. She's very proactive and headstrong, is Aileen.

It cost £47,500 – a bargain even by those days' standards. (I saw a similar property in an estate agent only last night, priced £387,500, which made my stomach turn.)


This was my second attempt at being a property magnate, the previous attempt, with Jane in Tottenham, having ended ignominiously with barely a jot of profit and a whole heap of heartache.

Aileen and I had been seeing each other for well over a year by that stage, and cracks were starting to appear in our relationship – small personality clashes – which we both duly papered over. But I've always been an in-for-a-penny, in-for-a-pound kinda guy and an offer was accepted on Chardmore Road and a completion date set.

I remember after one late-night row, stomping out of the house and walking to that flat while the neon streetlights did their stuff with not a soul around, gazing up at it and thinking, 'What am I doing?'

★

We moved in. A lot of decorative work was required, which I took to with gusto, and the experience of renovation bonded us. It felt pretty grown-up.

Aileen enjoyed choosing the colour schemes but I still managed to paint my office orange, and swiftly installed a pub quiz machine in there, which chipped paintwork on the way up the stairs.

My primary contribution to the ornaments were two papier maché fishes, balloon-sized, painted in day-glo colours, with eyes that said, 'Buy me!', so I did, from Camden Market at a tenner a piece, and named then Mr and Mrs Fish.

And I tried smooth-talking her into watching *Doctor Who* videos with me, with the usual only brief success.

When I said it felt pretty grown-up, maybe it was more Aileen.

Anyway, having a baby was talked about. If you're going to experience everything in life, that's in there. We made a list of Pros & Cons, and with a little unconscious manipulation, the Pros won hands down.

The night Dylan was conceived, I had this sixth-sense. I knew it had happened. Aileen peed on a stick and it was confirmed: my girlfriend was pregnant.

Cue strange times.

None of our friends had babies. I don't think I had ever even held one. Actually, I'm not certain I had even *seen* one close up.

I didn't know what one did with babies: how they fed, how the waste bit worked, what they ate, when they went to bed, when they got up, what one said to them, when they started to walk and talk, how they took their tea, what their favourite programmes were, at what age you could safely sit one in front of *Doctor Who*, why their little legs curved inwards, how you could stop gathered mothers banging on about how often their little angel pooped its nappy . . . I did not know a blummin' thing about babies – which very gradually dawned on me.

Frankly, truth told, I wasn't mature enough for father-hood, but I've always been up for a challenge. I was 28 when Aileen became pregnant; people half that age have had kids. Why couldn't I manage?

Those nine months do prepare a mother far better than a father. She lives with the child and feels it growing. He watches her belly expand and wonders what the hell is going on.

I wrote a slightly tongue-in-cheek piece for *New Woman*, titled 'Pregnancy is a Female Conspiracy', which included my single visit to an ante-natal class ('Would the men have those hideous joke-breasts and feign suckling Tiny Tears? No. We weren't expected to do anything except ask stupid questions like, 'Which way's the toilet?'') and the first scan ('Aileen lay on a couch. "Sit there," the nurse told me. She had opened an *A-Z* and was pointing in the direction of Chorleywood.')

The reality was starting to kick in and I felt unprepared.

At least I still had *Doctor Who*.

I'll tell you how bad my addiction became.

I started buying those Reeltime video interviews with the stars of the show. I collected: Katy Manning (Jo Grant), Tom Baker (twice) and the bloke who played UNIT's Sgt Benton, John Levene, who has a fantastically corny sense of humour.

I even bought two Reeltime videos of Panopticon *Doctor Who* conventions, so I could see what went on without actually having to be there. It's cowardly and it's hardly quality television.

I had some growing up to do. And fast.

*Coming up: My son is born, I realise that parenting is not easy; everything falls apart; on the career front, I start freelancing for* Radio Times, *something unexpected and amazing is about to happen . . .*

## Chapter Seven
### *Age 28–30*

# A Circle Closes

*'This is the moment when I get a real feeling of job satisfaction.'*
The Collector, The Sun Makers

The baby was late. With Aileen booked in for an induced
birth on Monday, I spent the Saturday evening in the pub
with sanctions, for one final wetting of the imminent child's
head.

At 4 a.m. she woke me and pointed out that her waters
had broken.

That early-morning drive from Chardmore Road to the
hospital in Hackney was among my more surreal. No one
about, Aileen calm, me confused but trying to do the stoical,
supportive thing. Romantically, I imagine myself being
stopped by the police, pouring out the story while Aileen
puffed largely in the passenger seat, and them escorting us
to our destination with blue lights flashing.

In fact, they might have nicked me for drink-driving.

I didn't really have a choice. Er, officer.

Aileen was taken into a delivery suite, her bag with nightwear
and baby things packed and ready.

I stood there like a twonk, wishing I had brought grapes,

feeling astonishingly sober. Six hours previously, I had been in a pub. Suddenly I was in a hospital. You mentally plan for the moment, of course, but as the months pan out time plays tricks and you wonder whether the wait might last forever. A midwife came and went, but mostly went.

I had imagined an instant hive of matronly activity, an awful lot of screaming, death-gripped hands and a long, long delivery. Instead, Aileen and I sat and chatted. Then the contractions kicked in. You don't need a degree in Medical Science to spot when that happens.

What on earth was I supposed to do? Holding someone's hand while they push out a baby through a hole the size of a willy seems somewhat half-hearted.

A midwife handed me a damp cloth, to wipe Aileen's forehead. I'd seen people do that on telly.

I'm a logical sort. My actually being a midwife would have been useful. Having a decent idea of the biological processes involved in childbirth would have helped. Dabbing someone's forehead with a small rag? I felt like I was being inveigled into some kind of delivery-room cliché. But what else was there? I dabbed.

I wasn't unduly worried about my uselessness because I have utter faith in medical professionals, and there's a baby born every second. Nothing was going to go wrong.

Then something did. No one stated it explicitly, but the atmosphere in the room palpably changed: from routine to concern.

A team of people pushing a new monitor marched through the door, set up their equipment and went about their business with efficiency, but this was worrying and I didn't understand.

I only remember a blur of fear.

It was explained that a cut would have to be made, to make the baby's exit wider. It happened without anaesthetic as far as I recall. It was beyond me. The respect I had for Aileen.

Though the birth took about four hours, the time gal-
loped like a steed.

'Does Daddy want to see Baby's head?' asked a midwife.

I certainly wished she had couched it in slightly more
grown-up terms. I was also reluctant to view something that
might look like a real-life operation, given my squeamish
nature. But you have to.

It was the most incredible scene I have witnessed. This
reddish matted-haired dome of a head, emerging.

Human birth.

That really is how it happens.

It was over quickly after that. This entire person slipped out,
a length of head and limbs, gunky and whole, to breathe its
first.

That was a very, very strange sensation. From the first
moment having a baby was lazily mooted, via the tiny
silvery, curled skeleton on the scan and that insane stomach,
to this: a real, small person – who would be heading home
with you, not hanging around at the hospital until he could
eat a square meal without requiring it to be dressed up as a
choo-choo train. Maybe that was when the enormity of the
responsibility I had taken on hit me.

Did I cut the umbilical chord? I guess so. I don't really
remember.

I do remember Dylan being weighed in some scales and
coming in over the eight-pound mark, and the hospital staff
afterwards wheeling out the placenta on a trolley, as if it
were breakfast, and my declining an inspection.

I'll be honest: I was kind of surprised we had an actual
baby.

Had he been a girl, he would have been Robyn Janine.
Instead he was Dylan, born October 1994, neither named
after the nasally troubadour nor the Welsh poet, but the
rabbit from *The Magic Roundabout*. Laid-back. The kind of

guy who has strings missing from his guitar and either fails to notice or doesn't care. (Boys' names are so generally dull that we couldn't decide on a second, so gave it a miss.)

I well remember turning up in the car to take Aileen and Dylan home, having first 'wet the baby's head', which must be the lamest of euphemisms for getting drunk with your mates.

I carried him upstairs into the house and sat him in the lounge in his Moses basket, and thought: 'Right, er, now what?'

Work wasn't going so well. *Select* had moved without me and I had eventually taken the hint. Being *Deadline*'s features editor had been fun, but the publisher had suddenly employed two new geezers, The Stud Brothers, I think they were called, and that was the end of that, too. Not long afterwards, the mag folded. Actually, lots of the magazines I have worked on bit the dust.

A coincidence?

At least I still had *New Woman* and some other TV bits, but they weren't going to pay the mortgage. Then I got some work from the *Young Telegraph* and ended up in their offices on Old Street.

A friendly bunch, their editor gave me weekly shifts, subbing and writing, about Ryan Giggs, the Wright brothers and playground crazes.

From writing for 18–35-year-olds during the music days, to writing primarily for teenagers on the computer-games mag . . . suddenly my readership had sugar rush off too many lemonades and drew people with preposterously sized hands.

Hmm.

Aileen and I ended up in Marriage Guidance, or Relate as it was renamed in honour of people who weren't married.

So much angst, so many hankies.

The counsellor never started with a question nor passed judgment. So we'd sit there in silence until someone said something, which didn't feel remotely awkward.

I think we both believed Relate would somehow draw us back together; instead, it did the opposite. Better to get it over with while Dylan was still very young, we reasoned, rather than drag it out.

Driving to Kent to inform my parents, face to face, was one of the hardest things I have ever done.

'AileenandIaresplittingup.' Curl into ball and die.

I should have known: there were no recriminations, only support and practicalities. I think they had seen what Aileen and I had only just worked out: we simply weren't suited.

I had brought a child into the world. Now I was going to have to leave his home and him behind. It's not something you can get your head around quickly. One thing I knew: I would always be there for that little boy, no matter what. I would live nearby, maintain regular contact, remain a father – but would it be enough?

Had I failed him already? It certainly felt like it. I recalled tales of broken families in which the child goes off the rails. And I hated myself.

How desperately I needed a crystal ball. Would he be happy in the future? If I knew that it would all work out, I could move on without shame or fear. I just didn't know.

Dylan was two years old, an adorable, easy-going little blond boy with a bowl haircut.

Those were bleak months.

I wore black every day because nothing else felt right, and subsisted largely on alcohol.

One night kind of sums it up.

Aileen had been for a rare night out, and when she returned we rowed briefly. I left the house, walked to the bus stop and took a night bus into town. To where exactly, I gave no thought. I was already lost.

I ended up wandering down The Strand as the sun came up. There were homeless people in shop doorways, asleep under cardboard and piled coats.

I walked towards King's College and turned right over Waterloo Bridge.

Those bridges towards the South Bank offer the most life-affirming views, of St Paul's, the Houses of Parliament, Big Ben, the City, London, its history and vibrancy and soul, with the Thames stretching though that clustered stone humanity, a defiant, natural statement of intent.

I was cold. My linen suit let the wind in. That was fine: I deserved whatever the elements threw at me.

I took a right along the South Bank and turned back over Hungerford Bridge towards Embankment. That's a disturbing little construction (happily now replaced); whenever I walked over it, beside the industrial, throbbing railway lines, I always imagined the terror if someone grabbed me and threw me over the railings into the shit-strewn waters.

As I came upon shops I window-browsed, and when I found myself on Piccadilly, I did something I had never done before: I went to an art gallery.

Really, I just wanted to get warm. I didn't much expect to enjoy the art.

Sensation, at the Royal Academy, was the controversial one, featuring the Young British Artists who riled the Establishment so: Damien Hirst, Tracey Emin, the Chapman brothers, Gavin Turk . . . That lot.

Please don't expect me to start reading deep things into the exhibits, clawing my way out of depression through art appreciation. But it did affect me.

Walking in between Hirst's sections of floaty cow ('Some Comfort Gained from the Acceptance of the Inherent Lies in Everything' – absolutely) was strangely moving, and his tiger shark, inexplicably powerful.

I loved 'Dead Dad' (weirdly lifelike wax model of naked, deceased father on slab) and 'Blue Minotaur' (vivid painting of toy) and the child's-hand-print picture of Myra Hindley.

When I left, I had done something new, opened my mind very slightly.

There was a potential for things to be different.

Funnily enough, it was Aileen again who arrived home with the estate agent details, of a property less than a mile from Chardmore Road, in Stoke Newington.

I really didn't want to make that final move out of the house and away from Dylan, having pictured in my mind countless times the act of closing the front door behind me. Aileen knew it and was keen for us to move on, find some normality where there was only the strain of cohabiting amid the ashes of a relationship.

To my surprise, things did turn around. Dylan stayed with his mother; I moved into Bethune Road and decorated until I dropped. The monotony compelled my battered mind elsewhere. Woodchip off, lining paper on. Carpets up, floorboards sanded. All new colours. Fresh start.

We drew up an arrangement where I saw my son one evening a week and one day every weekend, with the option of dropping by at other times.

I started to feel positive again. And then the break came.

Through a connection at the *Young Telegraph*, I was asked to spend two days at the *Radio Times*, writing for their Children's page. This would have been late 1995.

It was the first publication I had worked for where you were embraced, not pelted with small Germans, if you admitted to loving *Doctor Who*.

No one stays at *Radio Times* for just two days. The shifts continued, until I was in there five days a week.

If I'm honest, I didn't immediately make the connection between the magazine and my Who-phile days of yore.

It was work. And I would end up ghosting Andi Peters' and later Tim Vincent's columns for the kids' page, while interviewing the guys from *Chucklevision*.

As I said, it was work. But it was the BBC and, being solidly British, I was proud to walk into a building, for actual employment, bearing that celebrated logo.

My parents were happy, too. Shortly I'd be writing for the *Daily Mail*. Practically landed gentry. (I do sometimes wonder how *Mail* readers would feel if they saw how scruffy I am.)

If only they'd known, back when I was flogging Astley in Our Price.

Someone a few desks away mentioned a Tom Baker interview.

I wanted to run over there, fall at his feet and offer to clip his toenails for a fortnight, just for the chance. Were that not enough, I would have considered eating them.

But someone piped up with another freelancer's name, held in greater esteem than the bloke who wrote about *Blue Peter* viewers collecting ring-pulls for charity, and that was it. Moment passed. Perhaps for the best.

How I ached.

Slowly, though, as my face became known, and the fact that I could string a few words together, I was offered higher profile work.

My first ever *Radio Times* feature was a two-pager, interviewing Vic Reeves and Bob Mortimer about one of their sketch shows. They talked about chronic indigestion and wanting to eat the White Cliffs of Dover.

You can get blasé about seeing your work in print, but this was something else after the diminishing kudos of my magazine work. A career rebirth.

Then, from nowhere (or possibly Raxacoricofallapatorius, Who fans), *Doctor Who* came back. The magazine planned a

16-page pull-out Time Lord souvenir. By which time I was friends with Anne, the commissioning editor.

'Can I? Can I? Can I?'

Yes, I could!

AAAAAAAGH!

I researched the 'Timeline' that runs along the foot of each page, detailing moments in the show's history, which involved a trip to the RT boardroom where bound copies of every back issue are kept.

With reverence and mild awe, I turned the pages of the 1963 issue, detailing the debut story, An Unearthly Child.

I found the very first RT *Doctor Who* cover (22–28 February 1964), a black-and-white of William Hartnell with Marco Polo and minion in a hat.

Other covers: Cybermen, Pertwee, the Master, The Three Doctors, the Tenth Anniversary Special.

I adored that magazine. I read it so often that I could have specialised in it on *Mastermind* (no doubt while the other contestants, specialising in Shakespeare's sonnets, Every Insect Ever Known and Celebrated Scandinavians named Jurgen 1023–1866 muttered to each other about dumbing down). And here I was, in the *Radio Times* boardroom, working on a 1996 version of the very same thing.

Years tumbled, memories shimmered, significance hit, heart swelled.

It was so much fun, I even went into the office on a Sunday.

I didn't get the trip to Vancouver to meet Paul McGann, but I was commissioned to do the Q&A interviews with every surviving Doctor.

I would actually be talking to Jon Pertwee, Tom Baker, Peter Davison, Colin Baker and Sylvester McCoy! Me! To them! How amazing?

A few months earlier, I'd wondered whether I should cut my losses and drive a milk float for a living.

Tom Baker declined the interview. As he'd tell me when I finally stalked him down a year or so later, the moment has to be right.

It was a blow.

But I got Pertwee.

I still have his handwritten fax.

FROM:– Jon Pertwee
TO:– NICK GRIFFITHS, RADIO TIMES

WOULD BE DELIGHTED TO BE INTERVIEWED BY RT
TEL 0181 xxx xxxx

What a gent.

It was him, on the other end of the telephone line, those same soothing, undulating, fatherly tones, with the slightest of lisps.

It was a no-brainer interview. How easily did he fit into the role? When did he feel silliest? (Fighting the Minotaur in The Time Monster, when the stuntman couldn't see through the costume and kept running into walls.) Were there any hairy moments? When did he decide to leave? Favourite souvenir? Biggest *Doctor Who* regret? (The pay.)

And he talked about the show's future, and its remake by an American production company, with McGann in the lead role. (Pertwee 'blew his stack', evidently, when David Hasselhoff was at one time suggested as a reasonable Doctor.)

Then it was over, we said our goodbyes and I put the phone down. And I sighed and glazed over for a few seconds.

★

That 16-page *Doctor Who* supplement was dated 25–31 May 1996.

Jon Devon Roland Pertwee died on 20 May 1996, of a heart attack while holidaying in the States, aged 76.

I was privileged and not a little shocked to be invited to his Memorial Service, at St Giles in the Fields Church in Central London, that August. It opened with All Things Bright and Beautiful, typically unpretentious, and Nicholas Courtney, Bill Pertwee and David Jacobs, among others, offered reminiscences. It was a lovely occasion.

Mine may well have been the last interview that Pertwee gave, which offers me no pride. I'd rather he were still around today, still doing the odd convention, emerging from his Tardis in that velvet cape, throwing wide his arms, declaring, 'I AM THE DOCTOR!'

For this child of the seventies, much as I grew to love Tom Baker, he always will be 'my Doctor'. Bless him.

So the circle had closed. The Doctor I first fell in love with had passed away. My son had been born, whom I would soon be hassling with videos of those very same early-seventies stories. And I was writing for the very publication, about the show itself, which had cemented that love.

I got lucky.

# Postscript

## Some Things . . . That are Great About Doctor Who

- The imagination – Which other programme could offer you a lead character who travels time and space in a telephone box, proffering Jelly Babies and unconventional wisdom, with a supporting cast of characters that included a tin dog, a woman called Romanadvoratrelundar, some blokes wheeling themselves around on castors clutching sink plungers and more bubble-wrap, latex, sticky-back plastic and loo-roll holders than you could chuck at Anthea Turner?

  Note to self: Good idea. Consider throwing loo-roll holders at Anthea Turner.
- The Daleks – How on earth did they catch on? Really. Consider that list of stuff required to make your own Dalek: 28-lb bag modelling clay, 28 lbs fast-setting potter's plaster, 4 sq. yds hessian scrim, ½ pint PVA release agent . . . yes, that stuff. Somehow, when all put together in the correct way, it sent children scurrying behind the nearest soft furnishing, inspired merchandise that included thimbles, a cruet set, novelty hat and small boy's pants, and they never went away. Indeed, the Daleks are more popular now than they have ever been, 43 years since their first appearance.

- The formula – Whoever dreamed up the idea of a lead character who could regenerate, meaning that different actors could take on the role, hence *Doctor Who*'s remarkable longevity, should have been given an OBE, knighted, offered the keys to the city of Ripon and surreptitiously passed the telephone number of the world's sexiest person. Pure genius.

- The escapism – Fancy travelling to the planet Gallifrey in the constellation of Casterborus? No problem. All right, planet Gallifrey doesn't exist, and what you're seeing was knocked up by the BBC design department on a budget of sixpence, but that's where your own mind can get to work. Believe it and you will reap reward.

- The humour – *Doctor Who* rarely took itself too seriously (sometimes it didn't take itself seriously enough – Nicholas Parsons?!). There have been some great gags. And some stupid ones. Doctor: 'I'll call you Romana.' Romana: 'I don't like Romana.' Doctor: 'It's either Romana or Fred.'

- The quarries – People take the mickey out of the wobbly sets, the joins in the costumes and the fact that it was always being filmed in a quarry, but I love those aspects of the classic *Doctor Who*. Those people worked miracles with the resources to hand, creating joyous entertainment for generations of fans around the world. That spirit of kicking against adversity, the self-belief . . . the Britishness.

## Just a Handful of Things . . . That Weren't So Great

- The Loch Ness Monster – Oh dear, oh dear, oh dear. It appeared at the end of The Terror of the Zygons, looking like a glove puppet a small child knocked up using two gobstoppers, four lolly sticks and a hamster named Nigel.

- Colin Baker – He claims it wasn't his fault, that the producers wanted him to be grouchy. How does that excuse his hair? And what on earth were the costume people thinking? If someone had turned up for work like that on *Play School*, they'd have been laughed out of town by Big Ted and Hamble.
- Paradise Towers – I had the misfortune to buy this Sylvester McCoy-era video, by which time the show had become a pantomime. You've got Richard Briers dressed as a comedy Hitler, young-girl gangs called Kangs, psychotic pensioners and a monster that looks like something a child played with in the bath. Oh, and Bonnie Langford was in it.
- That monster – You know the one, in the Tom Baker story, which looked like a huge, shuffling lump attached to a large willy.

So here we are. Today's date is 12 May 2006 and I have a creeping sense of euphoria as the word-count reaches its conclusion. Writing this book has been not only a labour of love but actual hard work, such as I am unused to. I even made a bar graph, to chart my progress. That's how organised I was.

It will have been worth it. It has been a fantasy of mine for whole decades to somehow write a book and to see it published. I have honestly daydreamed of hearing the post arrive and watching the very first copy of such a tome thud on to the doormat, and I rip open the packaging and gaze at the cover, grinning like an idiot.

*That is actually going to happen.*

I have joined The Society of Authors. And they gave me a membership card.

Note to the Society of Authors: consider also giving out a

badge, plastic wallet (embossed) and perhaps a Society of Authors pendant.

When I was going out with Tammy, back in the days of Woodpecker cider and innocence, I always thought I would get married, have children, do the decent thing. Then she went, everyone else afterwards did the same, often gesticulating crudely, and I began to wonder. Cynicism crept in.

Actually, it didn't creep in, it broke the door down with a discarded cistern found on a building site and ran through the house shouting, 'YOU'LL NEVER LOVE AGAIN!'

But I got married last year, at the age of 40, in a fort on the Cornish coast, with my parents, one brother, Sinead's mum and numerous siblings, plus cast of friends in attendance.

At 38, I had found myself once again dumped and wondering whether my next girlfriend – should one even come along – might be Edna Doré.

Then Sinead Hanks appeared. Brains, personality, looks – people say she looks like Gillian Anderson, or Kate Winslet, which saves me from having to describe her here, which could end in a row – loves pub quizzes, is starting to love the new *Doctor Who*, enjoys a drink now and again, as do I, works for a charity, has dressed up as a nurse, won't eat oysters, makes me incredibly happy.

I think, at last, I have actually found someone I am suited to.

Dylan is 12 in October and it did work out, after all. His mother and I have become good friends – she came to the wedding – and I cannot fault her parenting skills. Our son is the funniest, brightest, sweetest child in the entire cosmos and I am so very proud of him.

And we sit together on a Saturday evening and we watch *Doctor Who*, huddled together on the sofa (ready for a quick leap backwards), I more scared than he, and the show exceeds our expectations.

Handily for him, he can go to school on the Monday morning and declare, 'I watched *Doctor Who* at the weekend', and far from being derided as a nerd he will be seen as some kind of fashion guru. (Handily for me, I can declare to friends, 'I watched *Doctor Who* at the weekend with my son,' and they merely think that I'm a paragon of fatherhood.)

As happened with the 1996 Paul McGann TV movie, this *Doctor Who* renaissance could have fizzled magnesium-bright and died just as swiftly. And that, without a doubt, would have been that. No more chances. This was the big one.

It didn't just work, it went stratospheric: vast ratings, glittering prizes, endless merchandising. Not only was there life in the Time Lord, there was even life in his old dog.

Credit is due to every soul on that show, from Russell T Davies, Doctors Eccleston and Tennant, companion Piper, through the producer, writers, directors, designers, costume and make-up to the gaffer, grip, best boy and other job titles that sound like they could do with some reinvention using the words 'executive' and 'technician'.

*Radio Times* gathered together as many as possible for a cast-and-crew shoot, which I witnessed, and there were 147 of them, with 50 or so others unavailable.

Thanks to that talented bunch, I've been able to watch Daleks again, and Autons – my very first *Doctor Who* monster. I've seen Earth explode, I've heard boggle-eyed aliens break wind and Queen Victoria admit she wasn't amused, I've watched Richard Wilson's face become engulfed by a gas mask – and *I* didn't believe it – the Doctor danced, Mickey pranced, Rose dashed, a mirror smashed, a werewolf howled, I've seen Krillitanes, acid rain, Billy Zane . . .

Sorry, got carried away at the end there. But that's great – like I used to get carried away, transported to other places and times where this wonderful man added fever and imagination to my childhood.

I got it all back, and my son shared it with me.

Tomorrow sees the return of the Cybermen.

We'll be waiting.

# Acknowledgements

This book would not exist without Jane Walker, whose idea it was. The same Jane I glimpsed at the Anarchist Society stall at the King's College Fresher's Fair, and went out with after college. I am indebted.

Thanks also to Simon Spanton, editorial director at Gollancz, for ideas, advice, support, Chinese, Thai and Indian for lunch, and for actually publishing the thing.

Dylan, my son, is always an inspiration to me. As is my wife, Sinead, who supported, advised and shared in the excitement. It wouldn't have been the same without her.

Without Anne Jowett, my favourite commissioning editor, I might never have written about *Doctor Who* for the *Radio Times*. Cheers.

Thanks also to Shelley Weiner, author and tutor, whose writing groups I attended and whose teaching was invaluable. And to Jane Hill, who has always been so supportive of my attempts at writing whole books.

I'm grateful to Shaun Phillips, formerly of *Sounds*, for rescuing me from editing *Business Education Today*, and to David Cavanagh, who asked me to join *Select* shortly before *Sounds* folded. It might have been so very different. 'What size do you wear, sir? . . . I think we have that.'

And finally, since I don't want to bang on weepily like Gwyneth Paltrow at an awards ceremony, to Norman and

Lynne Griffiths. I couldn't have wished for kinder, funnier, more supportive parents. I love them to bits. Without them, etc. No, really.